KALLIS' TOEFL iBT PATTERN

Listening 3

TOEFL® is a registered trademark of Educational Testing Services (ETS), Princeton, New Jersey, USA. The content in this text, including the practice questions, Hacking Strategy, and Quick Look, is created and designed exclusively by KALLIS. This publication is not endorsed or approved by ETS.

KALLIS' TOEFL iBT ® Pattern Listening 3

KALLIS EDU, INC.
7490 Opportunity Road, Suite 203
San Diego, CA 92111
info@kallisedu.com
www.kallisedu.com

Copyright © 2015 KALLIS EDU, INC.

All rights reserved. No part of this book may be reproduced, stored in a retrieval system, or transmitted in any form or by any means, electronic or mechanical, including photocopying, recording, or otherwise, without the prior written permission of the copyright owner.

ISBN-10: 0-9911657-9-9
ISBN-13: 978-0-9911657-9-7

TOEFL iBT ® Pattern - Listening III is the third of our three-level TOEFL iBT ® Listening Exam preparation book series.

Our **TOEFL iBT ® Pattern Listening** series simplifies each TOEFL Listening question type into a series of simple steps, which ensures that students do not become overwhelmed as they develop their listening skills. Moreover, our commitment to minimizing instruction and maximizing student practice assures that students have many opportunities to strengthen their listening skills.

KALLIS

KALLIS'
TOEFL® iBT
PATTERN
LISTENING 3
CONQUER

Getting Started

A study guide should familiarize the reader with the material found on the test, develop methods that can be used to solve various question types, and provide plenty of practice questions. *KALLIS' TOEFL iBT ® Pattern Series* aims to accomplish all these study tasks by presenting TOEFL iBT ® test material in an organized, comprehensive, and easy-to-understand way.

KALLIS' TOEFL iBT ® Pattern Listening Series shows students how to identify and solve each question type found on the TOEFL iBT Listening section. Thus, students can identify which types of question they find most challenging, and then develop strategies for solving them. Additionally, each book in our Pattern Listening Series contains hundreds of practice questions, ensuring that students can develop the skills they need to succeed on the TOEFL iBT.

Putting the Questions into Context

Chapter 1

▶ This chapter provides general information about what you will listen to during the TOEFL iBT Listening section.
▶ This chapter explains and provides examples for each type of multiple-choice questions found on the TOEFL iBT Listening section.

Enhancing Test-Taking Skills through Practice

Chapter 2

- Located in Chapter 2, **Actual Practices** provide dozens of listening passages (conversations and lectures) that include every type of multiple-choice question found on the TOEFL iBT Listening section. In order to complete these, you must use the skills that you reviewed in Chapter 1.
- A scaled scoring chart is located at the beginning of Chapter 2 , so you can grade yourself and get an idea of how you might score on the official TOEFL iBT Listening section.
- Each listening passage in these chapters includes **Key Terms** and **Notes** sections to help you organize your thoughts as you listen.

Checking Your Own Progress

Appendix and Answer Key

- The **Appendix** contains transcripts of all the conversations and lectures found throughout this book.
- The **Answer Key** contains the correct answers to all multiple-choice questions found throughout this book. It also includes answer explanations and example notes that can help guide your studies.
- If you do not want to repeatedly flip to the back of the book for answers, simply cut out the **Simple Answers** at the very back of the book. **Simple Answers** provides a quick reference so you can confirm that all your answers are correct.

Table of Contents

Chapter 1

General Information — 1
Type 1: Main Idea — 4
Type 2: Detail — 5
Type 3: Purpose — 6
Type 4: Inference — 7
Conversation: Main Idea Question — 8
Conversation: Detail Question — 9
Conversation: Purpose Question — 10
Conversation: Inference Question — 11
Lecture: Main Idea Question — 12
Lecture: Detail Question — 13
Lecture: Purpose Question — 14
Lecture: Inference Question — 15

Chapter 2

Actual Practices — 17
Actual Practice 1 — 18
Actual Practice 2 — 24
Actual Practice 3 — 30
Actual Practice 4 — 36
Actual Practice 5 — 42
Actual Practice 6 — 48
Actual Practice 7 — 54
Actual Practice 8 — 60
Actual Practice 9 — 66
Actual Practice 10 — 72
Actual Practice 11 — 78
Actual Practice 12 — 84

LISTENING 3 CONQUER

Actual Practice 13	90
Actual Practice 14	96
Actual Practice 15	102
Actual Practice 16	108
Actual Practice 17	114
Actual Practice 18	120
Actual Practice 19	126
Actual Practice 20	132
Actual Practice 21	138
Actual Practice 22	144
Actual Practice 23	150
Actual Practice 24	156
Actual Practice 25	162

Appendix

Listening Scripts	169
Chapter 2	170

Appendix

Answer Key	251
Chapter 2	252

Appendix

Simple Answers	295

Before You Begin...

OVERVIEW

The TOEFL iBT Listening section consists of four to six academic lectures and two to three campus-related conversations. At the end of each lecture, you must answer six multiple-choice questions, and at the end of each conversation, you must answer five multiple-choice questions. The Listening section takes 60 to 90 minutes to complete. Each lecture or conversation is 3 to 6 minutes long.

 Because this is the advanced book in the series, the conversations and lectures in this book are similar to those you will encounter on the TOEFL iBT.

LISTENING CONTENT

The lecture portions of the Listening section will consist of a professor discussing a topic that you might hear in an introductory-level university course. Because these Listening-section lectures replicate lectures that you might hear at an American university, you should expect the professor to pause, stammer, digress, and repeat himself or herself.

The conversation portions of the Listening section will consist of a dialogue between a student and a professor or some other university employee. If students are speaking to a professor, they will discuss something related to the professor's class, such as a student's project. If students are talking to any other university employee, they will discuss something related to campus life, such as class registration. The speakers in the conversations will use normal speech patterns, including pauses, stammers, and repetition.

LISTENING SECTION QUESTIONS

Once you have finished listening to a lecture/conversation, you will be asked to answer several multiple-choice questions. Some questions will ask you to select one correct answer, some will ask you to select more than one correct answer, and others will ask you to fill out a small table or chart. Each question will fall under one of four broad categories: Main Idea Question, Detail Questions, Purpose Questions, or Inference Questions.

TAKING NOTES

Because you will only hear each lecture or conversation once, taking notes is important. But trying to write down everything you hear will reduce your comprehension of the lecture or conversation. Make sure to picture the speakers in your head and follow their meanings clearly. Your job as to understand:

1) What is the lecture or conversation mainly about?
2) Why is the speaker including particular details?

SYMBOLS AND ABBREVIATIONS

When taking notes, save time by using **symbols** instead of words. In addition to using the symbols in the chart that follows, you can create your own symbols.

SYMBOLS AND ABBREVIATIONS

When taking notes, save time by using **symbols and abbreviations** instead of some words. In addition to using the symbols in the chart that follows, you can create your own symbols.

Symbol	Meaning	Symbol	Meaning
&	and	=	equals, is
%	percent	>	more than
#	number	<	less than
@	at	→	resulting in
↓	decreasing	↑	increasing

ABBREVIATIONS FOR UNIVERSITY ACTIVITIES

Abbreviation	Meaning	Abbreviation	Meaning
edu.	education	RA	resident assistant
GE	general education	stu.	student
GPA	grade point average	TA	teaching assistant
prof.	professor	univ.	university

ABBREVIATIONS FOR ACADEMIC TOPICS

Abbreviation	Meaning	Abbreviation	Meaning
BCE	before common era	info.	information
bio.	biology/biological	gov.	government
CE	common era	lit.	literature
chem.	chemistry/chemical	poli. sci.	political science
econ.	economics/economy	psych.	psychology
env.	environment	vocab.	vocabulary

OTHER ABBREVIATIONS

Abbreviation	Meaning	Abbreviation	Meaning
b/c	because	ppl.	people
ex.	example	pro.	professional
H2O	water	pt.	point
hr.	hour	ques.	question
int'l	international	sec.	second
nat'l	national	w/	with
min.	minute	w/o	without

CHAPTER 1

General Information

Chapter 1: Listening Section: General Information

EXPLANATION OF THE LISTENING SECTION

The Listening section tests your abilities to comprehend and analyze spoken English in both social and academic settings. Thus, the Listening section of the TOEFL iBT consists of both campus-related conversations and academic lectures.

CAMPUS-RELATED CONVERSATIONS

Each Listening section will include two or three campus-related conversations. The speakers in these conversations will discuss issues that you may encounter as a student at an American university. The conversations are generally between a university student and a university employee or faculty member. Some common conversation topics include:

- students asking their professors about project or research-paper requirements
- students asking their professors about matters related to their classes
- students asking university employees for advice on academic, financial, or housing problems

ACADEMIC LECTURES

Each Listening section will include four to six academic lectures. These lectures will discuss topics that you are likely to encounter as a student at an American university. The topics are drawn from a range of academic fields, including psychology, biology, chemistry, the social sciences, and literature. In addition to formal lectures, you may also hear a back-and-forth discussion between a professor and his or her students.

After you have listened to the lecture, you must answer six multiple-choice questions that relate to the lecture information. These questions will be related to the main idea, purpose, organization, or implications of the lecture.

NECESSARY SKILLS

In order to successfully complete the Listening section, you must be able to:

- comprehend vocabulary regarding a variety of campus and academic topics
- summarize and take notes on campus and academic material
- recognize the main ideas and details of spoken information
- determine a speaker's purpose for saying something
- make inferences about speakers' meanings and attitudes

Question Types

The TOEFL iBT Listening section consists of four main types of questions.

1 Main Idea Questions

These questions require you to identify the main topic of the conversation or lecture.

2 Detail Questions

These questions require you to identify a detail, an example, or an explanation related to the main idea of the conversation or lecture.

3 Purpose Questions

These questions require you to identify *why* a speaker makes a particular statement or reference, or asks a particular question.

4 Inference Questions

These questions require you make an *inference*, or assumption, based on the contents of the conversation or lecture.

Question Type 1: Main Idea

WHAT IS A MAIN IDEA QUESTION?

The *main idea*, or topic, is the overall subject of the conversation or lecture. The speakers will not always directly state their main ideas; you may have to infer them. If it appears, the **Main Idea Question** will be the first question you are asked.

Common formats for **Main Idea Questions** include:

> *What is the conversation/lecture mainly about?*
> *What is the professor mainly talking about?*
> *Why does the student visit the professor/advisor/university employee?*
> *What is the main issue being discussed in the conversation?*

Note **Main Idea Questions** that begin with "why" are very similar in structure to **Purpose Questions** (page 6). But **Main Idea Questions** that begin with "why" ask for the main purpose of the conversation, while **Purpose Questions** ask *why* the speaker discusses certain details and examples.

TIPS

Listening Tips: The beginning of the conversation or lecture usually includes the main idea. Listen for words, phrases, and sentences that introduce topics, such as, "Today I want to talk about_____."

Answer Tips: In questions about the topic, main idea, or main purpose, the correct answer will deal with the overall subject of the conversation or lecture. Incorrect answer choices will be:

- broader than the focus of the discussion
- details from the conversation or lecture, not the main idea
- inaccurate or untrue according to the speaker
- about a subject not mentioned in the discussion

Question Type 2: Detail

WHAT IS A DETAIL QUESTION?

Details are specific pieces of information that relate to a larger topic. These pieces of information can be facts, descriptions, reasons, examples, or opinions. **Detail Questions** will ask you to recall specific information from the conversation or lecture. There will be one to three **Detail Questions** in each conversation or lecture. As you listen, ask yourself, "**WHICH** details contribute to the main idea?" Answering this question will make identifying and answering the **Detail Questions** easier.

Common formats for **Detail Questions** include:

What does the speaker say about _____ in the conversation?
According to the speaker, what/why/where/when/how _____?

Whereas a **Main Idea Question** will always appear as multiple-choice question with one correct answer, a **Detail Question** may have more than one correct answer.

TIPS

Listening Tips: When listening, notice information that contributes to the main idea of the conversation or lecture. These may be facts, explanations, examples, connections, or processes.

Answer Tips: In questions about details, the correct answer will match information in the conversation or lecture. When you answer **Detail Questions**, try to recall exactly what was said by the speaker. Use your notes. Incorrect answers may:

- repeat some of the speaker's words but convey a different meaning
- use words that sound like, but are actually different from, the speaker's words
- be inaccurate or irrelevant based on what you hear in the discussion

Question Type 3: Purpose

WHAT IS A PURPOSE QUESTION?

The "purpose" of a statement is the speaker's intention; you must infer it. In some **Purpose Questions**, you will listen to part of the conversation again before answering. There are usually one or two **Purpose Questions** that accompany each conversation or lecture. As you listen to the conversation or lecture, pay close attention to the speaker's explanations and supporting information. Notice how the information connects to the speaker's main claim or question.

Common formats for **Purpose Questions** include:

> *Why does the student/professor mention _____?*
> *Why does the student/professor say this?*

TIPS

Listening Tips: When listening for the purpose of a statement or a claim, you must rely on your ability to draw logical conclusions as to *why* the conversation is taking place or *why* a statement is being made. Use your notes to help you piece together information.

Answer Tips: The correct answers to **Purpose Questions** may be implied. When answering **Purpose Questions**, eliminate choices that conflict with the speaker's main ideas or attitudes. Incorrect answer choices may:

- repeat some of the speaker's words but convey a different meaning
- be inaccurate based on what you hear in the conversation or lecture
- be irrelevant and not about anything mentioned in the discussion

Question Type 4: Inference

WHAT IS AN INFERENCE QUESTION?

Inference Questions will ask you to identify an idea that was hinted at, but not directly stated, in a conversation or lecture. Below are several types of inference questions that you might encounter.

Inferences: An *inference* is a conclusion that is drawn from implications. Pay attention to what the speaker means. Common formats for **Inference Questions** include:

> *What does the speaker suggest about _____ in the conversation/lecture?*
> *What can be inferred from this?*

Predictions: Prediction Questions ask you to identify what a speaker might do after a conversation or lecture based upon what he or she says. Common formats for **Prediction Questions** include:

> *What will "speaker 1" probably do after talking to "speaker 2"?*

Organization: Organization Questions ask you to analyze the structure of the conversation or lecture. **Organization Questions** ask you *how* the speaker presents the information. Common formats for **Organization Questions** include:

> *How does the speaker organize the lecture information?*
> *How does the speaker clarify the points he/she made about _____?*

Attitude: Speakers often reveal a particular attitude toward topics. For example, a speaker may feel approval, disapproval, excitement, confusion, or surprise toward what is being discussed. Many times the speakers communicate attitudes indirectly. Common formats for **Attitude Questions** include:

> *What is the speaker's opinion of _____?*
> *Which choice best describes the speaker's attitude toward _____?*

Connecting Information: Some lectures will include a **Connecting Information Chart**. To complete these, you must categorize information presented in the lecture. You must reflect upon the characteristics that are described.

Listening Tips: In order to infer or analyze, pay attention to phrases that convey emotions, opinions, and connections.

Conversation: Main Idea Question — Example

In the example below, phrases and terms that help identify the main idea have been underlined. The notes summarize the main concepts of the lecture.

> **Male Student (MS):** Hi, Professor Lynn. Can I talk to you for a minute?
> **Female Professor (FP):** Yes, of course, Andrew. What can I do for you?
> **MS:** Well, <u>it's about the test that you gave back today. I did really badly on it</u>.
> **FP:** I was surprised to see that. You don't seem like the kind of student who scores poorly on tests. What happened?
> **MS:** I couldn't really study for it, to be honest. My dad was having some chest pains, so I drove him to the hospital and stayed with him while they ran tests for a couple of days. He's okay now, but <u>I didn't really get to prepare for the test like I normally would. I was wondering if there was any way I could retake it.</u>
> **FP:** Oh, I'm sorry to hear you had such a scare. Well, normally I would never do this, but I understand that a family emergency takes priority over studying chemistry. <u>I'll let you retake the test this Friday</u>. That way you have a couple of days to prepare. But the make-up test will be harder than the original, so make sure you're prepared this time.
> **MS:** I will. Thanks so much for understanding, professor. You're a life-saver!

Notes

WHAT is the conversation about?

stud. did badly on test, wants to retake → prof. allows him to retake, Fri.

When you answer a main idea question, use any notes that you have taken to help you identify key topics and ideas.

Why does the student talk to the professor?
(A) To ask for a better grade on a recent test
(B) To discuss the professor's grading system
(C) To explain why he missed a recent lecture
(D) To see if he can retake a test

Answer Explanation

The student begins by mentioning that he did poorly on a recent test. We can infer that the main idea of the conversation has to do with his test score. After explaining why he did poorly on the test, the student asks if he can retake it. The only answer that mentions retaking a test is **Choice D**.

Conversation: Detail Question — Example

In the example below, phrases and terms related to important details have been underlined. The notes summarize the details and examples mentioned in the lecture.

Male Student (MS): Hi, Professor Lynn. Can I talk to you for a minute?

Female Professor (FP): Yes, of course, Andrew. What can I do for you?

MS: Well, <u>it's about the test that you gave back today. I did really badly on it.</u>

FP: I was surprised to see that. You don't seem like the kind of student who scores poorly on tests. What happened?

MS: I couldn't really study for it, to be honest. <u>My dad was having some chest pains, so I drove him to the hospital and stayed with him while they ran tests for a couple of days</u>. He's okay now, but I didn't really get to prepare for the test like I normally would. I was wondering if there was any way I could retake it.

FP: Oh, I'm sorry to hear you had such a scare. Well, normally I would never do this, but I understand that a family emergency takes priority over studying chemistry. <u>I'll let you retake the test this Friday</u>. That way you have a couple of days to prepare. <u>But the make-up test will be harder than the original, so make sure you're prepared this time.</u>

MS: I will. Thanks so much for understanding, professor. You're a life-saver!

Notes

WHAT details contribute to the main idea of the conversation?

stud. did badly on test, wants to retake → *had to care for dad in hosp. (chest pains)*

→ *prof. allows him to retake, Fri., make-up test ↑ diff.*

When you answer a detail question, use any notes that you have taken to help you identify key terms and details.

What does the professor say about the make-up test that the student will take?

(A) It will be more difficult than the original test.

(B) It will be twice as long as the original test.

(C) It will include information not discussed in class.

(D) It will include questions on hospital procedures.

Answer Explanation

After the professor says that she will allow the student to retake the test, she says, "the make-up test will be harder than the original, so make sure you're prepared this time." Because it mentions the difficulty of the make-up test, **Choice A** is the correct answer.

Conversation: Purpose Question — Example

In the example below, phrases and terms that relate to the purpose have been underlined. The notes summarize the speakers' reasons for making certain statements.

> **Male Student (MS):** Hi, Professor Lynn. Can I talk to you for a minute?
> **Female Professor (FP):** Yes, of course, Andrew. What can I do for you?
> **MS:** Well, it's about the test that you gave back today. I did really badly on it.
> **FP:** I was surprised to see that. <u>You don't seem like the kind of student who scores poorly on tests. What happened?</u>
> **MS:** <u>I couldn't really study for it, to be honest. My dad was having some chest pains, so I drove him to the hospital and stayed with him while they ran tests for a couple of days. He's okay now, but I didn't really get to prepare for the test like I normally would.</u> I was wondering if there was any way I could retake it.
> **FP:** Oh, I'm sorry to hear you had such a scare. Well, normally I would never do this, but I understand that a family emergency takes priority over studying chemistry. I'll let you retake the test this Friday. That way you have a couple of days to prepare. But the make-up test will be harder than the original, so make sure you're prepared this time.
> **MS:** I will. Thanks so much for understanding, professor. You're a life-saver!

Notes

WHY are the speakers having the conversation?

stud. did badly on test, wants to retake

　→ *stud. didn't study b/c he had to care for dad in hosp. (chest pains)*

When you answer a purpose question, use any notes that you have taken to help you identify reasons and motivation.

Why does the student talk about staying at the hospital with his father?

(A) To relate information on a test to a real-life experience
(B) To explain why he was unable to study for a test
(C) To describe the event that inspired him to study medicine
(D) To give a reason for falling asleep during class

Answer Explanation

When the professor asks the student why he did poorly on the test, the student claims that he was unable to prepare for the test because he had to care for his father. Only **Choice B** accurately summarizes this idea.

Conversation: Inference Question — Example

In the example below, phrases and terms that help answer the inference question below have been underlined. The notes summarize information that can be inferred from the conversation.

> **Male Student (MS):** Hi, Professor Lynn. Can I talk to you for a minute?
> **Female Professor (FP):** Yes, of course, Andrew. What can I do for you?
> **MS:** Well, it's about the test that you gave back today. I did really badly on it.
> **FP:** I was surprised to see that. You don't seem like the kind of student who scores poorly on tests. What happened?
> **MS:** I couldn't really study for it, to be honest. My dad was having some chest pains, so I drove him to the hospital and stayed with him while they ran tests for a couple of days. He's okay now, but I didn't really get to prepare for the test like I normally would. I was wondering if there was any way I could retake it.
> **FP:** Oh, I'm sorry to hear you had such a scare. Well, normally I would never do this, but I understand that a family emergency takes priority over studying chemistry. I'll let you retake the test this Friday. That way you have a couple of days to prepare. But the make-up test will be harder than the original, so make sure you're prepared this time.
> **MS:** I will. Thanks so much for understanding, professor. You're a life-saver!

Notes

WHAT does the speaker imply or suggest in the lecture?

stud. did badly on test, wants to retake

→ prof. surprised by stud. bad grade, stud. usually gets good grades

→ prof. makes exception (family emergency), allows make-up test

When you answer an inference question, use any notes that you have taken to help you identify suggestions and implications.

What does the professor imply about the student's academic performance in the professor's class?

(A) He is likely to fail the professor's class.
(B) He does not put enough effort into the professor's class.
(C) He usually does well in the professor's class.
(D) He is having trouble with some new concepts discussed in class.

Answer Explanation

After the student says that he did badly on a recent test, the professor responds, "I was surprised to see that. You don't seem like the kind of student who scores poorly on tests." From this statement, we can infer that the student normally does well on the professor's tests. Therefore, **Choice C** must be the correct answer.

Lecture: Main Idea Question

Example

In the example below, phrases and terms that help identify the main idea have been underlined. The notes summarize the main concepts of the lecture.

> **Male Professor (MP):** As part of our discussion about rituals within communities, let's consider the Pledge of Allegiance. <u>As most of you know, standing to recite loyalty to the American flag and "to the republic for which it stands" is a daily ritual in most U.S. public schools. But why is that the case? Well, I would argue that adults and children like saying it.</u>
>
> Usually, school principals come on the intercom and say, "Please stand for the Pledge of Allegiance," and most children probably believe that they have to say it. But they do not. In 1943, the U.S. Supreme Court ruled that the Constitution does not permit forcing people to say anything, including the Pledge.
>
> Now the interesting thing is, kids don't really complain. It is parents who argue about the Pledge, almost exclusively about the phrase "under God." You know, "One nation, under God…" Some people want it out; some want it in. However, when the Supreme Court considered the Pledge in 1943, "under God" wasn't even included in the Pledge yet. That happened later. So the Supreme Court ruled on the broader question of whether people can be forced to say anything, and the court said that no, they can't.
>
> Yet schools continue to make the pledge a part of the daily routine. After all, saying the Pledge gives people a sense of connection to something larger than themselves. I would argue that if they disliked it, the ritual would fade away.

Notes

WHAT is the lecture mainly about?

Pledge of Allegiance a daily ritual in U.S. schools. Why? Prof: adults, children, like saying it

When you answer a main idea question, use any notes that you have taken to help you identify key topics and ideas.

What is the main topic of the lecture?

(A) People feel loyal to most cultural rituals.

(B) Cultural rituals become routine if people like them.

(C) Education should include learning the Pledge of Allegiance.

(D) Reciting loyalty to the flag happens once a day in most schools.

Answer Explanation

At the beginning of the lecture, the professor raises the question of why U.S. schools continue having students recite the Pledge of Allegiance. The professor points out that people do not have to say it, but do so anyway. Therefore, the main idea of the lecture is to explain something about why cultural rituals continue. The answer that best summarizes this point is Choice B.

Lecture: Detail Question

Example

In the example below, phrases and terms related to important details have been underlined. The notes summarize the details and examples mentioned in the lecture.

> **Male Professor (MP):** As part of our discussion about rituals within communities, let's consider the Pledge of Allegiance. As most of you know, standing to recite loyalty to the American flag and "to the republic for which it stands" is a daily ritual in most U.S. public schools. But why is that the case? Well, I would argue that adults and children like saying it.
>
> Usually, school principals come on the intercom and say, "Please stand for the Pledge of Allegiance," and most children probably believe that they have to say it. But they do not. In 1943, the U.S. Supreme Court ruled that the Constitution does not permit forcing people to say anything, including the Pledge.
>
> Now the interesting thing is, kids don't really complain. It is parents who argue about the Pledge, almost exclusively about the phrase "under God." You know, "One nation, under God…" Some people want it out; some want it in. However, when the Supreme Court considered the Pledge in 1943, "under God" wasn't even included in the Pledge yet. That happened later. So the Supreme Court ruled on the broader question of whether people can be forced to say anything, and the court said that no, they can't.
>
> Yet schools continue to make the pledge a part of the daily routine. After all, saying the Pledge gives people a sense of connection to something larger than themselves. I would argue that if they disliked it, the ritual would fade away.

Notes

WHICH details contribute to the main idea of the lecture?

Principals give directions for Pledge, children believe have to say?

1943, Supreme Court: unconstitutional to make them

Now parents debate "under God" phrase (not included in 1943)

When you answer a detail question, use any notes that you have taken to help you identify key terms and details.

According to the lecture, how has the Pledge of Allegiance changed over time?

(A) A phrase was added.

(B) A phrase was amended.

(C) It became controversial.

(D) It became mandatory.

Answer Explanation

Detail questions draw particular information directly from the passage. In the lecture, the professor says that the phrase "under God" was not included in the Pledge in 1943, but "That happened later." In other words, the phrase was included or added later; the answer is Choice A.

Lecture: Purpose Question

Example

In the example below, phrases and terms that help identify the purpose have been underlined. The notes summarize the speaker's reasons for making certain statements.

> **Male Professor (MP):** As part of our discussion about rituals within communities, let's consider the Pledge of Allegiance. As most of you know, standing to recite loyalty to the American flag and "to the republic for which it stands" is a daily ritual in most U.S. public schools. But why is that the case? Well, <u>I would argue that adults and children like saying it.</u>
>
> Usually, school principals come on the intercom and say, "Please stand for the Pledge of Allegiance," and most children probably believe that they have to say it. But they do not. <u>In 1943, the U.S. Supreme Court ruled that the Constitution does not permit forcing people to say anything, including the Pledge.</u>
>
> Now the interesting thing is, kids don't really complain. It is parents who argue about the Pledge, almost exclusively about the phrase "under God." You know, "One nation, under God…" Some people want it out; some want it in. However, when the Supreme Court considered the Pledge in 1943, "under God" wasn't even included in the Pledge yet. That happened later. So <u>the Supreme Court ruled on the broader question of whether people can be forced to say anything, and the court said that no, they can't.</u>
>
> Yet schools continue to make the pledge a part of the daily routine. After all, saying the Pledge gives people a sense of connection to something larger than themselves. <u>I would argue that if they disliked it, the ritual would fade away.</u>

Notes
WHAT information does the speaker use to support his point?

Prof: adults, children like saying Pledge

Sup. Court: Constitution says speech can't be forced (incl. Pledge)

Pledge gives ppl. sense of connect. (something larger)

When you answer the purpose question, use any notes you have taken to help you identify reasons and motivations.

Why does the professor mention the U.S. Constitution?

(A) To explain why students are not legally required to say the Pledge of Allegiance

(B) To criticize the structure of the U.S. government

(C) To argue that reciting the Pledge of Allegiance is the most important American tradition

(D) To point out an important law in U.S. history

Answer Explanation

The professor's overall purpose is to explain that cultural rituals tend to last only if people like them. He mentions the Constitution to explain that the law protects people's right not to say the Pledge, in order to build his case that they continue to say it because they like it. **Choice A** is correct.

Lecture: Inference Question

Example

In the example lecture, phrases and terms that help identify the answer to the inference question below have been underlined. In the example notes, information that can be inferred from the lecture have been summarized.

> **Male Professor (MP):** As part of our discussion about rituals within communities, let's consider the Pledge of Allegiance. As most of you know, standing to recite loyalty to the American flag and "to the republic for which it stands" is a daily ritual in most U.S. public schools. But why is that the case? Well, <u>I would argue that adults and children like saying it.</u>
>
> Usually, school principals come on the intercom and say, "Please stand for the Pledge of Allegiance," and <u>most children probably believe that they have to say it.</u> But they do not. In 1943, the U.S. Supreme Court ruled that the Constitution does not permit forcing people to say anything, including the Pledge.
>
> Now the interesting thing is, <u>kids don't really complain.</u> It is parents who argue about the Pledge, almost exclusively about the phrase "under God." You know, "One nation, under God…" Some people want it out; some want it in. However, when the Supreme Court considered the Pledge in 1943, "under God" wasn't even included in the Pledge yet. That happened later. So the Supreme Court ruled on the broader question of whether people can be forced to say anything, and the court said that no, they can't.
>
> <u>Yet schools continue to make the pledge a part of the daily routine. After all, saying the Pledge gives people a sense of connection to something larger than themselves. I would argue that if they disliked it, the ritual would fade away.</u>

Notes

WHAT does the speaker imply or suggest in the lecture?

Children prob. think they have to say Pledge

not kids, but parents complain;

schools continue routine b/c ppl. feel connected to something bigger; if disliked, it would fade

When you answer an inference question, use any notes that you have taken to help you identify suggestions and implications.

What does the professor imply about cultural rituals?

(A) They are usually established in a nation's constitution.

(B) They are ignored if they are not legally required.

(C) They tend to have positive emotional effects.

(D) They often conflict with common sense.

Answer Explanation

In the final part of the lecture, the professor argues that the Pledge of Allegiance continues to be said in U.S. schools because it "gives people a sense of connection to something larger than themselves." We can infer his point that cultural rituals become traditional if they make people feel better, indicating that the correct answer is **Choice C**.

Actual Practices

CHAPTER 2

Actual Practice Information

In this section, you will listen to a series of academic lectures and campus-related conversations. After each lecture and conversation, you will answer a series of multiple-choice questions about what you have just heard. Multiple-choice questions are worth one point each, and chart-based, "organizing information" questions are worth two points each.

When you take the official TOEFL iBT, you will have 60 to 90 minutes to listen to the lectures and conversations and to answer all the corresponding questions. Because this is the advanced book in the series, you should plan to spend the full 60 to 90 minutes on the Actual Test portion of this book.

	Very Poor	Poor	Good	Very Good	Excellent
Points	1 - 10	11 - 16	17 - 23	24 - 29	30 - 34
Scale	1 - 9	10 - 14	15 - 21	22 - 26	27 - 30

Take notes as you listen to the conversation on **Track 1**. Then answer the multiple-choice questions that follow.

research paper   rough draft

Notes

Circle the letter next to the correct answer or answers to each of the multiple-choice questions below.

1) What are the student and the teaching assistant mainly discussing?
   (A) The student's progress on a research paper
   (B) The teaching assistant's grading policy for work that is turned in late
   (C) Some methods to help the student outline his research paper
   (D) Some recent research that might help the student finish his research paper

2) What problem is the student having with his research paper?
   (A) He lost the rough draft of his research paper.
   (B) He cannot find any books on the topic of his research paper.
   (C) He is having trouble narrowing down his research topic.
   (D) He is finding it difficult to edit his paper down to an appropriate length.

3) Listen to **Track 2**.
   What is the teaching assistant's attitude when she says this?
   (A) Confused
   (B) Overjoyed
   (C) Furious
   (D) Concerned

4) Why does the teaching assistant want to see the student's rough draft?
   (A) To suggest parts that the student could use
   (B) To give the student a grade for the rough draft
   (C) To determine whether or not the student has done enough research
   (D) To proofread the paper for grammar and spelling mistakes

5) What will the student do next?
   (A) Bring his rough draft to the teaching assistant
   (B) Describe the history of minimum wage in the U.S.
   (C) Go to the library to find books for his research paper
   (D) Listen to the teaching assistant describe good writing techniques

Take notes as you listen to the lecture on **Track 3**. Then answer the multiple-choice questions that follow.

Visual Arts

- finger painting
- Ruth Faison Shaw
- liquid starch
- pigment
- iodine

Notes

Circle the letter next to the correct answer or answers to each of the multiple-choice questions below.

1) What is the main topic of the lecture?
   (A) The artwork of America's most famous finger painter
   (B) The history and techniques of finger painting
   (C) How finger painting differs from other styles of painting
   (D) An evaluation of a painting project the class has just completed

2) According the professor, why has finger painting become a popular hobby with adults?
   Choose 2 answers.
   (A) It gives people a chance to spend time with their children.
   (B) It helps people learn to complete sweeping motions with their arms.
   (C) It does not require any training or mastery of technique.
   (D) It allows people to express themselves creatively.

3) According to the professor, what gave Ruth Faison Shaw the idea for finger painting?
   (A) She saw a student put iodine on a bathroom wall with his fingers.
   (B) She saw graffiti on the classroom walls of the school where she taught.
   (C) She used the art form as a type of rehabilitation for her hands.
   (D) She noticed that children's hands were too small to use paint brushes.

4) Listen to **Track 4**.
   What does the professor imply about the technique of finger painting when she says this?
   (A) It is not something of interest to her.
   (B) It goes well with other art styles and forms.
   (C) It requires a lot of work and dedication.
   (D) It is a free and spontaneous activity.

5) According to the professor, which of the following are "guidelines" for finger painting?
   Choose 3 answers.
   (A) Spreading the paint using sweeping movements
   (B) Using as many different colors as possible
   (C) Standing up rather than sitting down while painting
   (D) Making a variety of movements rather than just one movement
   (E) Washing hands, arms, and clothing as soon as possible

6) What does the professor imply about the paint on the students' desks?
   (A) Students who get the paint in their eyes or mouth will become sick.
   (B) It is more colorful and bright than paints used for other art.
   (C) It dries out fairly quickly when uncovered.
   (D) It is difficult to apply to dry paper.

ACTUAL PRACTICE 1

Take notes as you listen to the lecture on **Track 5**. Then answer the multiple-choice questions that follow.

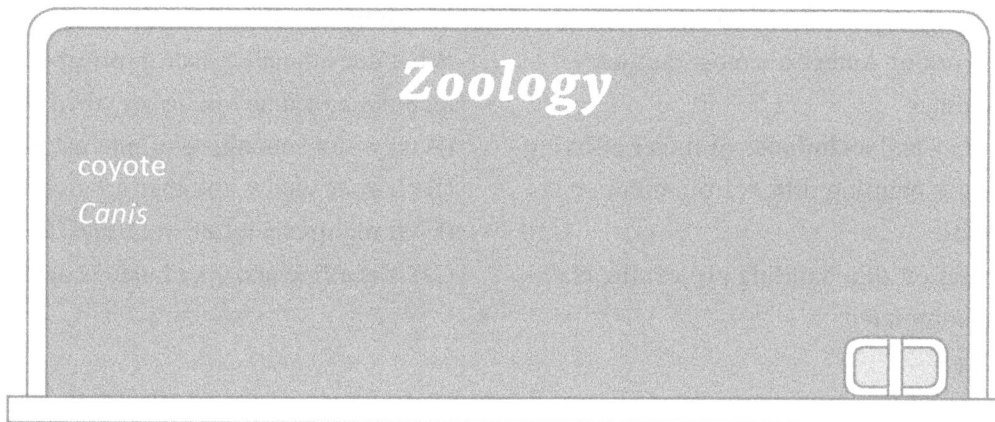

Notes

Circle the letter next to the correct answer or answers to each of the multiple-choice questions below.

1) What is the main topic of the lecture?
   (A) Representations of coyotes in films and legends
   (B) The types of relationships that form between wolves and coyotes
   (C) The types of social groups formed by pack animals
   (D) The physique, environment, and behavior of the coyote

2) According to the professor, what are some similarities between wolves and coyotes?
   Choose 2 answers.
   (A) Both types of animal are approximately the same size and weight.
   (B) Both types of animal belong to the same genus.
   (C) Both types of animal live in similar social groups.
   (D) Both types of animal are nocturnal predators.

3) Why does the professor mention that popular culture often depicts coyotes as solitary predators?
   (A) To address a common misconception about coyotes' social behavior
   (B) To compare the coyote's solitary lifestyle to the wolf's large social groups
   (C) To suggest that coyotes are ineffective predators because they hunt alone
   (D) To describe a characteristic common to many species of nocturnal predators

4) Listen to **Track 6**.
   What does the professor suggest when she says this?
   (A) Arizona and California are home to the largest number of coyote subspecies.
   (B) Coyotes prefer to live near large human populations because they are social animals.
   (C) Coyotes are increasing because they prey on rats and mice in cities.
   (D) The professor has previously discussed the ecological effects of human developments.

5) Based on the lecture, how do coyotes survive successfully in so many different environments?
   (A) They often work with wolves to hunt large prey.
   (B) Their solitary lifestyle means they require little food to survive.
   (C) They have diverse diets and flexible social groups.
   (D) Their nocturnal lifestyle allows them to avoid large predators.

6) According to the student, why are coyote populations increasing today?
   (A) They are well taken care of by nature conservationists.
   (B) They lack natural predators because of human activities.
   (C) They are better at adapting to difficult environments than other predators.
   (D) They are multiplying in the warm climate of the American southwest.

Take notes as you listen to the conversation on **Track 7**. Then answer the multiple-choice questions that follow.

anxiety Advanced Spanish Conversation
sweaty class presentations
transition

Notes

Circle the letter next to the correct answer or answers to each of the multiple-choice questions below.

1) Why does the student visit the professor?
   (A) To ask a question about an upcoming presentation
   (B) To tell her that he finds the class too difficult
   (C) To complain about the rude behavior of another student
   (D) To explain why he has been leaving class early

2) What is the student's opinion of other students in the class?
   (A) He feels that they are not very good at speaking Spanish.
   (B) He finds them intimidating because they are older than he is.
   (C) He thinks that they are rude because they speak too quickly.
   (D) He feels comfortable with them most of the time.

3) Listen to **Track 8**.
   Why does the professor say this?
   (A) To encourage the student to keep putting effort into her class
   (B) To tell the student how he can raise his failing grade
   (C) To explain how to make up for missed class time
   (D) To list some upcoming extra credit opportunities

4) What does the professor recommend that the student do to help with his anxiety?
   Choose 2 answers.
   (A) Arrive to class earlier
   (B) Sit close to the door
   (C) Interact with his classmates
   (D) Retake the class next year

5) What is the professor's attitude toward the student's anxiety issues?
   (A) Alarmed and fearful
   (B) Cold and uncaring
   (C) Sympathetic and understanding
   (D) Angry and reproachful

ACTUAL PRACTICE 2

Take notes as you listen to the lecture on **Track 9**. Then answer the multiple-choice questions that follow.

Ecology

- New Zealand
- endemic
- avian
- flora
- ecological niche
- Maori people
- extinct
- decimation

Notes

Circle the letter next to the correct answer or answers to each of the multiple-choice questions below.

1) What is the main topic of the lecture?
   (A) The effects of an invasive species on an ecosystem
   (B) The differences between Maori and European settlements in New Zealand
   (C) The untimely extinction of the moa bird
   (D) The ecological history of New Zealand

2) Why does the professor mention the Galapagos tortoise at the beginning of the lecture?
   (A) To discuss a species that fills a certain ecological niche
   (B) To give an example of an endemic, island-dwelling species
   (C) To point out ecological similarities between the Galapagos Islands and New Zealand
   (D) To argue that conservation efforts for endangered animals are largely ineffective

3) Why is New Zealand home to numerous endemic species?
   (A) Its extreme temperatures
   (B) Its geographic isolation
   (C) Its small size
   (D) Its abundance of natural resources

4) Why does the professor mention the moa?
   (A) To name an endemic bird species that was driven to extinction by human activities
   (B) To explain why so many bird species thrived in New Zealand
   (C) To name an invasive species that was introduced to New Zealand by European settlers
   (D) To name a type of bird that is of particular interest to modern ecologists

5) According to the lecture, which of the following are causes of extinction for endemic bird species in New Zealand?
   Choose 3 answers.
   (A) Spread of disease
   (B) Overhunting
   (C) Habitat loss
   (D) Climate change
   (E) Invasive species

6) What is the professor's opinion of humans' impact on New Zealand's ecosystem?
   (A) Human settlement of New Zealand has affected a few native bird species.
   (B) Humans' introduction of invasive species has actually improved conditions for some native species.
   (C) Recent conservation efforts have reversed nearly all the damage done by early settlers.
   (D) Maori and European settlers have irreversibly damaged New Zealand's ecosystem.

Take notes as you listen to the lecture on **Track 10**. Then answer the multiple-choice questions that follow.

Music History

jazz music
syncopation
a solo

improvisation
the Gettysburg Address

Notes

Circle the letter next to the correct answer or answers to each of the multiple-choice questions below.

1) What is the main purpose of the lecture?
   (A) To discuss the reasons for jazz's increasing popularity
   (B) To point out common features of most jazz compositions
   (C) To describe some unique characteristics of jazz music
   (D) To argue that jazz is the most diverse genre of music

2) Listen to **Track 11**.
   What does the professor suggest when he says this?
   (A) He does not think that many students understand the definition of art.
   (B) Hamburgers and French fries are often associated with the United States.
   (C) Hamburgers and French fries are often depicted in American art.
   (D) Creating good fast food is similar to creating good art.

3) Listen to **Track 12**.
   Why does the professor say this?
   (A) To point out reasons that jazz appeals to many people
   (B) To show that jazz fusion is very similar to rock 'n roll
   (C) To argue that the quality of jazz music declined in the 1970s
   (D) To explain that jazz music uses a wide variety of instruments

4) Why does the professor mention President Lincoln's Gettysburg Address in the discussion?
   (A) To talk about the period in American history when jazz music began
   (B) To help students understand a feature of jazz music
   (C) To discuss a famous American who appreciated jazz music
   (D) To show the similarities between public speaking and jazz music

5) How is improvisation in jazz different from improvisation in other musical styles?
   (A) It is based on more complex ideas.
   (B) It is more central to jazz compositions.
   (C) It has no relationship to the song itself.
   (D) It is only played by one musician.

6) How does the professor illustrate the concept of improvisation?
   (A) He plays a piece of jazz music for the class.
   (B) He talks about a famous American speech.
   (C) He reads a passage from a textbook.
   (D) He encourages one of his students to create a solo.

Take notes as you listen to the conversation on **Track 13**. Then answer the multiple-choice questions that follow.

- upper-division class
- homework schedule
- veterinarian (vet)
- lower-division class
- prerequisites
- self-discipline

Notes

Circle the letter next to the correct answer or answers to each of the multiple-choice questions below..

1) Why does the student go to see the professor?
   (A) To ask about extra credit opportunities to raise her grade
   (B) To ask for a letter of recommendation for veterinary school
   (C) To talk about dropping the professor's difficult class
   (D) To ask for advice about improving her grade in the class

2) Listen to **Track 14**.
   What does the professor mean when he says this?
   (A) Sophia should study rather than walk in the park.
   (B) The lower-division classes are difficult.
   (C) The lower-division classes are as easy as walking.
   (D) The University has many nice parks.

3) Why does the student want to do well in the professor's chemistry class?
   (A) To keep her academic scholarship
   (B) To impress the professor
   (C) To get a PhD in chemistry
   (D) To get into veterinary school

4) What does the professor suggest that Sophia do to succeed in his class?
   (A) She should drop the class now and enroll when she feels better prepared.
   (B) She should come to his office hours to receive extra help and tutoring.
   (C) She should break down the assignments into a study plan and follow it carefully.
   (D) She should form a study group with other students from the class.

5) What does the professor imply about his upper-division class, Chemistry 201?
   (A) Most students drop the class.
   (B) Most students find it very difficult.
   (C) It is only available to graduate students.
   (D) It is as easy as some lower-division classes.

Take notes as you listen to the lecture on **Track 15**. Then answer the multiple-choice questions that follow.

Education

- progressive education
- slate
- manuscript
- schoolhouse
- monastery
- John Dewey

Notes

Circle the letter next to the correct answer or answers to each of the multiple-choice questions below.

1) What is the main topic of the lecture?
   (A) Radical changes brought about by steam-powered technology
   (B) Typical American education in the 19th century
   (C) The ideas of American philosopher John Dewey
   (D) Two opposing approaches to education in the U.S. since 1880

2) According to the professor, how did 19th century students use slates?
   (A) They practiced penmanship and arithmetic.
   (B) They wrote their own songs and poems.
   (C) They practiced Latin and copied ancient manuscripts.
   (D) They took notes on information from lectures.

3) In the lecture, why does the professor mention medieval European monasteries?
   (A) To suggest that strict school discipline started in monasteries
   (B) To explain a historical source of the 19th century emphasis on rote learning
   (C) To imply that American 19th century schools were overly religious
   (D) To express the atmosphere and feeling of 19th century schools in the U.S.

4) What can be inferred about supporters of progressive education and democracy?
   (A) They wanted American classrooms to teach more democratic principles.
   (B) They thought that American democracy was weak.
   (C) They believed that progressive education would help citizens vote wisely.
   (D) They thought progressive education was called for in the U.S. Constitution.

5) According to the lecture, which of the following societal changes contributed to the Progressive Education movement?
   Choose 3 answers.
   (A) People were educating their daughters as well as their sons.
   (B) More people were living in cities.
   (C) More than ever, people needed to know how to read.
   (D) Paper, pencils, and books were more available.

6) How does the professor organize the lecture?
   (A) He describes how teachers can use a particular educational approach.
   (B) He provides data about outcomes, and then he draws a conclusion.
   (C) He gives his own opinion about an issue and explains his personal experiences.
   (D) He gives a brief historical background of an issue, and asks for current examples.

Take notes as you listen to the lecture on **Track 16**. Then answer the multiple-choice questions that follow.

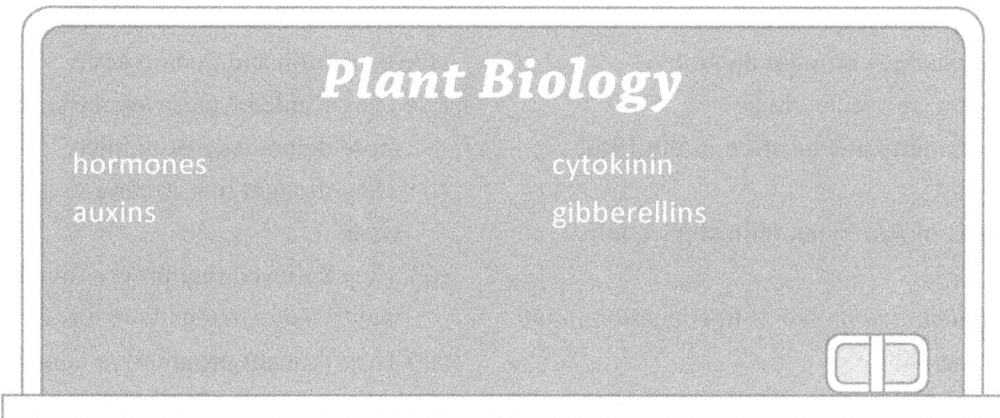

Notes

Circle the letter next to the correct answer or answers to each of the multiple-choice questions below.

1) What is the main purpose of the lecture?
   (A) To differentiate hormones from other chemical messengers
   (B) To discuss the functions of hormones in plants
   (C) To argue that plant growth is possible without hormones
   (D) To show that hormones affect every plant differently

2) According to the professor, what is true of hormones?
   (A) They are produced in one part of an organism but affect a different part.
   (B) They are most active when the plant begins its reproductive cycle.
   (C) They are usually produced artificially by scientists in laboratories.
   (D) They function like chemicals but are actually cells.

3) What can be inferred about cytokinins from the lecture information?
   (A) They are produced in a plant's leaf cells.
   (B) They are only active in plants that do not receive sufficient sunlight.
   (C) They are most active in young, developing plants.
   (D) They were the last type of hormone to be identified by scientists.

4) Why does the professor mention career and guidance counselors in the discussion?
   (A) To compare a plant hormone to something more familiar to students
   (B) To encourage his students to seek guidance before choosing a job
   (C) To claim that working with hormones in any organism can be dangerous
   (D) To tell the students how he first became interested in studying hormones

5) The professor talks about three main types of hormones found in plants.

Check each box where the description in the left column matches the hormone in the top row.

	Auxins	Cytokinins	Gibberellins
Cause the seeds and flowers of plants to grow			
Cause the stems and roots of plants to grow			
Control and direct cell division in plants			

Take notes as you listen to the conversation on **Track 17**. Then answer the multiple-choice questions that follow.

- internship
- public policy
- letter of recommendation
- non-profit agency
- Geneva, Switzerland
- microcosm

Notes

Circle the letter next to the correct answer or answers to each of the multiple-choice questions below.

1) Why does the student need to see the professor?
   (A) To complain about a grade he received in a class
   (B) To ask the professor for a letter of recommendation
   (C) To receive help on a paper for the professor's class
   (D) To apply for an upcoming internship

2) What does the student tell the professor about his major at the university?
   (A) He has changed his major from psychology to political science.
   (B) He has changed his major from political science to environmental science.
   (C) He is majoring in language studies, with an emphasis on the Korean language.
   (D) He is currently majoring in anthropology, but he wants to switch to sociology.

3) What does the professor imply about Geneva, Switzerland?
   (A) It currently faces many environmental issues.
   (B) Most people there speak Korean and French.
   (C) It is a good place to study political science.
   (D) Most people there are political science students.

4) How is the student preparing for the study abroad program and internship in Switzerland?
   Choose 2 answers.
   (A) He is volunteering at a local nonprofit organization
   (B) He is learning to speak French.
   (C) He is learning to speak Korean.
   (D) He is applying for scholarships and financial aid.

5) Listen to **Track 18**.
   Why does the student say this?
   (A) To tell the professor that he enjoys gambling
   (B) To shift the topic of discussion back to Geneva
   (C) To imply that he has already taken the professor's class
   (D) To express enthusiasm regarding the professor's upcoming class

Take notes as you listen to the lecture on **Track 19**. Then answer the multiple-choice questions that follow.

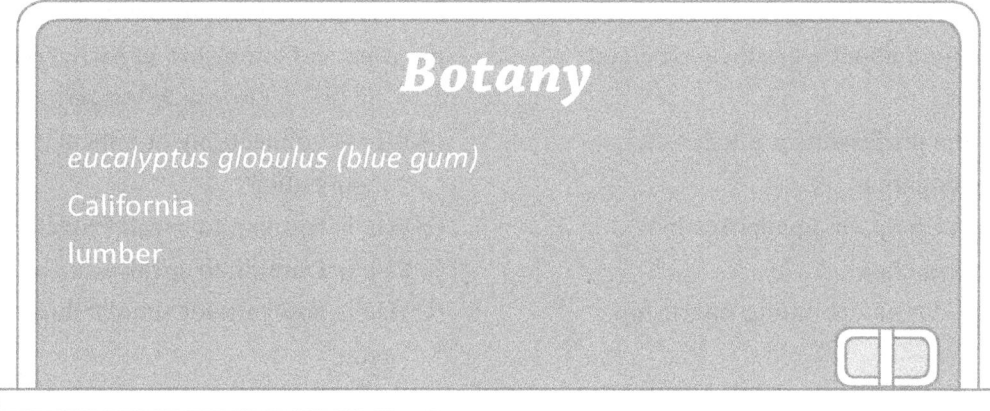

Botany

eucalyptus globulus (blue gum)
California
lumber

Notes

Circle the letter next to the correct answer or answers to each of the multiple-choice questions below.

1) What is the main topic of the discussion?
   (A) The places that the eucalyptus tree grows outside of Australia
   (B) The reasons that Australian immigrants brought eucalyptus trees to California
   (C) The botanical characteristics and industrial uses of eucalyptus trees
   (D) The differences among redwoods, Douglas firs, and eucalyptus trees

2) Why does the professor mention Douglas fir pine and redwood trees?
   (A) To contrast the growth of these trees to that of eucalyptus trees
   (B) To name types of trees planted on campus near eucalyptus trees
   (C) To show which trees are in the same genealogical family as eucalyptus trees
   (D) To relate information from another lecture to information in today's lecture

3) Listen to **Track 20**.
   What does the professor mean when he says this?
   (A) Eucalyptus trees are dangerous and should be avoided.
   (B) Eucalyptus trees poison the water that they save.
   (C) Adaptations for saving water have made the tree dangerous.
   (D) Eucalyptus trees are important in California because they save water.

4) According to the lecture, which feature of eucalyptus trees helps them prevent evaporation?
   (A) Their thick bark
   (B) The caps on their flowers
   (C) The depth of their roots
   (D) The direction of their leaves

5) Why did many people stop planting blue gum eucalyptus trees in the early 20th century?
   (A) Blue gums required too much water to keep alive.
   (B) The wood from blue gums made for inadequate lumber.
   (C) Blue gums could not withstand the hot, dry conditions in California.
   (D) The wood from blue gums was too heavy to ship long distances.

6) Why did settlers plant eucalyptus trees in California during the 19th and 20th centuries?
   Choose 2 answers.
   (A) To replace wood that had burned down in forest fires
   (B) To shield crops from intense sunlight
   (C) To protect crops and buildings from strong winds
   (D) To extract oils that can be used in certain medicines

Take notes as you listen to the lecture on **Track 21**. Then answer the multiple-choice questions that follow.

Paleontology

Laetoli
Australopithecus afarensis
hominid
hominidae

Notes

Circle the letter next to the correct answer or answers to each of the multiple-choice questions below.

1) What is the main topic of the lecture?
   (A) The stages of evolution that led to bipedal locomotion in hominids
   (B) A biography of influential archaeologist Mary Leakey
   (C) The discovery of fossils that may help explain hominid evolution
   (D) The environmental impact of volcanic eruptions in Tanzania on hominid species

2) Which of the following are true about the fossilized footprints found at Laetoli?
   Choose 2 answers.
   (A) They were preserved by an unusual series of events.
   (B) They were probably made by more than one hominid creature.
   (C) They are approximately 6 million years old.
   (D) They are older than the hominid fossils found at the same site.

3) Which captures the correct series of events at the Laetoli site, according to the professor?
   (A) Animals walked—sun came out—volcano erupted—rain fell—volcano erupted
   (B) Sun came out—animals walked—rain fell—volcano erupted—volcano erupted
   (C) Volcano erupted—rain fell—Animals walked—sun came out—volcano erupted
   (D) Rain fell—animals walked—volcano erupted—sun came out—volcano erupted

4) Why does the professor mention bipedal locomotion in the passage?
   (A) To explain how *Australopithecus afarensis* survived Tanzania's volcanic eruptions
   (B) To point out that Leakey was the first person to use this term in her research
   (C) To differentiate *Australopithecus afarensis* from modern humans
   (D) To highlight an important characteristic of the fossilized footprints

5) Why did Mary Leakey cover the Laetoli site with sand in 1979?
   (A) To prevent other scientists from taking pictures of it
   (B) To keep it a secret from the world until she was ready to share it
   (C) To maintain the site for future investigation
   (D) To utilize a new technology that required the site to be covered

6) Listen to **Track 22**.
   What does the professor suggest when he says this?
   (A) Vegetation is the biggest threat to all fossil sites.
   (B) Once uncovered, fossil sites are difficult to preserve.
   (C) Rival archaeologists attempted to steal the fossil evidence.
   (D) Leakey did not care about preserving the hominid footprints.

Take notes as you listen to the conversation on **Track 23**. Then answer the multiple-choice questions that follow.

shared rental dormitories
utilities landlord
bus route parking permit
cleaning deposit

Notes

Circle the letter next to the correct answer or answers to each of the multiple-choice questions below.

1) Why does the man start a conversation with the woman?
   (A) To find out about living in the dormitories
   (B) To suggest that they share a rented house
   (C) To talk about what costs to consider when renting
   (D) To ask about another friend named Ashley

2) Listen to **Track 24.**
   What does the woman imply when she says this?
   (A) The two speakers are completely alike.
   (B) The two speakers would be able to do their homework together.
   (C) The two speakers should be able to live together peacefully.
   (D) The two speakers have known each other well for a long time.

3) Why does the man suggest looking for a three-bedroom house instead of an apartment?
   (A) To split expenses between three or four people
   (B) To get a rental closer to campus
   (C) To have a place for both speakers to park their cars
   (D) To have a dining room or a study room

4) What does the woman imply about choosing where to live?
   (A) Few rentals are near bus stops.
   (B) Some rentals are along streets with too much traffic.
   (C) Places with free parking might be better deals.
   (D) Rents may be higher closer to campus.

5) Why does the woman's friend, Ashley, want to move?

   Choose 2 answers.

   (A) Her roommates are graduating and moving away.
   (B) She needs to find a place with lower rent.
   (C) She wants to live with different friends.
   (D) She wants to live in a pet-friendly place.

6) What does the man say about cats?
   (A) They require a bigger cleaning deposit and too many other expenses.
   (B) They are very cute, and they act bossy.
   (C) They seem wild, but they like attention from their owners.
   (D) They are mysterious, and they are fun to watch.

Take notes as you listen to the lecture on **Track 25**. Then answer the multiple-choice questions that follow.

U.S. History

indentured servitude   Powhatan Confederacy
debtor's prison

Notes

Circle the letter next to the correct answer or answers to each of the multiple-choice questions below.

1) What is the lecture mainly about?
   (A) The history of tobacco farming
   (B) Life in 17th century British colonies
   (C) Why and how a labor system developed
   (D) Consequences of a population explosion

2) Why does the professor mention labor-intensive crops?
   (A) To explain the demand for indentured servants
   (B) To describe effects of crops introduced by native tribes
   (C) To emphasize the difficulty of the indentured servants' work
   (D) To illustrate the challenges of living in a colony

3) Listen to **Track 26**.
   Why does the professor say this?
   (A) To criticize a political speech
   (B) To point out the importance of freedom
   (C) To praise a historical labor system
   (D) To exclaim about an irony

4) What was one reason people chose to become indentured servants?
   (A) They could learn a useful trade
   (B) They could avoid prison
   (C) They could experience a new culture
   (D) They could become wealthy

5) Listen to **Track 27**.
   What can be inferred about indentured servants from this?
   (A) They were often seasick during the journey.
   (B) They assumed they would outlive their contracts.
   (C) They began their work before they left Europe.
   (D) They wanted to become Americans.

6) Why did indentured servants often die before they earned their freedom?
   Choose 2 answers.
   (A) Their masters farmed tobacco instead of food.
   (B) Their freedom was delayed as a form of punishment.
   (C) Their needs for food, shelter, and rest were not met.
   (D) They received land that was not very fertile for farming.

Take notes as you listen to the lecture on **Track 28**. Then answer the multiple-choice questions that follow.

Geology

- solution cave
- Mammoth-Flint Ridge Cave
- limestone
- saturated
- susceptible

Notes

Circle the letter next to the correct answer or answers to each of the multiple-choice questions below.

1) What is the main topic of the lecture?
   (A) Why caves collapse over long periods of time
   (B) How a certain type of cave is formed
   (C) The difference between small caves and large caves
   (D) The kinds of rocks and minerals found in caves

2) Listen to **Track 29**.
   What does the professor suggest when she says this?
   (A) People did not explore or use caves until recently.
   (B) Caves are difficult to explore because of their darkness.
   (C) Many cave systems remain undiscovered.
   (D) Frequent tunnel collapses make mapping caves difficult.

3) What do scientists call caves that form in limestone?
   (A) Mammoth-Flint systems
   (B) Saturated zones
   (C) Carbon dioxide caves
   (D) Solution caves

4) Listen to **Track 30**.
   Why does the professor say this?
   (A) To address a common misconception about cave formation
   (B) To show that most people are fairly knowledgeable about cave formation
   (C) To suggest that limestone is a special type of rock
   (D) To compare limestone to other rocks that are involved in cave formation

5) According to the professor, how do entrances to caves form?
   Choose 2 answers.
   (A) The rock part above a cave collapses and forms a sinkhole.
   (B) A stream flows through the side of a cave on a hillside.
   (C) The water table floods the cave creating many entrances.
   (D) An animal makes a hole in a cave for its home.

6) Based on the lecture information, what is probably true about limestone?
   (A) It is often used to build houses.
   (B) It is a fairly common type of rock.
   (C) It is an extremely valuable type of rock.
   (D) It is found in abundance near all cave systems.

Take notes as you listen to the conversation on **Track 31**. Then answer the multiple-choice questions that follow.

emergency surgery independent study
studio arts dean
appendix

Notes

Circle the letter next to the correct answer or answers to each of the multiple-choice questions below.

1) Why does the student visit the professor?
   (A) To tell him that she must drop his class
   (B) To explain why she will miss his class next week
   (C) To ask him if she can enroll in his art class
   (D) To complain about the class's difficult enrollment process

2) Why does the student mention her recent surgery?
   (A) To explain why she has been leaving his class early
   (B) To explain why she did not submit a project
   (C) To explain why her paintings have been inadequate
   (D) To explain why she has not sorted out her scheduling issues

3) What does the professor imply about his painting class, Art 209-A?
   (A) It is a very popular class.
   (B) It is offered twice yearly.
   (C) It is a very time-consuming class.
   (D) It is the first class in a two-year series.

4) Listen to **Track 32**.
   What is the professor's tone in this part of the conversation?
   (A) Apathetic
   (B) Apologetic
   (C) Defensive
   (D) Confused

5) Why does the student want to take the professor's class?
   Choose 2 answers.
   (A) The class is part of a series that the student wants to take.
   (B) The class is worth more credits than other art classes.
   (C) The student must take the class in order to graduate.
   (D) The student has heard that the professor is an excellent teacher.

Take notes as you listen to the lecture on **Track 33**. Then answer the multiple-choice questions that follow.

American Literature

- postmodernism
- music videos
- "Thriller"
- "Vogue"
- MTV
- Michael Jackson
- Madonna
- YouTube

Notes

Circle the letter next to the correct answer or answers to each of the multiple-choice questions below.

1) What is the main topic of the lecture?
   (A) The popularity of MTV
   (B) Groundbreaking music videos
   (C) A definition of "postmodern"
   (D) A short history of television

2) Why does the professor mention the publication of *TV Guide*?
   (A) To illustrate the limited choices available at the time
   (B) To discuss an example of postmodern expression
   (C) To point to the source of new ideas in television programming
   (D) To describe how MTV communicated with its audience

3) According to the professor, how are talk shows and omniscient narrators alike?
   (A) They both must make use of emotional language.
   (B) They interact with multiple people.
   (C) They stay in the background of more colorful celebrities and characters.
   (D) They make selections and decisions for the audience.

4) What does the professor say about images in music videos?
   (A) Their meaning is often unclear.
   (B) They tend to be blurry and shadowy.
   (C) They often involve mimicking movie stars.
   (D) They became more linear over time.

5) Why does the professor discuss the Internet?
   (A) To introduce a new topic
   (B) To expand a metaphor
   (C) To voice his support and enthusiasm for websites such as YouTube
   (D) To predict the post-Internet frontier

6) What is the professor's attitude toward postmodernism?
   (A) bewildered
   (B) pessimistic
   (C) bored
   (D) enthusiastic

Take notes as you listen to the lecture on **Track 34**. Then answer the multiple-choice questions that follow.

Notes

Circle the letter next to the correct answer or answers to each of the multiple-choice questions below.

1) What is the main topic of the lecture?
   (A) Different species of parasitic wasps
   (B) Diseases that affect moths and butterflies
   (C) A rare protozoan that infests fleas
   (D) Epiparasites and their hosts

2) Why does the professor mention fleas?
   (A) To give an example of a parasite with its own parasites
   (B) To explain why cats and dogs have persistent itching problems
   (C) To make an analogy to the braconid and chalcid wasps
   (D) To urge his students to treat their pets with flea medication

3) According to the professor, why are braconid wasps successful?
   (A) They have parasites of their own.
   (B) They infest a wide-ranging order of insects.
   (C) They have evolved to prevent parasitic infestation.
   (D) They are a reliable source of energy.

4) What does the professor imply about mistletoe?
   (A) It is a rare parasitic plant.
   (B) It has a large number of host plants.
   (C) All varieties are epiparasites.
   (D) Some varieties are not parasites.

5) Match each description with the correct term.

Write a check in each box where the characteristic matches the term.

	Lepidoptera	Braconid Wasp	Chalcid Wasp
Hosts parasites			
Is a parasite			
Its host is a parasite			

Take notes as you listen to the conversation on **Track 35**. Then answer the multiple-choice questions that follow.

- discussion section
- syllabus
- recuperate
- Portuguese empire
- research paper
- sugar cane
- Portugal

Notes

Circle the letter next to the correct answer or answers to each of the multiple-choice questions below.

1) Why does the student visit the teaching assistant?
   (A) To find out what was discussed in a lecture that she missed
   (B) To tell him that she must miss a large amount of class
   (C) To ask for a copy of the class syllabus
   (D) To discuss the length of an upcoming paper

2) Listen to **Track 36**.
   Why does the teaching assistant say this?
   (A) To complain about the university's scheduling system
   (B) To explain how many weeks of class are left
   (C) To make sure that the student understands the university's scheduling system
   (D) To emphasize how much class time the student will miss

3) Where does the teaching assistant tell the student to find look for assignments?
   (A) The class syllabus
   (B) The professor's Power Point presentations
   (C) The class textbook
   (D) The email sent by the teaching assistant

4) What does the teaching assistant imply about writing a paper on sugar cane production?
   (A) He finds the topic tedious and boring.
   (B) Some students' papers will be hundreds of pages long.
   (C) There is an abundance of information on the topic.
   (D) All necessary information on the topic is in a Power Point presentation.

5) Why does the student need to maintain good grades?
   (A) To keep her scholarship
   (B) To apply to law schools
   (C) To please her injured mother
   (D) To go to graduate school for history

Take notes as you listen to the lecture on **Track 37**. Then answer the multiple-choice questions that follow.

Environmental Studies

- flood irrigation
- sprinkler irrigation
- desalination
- subirrigation
- water table

Notes

Circle the letter next to the correct answer or answers to each of the multiple-choice questions below.

1) What is the professor mainly discussing?
   (A) How to grow rice and alfalfa
   (B) Methods for diverting a resource
   (C) Reasons that people should not irrigate crops
   (D) Smarter ways to irrigate during a drought

2) What conditions make flood irrigation undesirable?

   Choose 2 answers.

   (A) Salts in the soil
   (B) Heavy clay soil
   (C) Expensive water
   (D) Light rainfall

3) Why does the professor mention "huge wheels"?
   (A) To discuss how a power source functions in sprinkler systems
   (B) To illustrate the concept of sprinkler system radius
   (C) To emphasize on of the main benefits of sprinkler irrigation
   (D) To describe how elevated sprinkler systems are moved

4) What can be inferred about places where sprinklers are "not feasible"?
   (A) They are always flooded
   (B) They are planted with crops susceptible to mold.
   (C) They have too many trenches.
   (D) They have less modern infrastructure.

5) Why does the student mention strawberry crops?
   (A) To ask about the best method for irrigating strawberries
   (B) To suggest an example of horizontal subirrigation
   (C) To introduce a new topic in the discussion
   (D) To explain why he thinks subirrigation is better than sprinkler irrigation

6) What does the professor suggest about irrigation?
   (A) It should only be used where the soil is sandy.
   (B) Subirrigation is a fairly wasteful method.
   (C) In general, farms should avoid irrigating and only plant where rain is plentiful.
   (D) The "best" system for a given farm depends on many factors.

Take notes as you listen to the lecture on **Track 38**. Then answer the multiple-choice questions that follow.

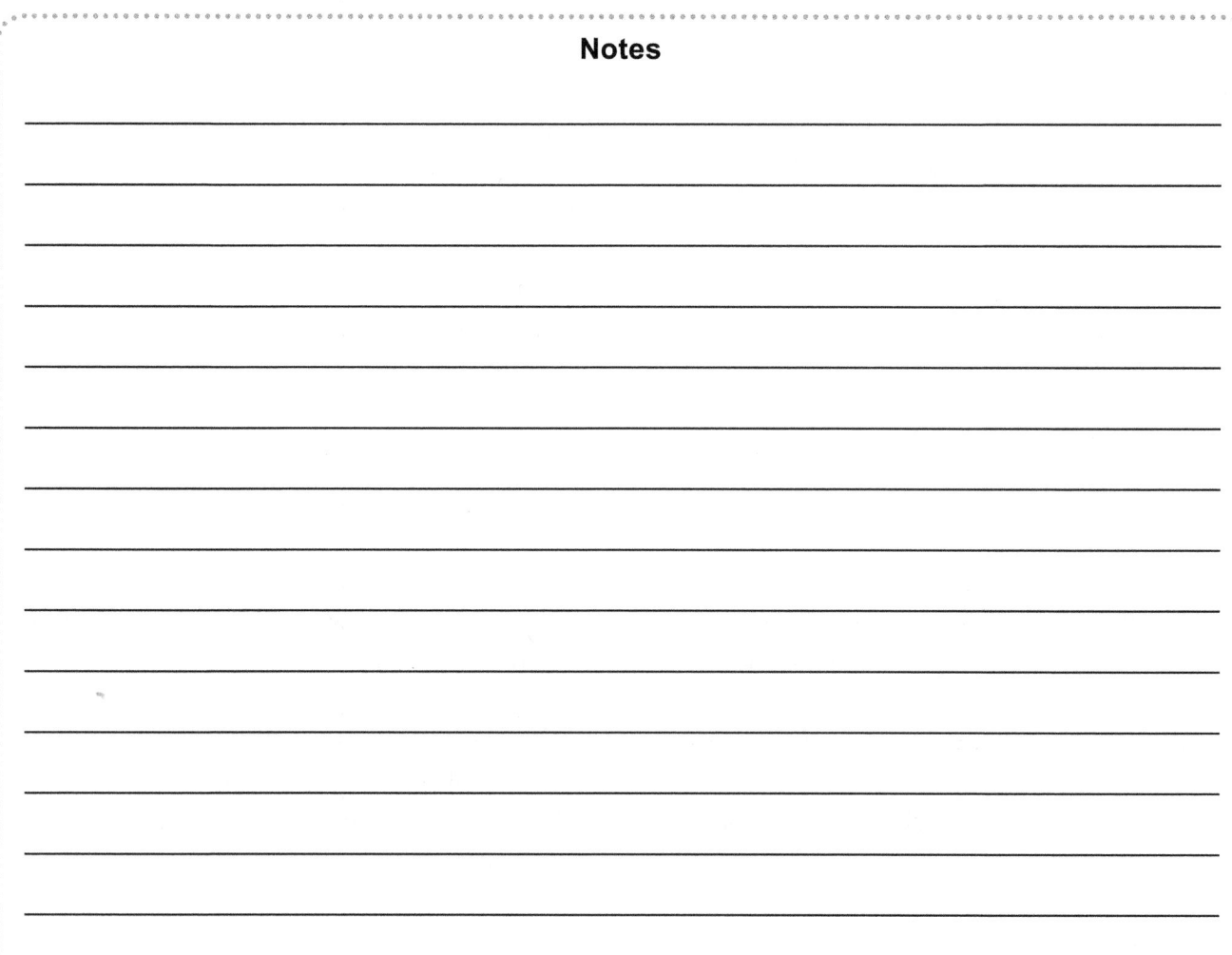

Business

Arcadia, California
hot dog stand
McDonald brothers
"Speedee Service System"

San Bernadino, California
Baby Boom
Ray Kroc
franchise

Notes

Circle the letter next to the correct answer or answers to each of the multiple-choice questions below.

1) What topic does the professor mainly discuss?
   (A) The origins of a specific fast food restaurant in the United States
   (B) How fast food restaurants changed under the franchise system
   (C) What happens when fast food restaurants are owned by family members
   (D) The use of bargaining in the original fast food model

2) Why does the professor mention the automaker Henry Ford in the lecture?
   (A) To compare the McDonald brothers to another great business leader
   (B) To explain that the McDonald brothers original restaurant revolved around cars
   (C) To tell who inspired the McDonald brothers to create their fast food concept
   (D) To give an example of someone who bought a McDonald's franchise

3) Which of the following are features of the original McDonald's fast food restaurant?
   Choose 2 answers.
   (A) Its limited number of menu items were prepared in advance.
   (B) It served only chicken, which was prepared in several different ways.
   (C) It used paper bags and cups instead of silver utensils and china plates.
   (D) It served all menu items in an all-you-can-eat buffet style.

4) What is the professor's opinion of Ray Kroc in the lecture?
   (A) He was a kind salesman who helped McDonald's succeed.
   (B) He was an ambitious and aggressive businessman.
   (C) He was a creative businessman who was cheated by the McDonald brothers.
   (D) He was responsible for investing in the first McDonald's restaurant.

5) Why did the McDonald brothers have a difficult relationship with Ray Kroc?
   Choose 2 answers.
   (A) He never paid them for the first franchise that he opened.
   (B) He unsuccessfully tried to place a McDonald's in Disneyland.
   (C) He recreated a new history of McDonald's, leaving the brothers out of it.
   (D) He purposely competed with their original store.

6) Listen to **Track 39**.
   What does the professor mean when she says this?
   (A) She does not think she can fill the class period with this topic.
   (B) She has a great deal of information to share.
   (C) She needs to know if the students have any questions.
   (D) She wants to include details that students may not know.

Take notes as you listen to the conversation on **Track 40**. Then answer the multiple-choice questions that follow.

Mandarin
course description
department chair
declare a minor

Notes

Circle the letter next to the correct answer or answers to each of the multiple-choice questions below.

1) Why does the student visit the advisor?
   (A) To ask about changing her major
   (B) To complain about the chemistry department
   (C) To submit a review of her recent course
   (D) To file an application to drop a class

2) What does the advisor imply about declaring a minor?
   (A) Declaring a minor will allow the student to graduate early.
   (B) It is a difficult and tedious process.
   (C) It will require the student to change her courses.
   (D) It might be easier than changing majors.

3) Which of the following classes does the student need to take in order to complete the Chinese Studies major?
   Choose 2 answers.
   (A) Advanced Mandarin
   (B) Introductory Mandarin
   (C) Consumer Chemistry
   (D) Modern Chinese Culture

4) Listen to **Track 41**.
   Why does the student say this?
   (A) To explain the reasons she wants to change majors
   (B) To suggest that the course description was incomplete
   (C) To complain about the general education requirements at the university
   (D) To emphasize her concern about being able to graduate on time

5) Why is the student interested in studying Chinese?
   (A) She has many family members who speak Mandarin.
   (B) She plans to move to China after graduating from the university.
   (C) She was bored with the English Literature major.
   (D) She thinks it will be helpful for her future career.

Take notes as you listen to the lecture on **Track 42**. Then answer the multiple-choice questions that follow.

Geography

the Dead Sea
the Jordan River

Notes

Circle the letter next to the correct answer or answers to each of the multiple-choice questions below.

1) What is the main topic of the lecture?
   (A) The processes that lead to the formation of seas
   (B) The physical makeup and historical background of the Dead Sea
   (C) The reasons that the Dead Sea interests global warming climatologists
   (D) The ways that the Dead Sea supports local economies

2) Why does the professor mention Death Valley in the lecture?
   (A) To give students an idea of how far below sea level the Dead Sea lies
   (B) To compare the climate of the Dead Sea to that of Death Valley
   (C) To explain that Death Valley and the Dead Sea formed at same time
   (D) To compare tourism of Death Valley to that of the Dead Sea

3) Which of the following have resulted from the high mineral content of the Dead Sea?
   Choose 2 answers.
   (A) People believe that the Dead Sea's waters have health-promoting qualities.
   (B) Large, mineral-absorbing plants grow on the Dead Sea's shores.
   (C) Few fish or plants can survive in the Dead Sea's mineral-rich waters.
   (D) Swimming in the Dead Sea darkens a person's skin.

4) What does the professor imply about the water level of the Dead Sea?
   (A) It is rapidly increasing because of the flooding of the Jordan River.
   (B) It is gradually decreasing because of global warming.
   (C) It has remained unchanged since Biblical times.
   (D) It is rapidly decreasing due to rising salt and mineral levels.

5) According to the professor, how did the Dead Sea probably form?
   (A) A glacier melted during the last ice age, creating a new feature in the area.
   (B) Intense rainfall 2,000 years ago created a landlocked body of water.
   (C) A volcanic explosion millions of years ago produced a split in Earth's crust.
   (D) An earthquake 10,000 years ago forced the Jordan River to change course.

6) What point does the professor make when he mentions the story of Sodom and Gomorrah?
   (A) Archeologists have discovered remains of those cities near the Dead Sea.
   (B) The Dead Sea received its name because of the events relayed in the story.
   (C) Christians often visit the Dead Sea because they believe that it is a sacred location.
   (D) Salt formations near the Dead Sea help explain the origin of one aspect of the story.

Take notes as you listen to the lecture on **Track 43**. Then answer the multiple-choice questions that follow.

World History

Spanish Flu pandemic

World War I

Notes

Circle the letter next to the correct answer or answers to each of the multiple-choice questions below.

1) What is the main topic of the lecture?
   (A) The development of the first successful vaccine
   (B) An epidemic during the early 20th century
   (C) An overview of common viral infections
   (D) The relationship between international conflict and disease

2) What made the Spanish flu unique among influenza viruses?
   (A) It mostly affected the very old and the very young.
   (B) It affected more men than women.
   (C) It did not affect humans but was deadly to pigs and chickens.
   (D) It most strongly affected healthy adults with good immune systems.

3) Listen to **Track 44**.
   Why does the professor say this?
   (A) To explain that the Spanish Flu caused the Bubonic Plague
   (B) To emphasize the deadliness of the Spanish Flu
   (C) To argue that the Bubonic Plague was not very serious
   (D) To point out that the Bubonic Plague occurred 100 years after the Spanish Flu

4) How did the Spanish Flu probably first infect soldiers fighting in World War I?
   (A) It thrived in the unsanitary conditions of most military hospitals.
   (B) It was transmitted by birds, and it mutated to affect humans.
   (C) It grew in soldiers' food rations, causing illness when consumed.
   (D) It was accidentally spread during attempts to vaccinate soldiers.

5) Why did the Spanish Flu move so quickly around the world?
   (A) Strong winds spread the virus across the oceans
   (B) The countries in World War I were experimenting with biological germ warfare.
   (C) The virus was transmitted in letters that soldiers sent to their families.
   (D) New methods of transportation were moving people around more quickly.

6) What does the professor imply about the Spanish Flu?
   (A) It was most harmful to young children and pregnant women.
   (B) It could have been controlled by eliminating chicken and pigs from diets.
   (C) Doctors and scientists still do not know a lot about it.
   (D) Military doctors are responsible for its spreading to the United States.

Take notes as you listen to the conversation on **Track 45**. Then answer the multiple-choice questions that follow.

Recreation Department   spring break

Notes

Circle the letter next to the correct answer or answers to each of the multiple-choice questions below.

1) Why does the student visit the university employee?
   (A) To sign up for a recreation class for the spring semester
   (B) To get a locker and a lock so she can use the campus recreation facilities
   (C) To ask about trips sponsored by the recreation department
   (D) To change her major to Parks and Recreation Management

2) How did the student learn about the spring break trips?
   (A) She saw an advertisement on the campus website.
   (B) Her mother went on similar trips when she was a student.
   (C) She and her friend heard someone talking about the trips.
   (D) Her English professor suggested that students take a trip to relax.

3) What type of trip is the student interested in?
   (A) A trip to a warm location
   (B) A trip to the rainforest to watch birds
   (C) A trip to the mountains for skiing
   (D) A trip to Greece to see Greek ruins

4) According to the staff person, what is the most important factor for most students when deciding where to travel?
   (A) How much the trip costs
   (B) If the trip requires inoculations
   (C) Which language is spoken in the place they will be visiting
   (D) How many students are going on the trip

5) Why does the university employee mention trips to Florida, North Carolina, and California?
   (A) To list his favorite trips
   (B) To list all the trips located near beaches
   (C) To list the trips located in the warmest locations.
   (D) To list some of the most affordable trips

Take notes as you listen to the lecture on **Track 46**. Then answer the multiple-choice questions that follow.

Art History

Post-Impressionist   Paul Jordan-Smith
Pavel Jerdanowitch   "Disumbrationist" art
Exaltation   *Aspiration*
Illumination

Notes

Circle the letter next to the correct answer or answers to each of the multiple-choice questions below.

1) What is the main topic of the discussion?
   (A) People being fooled into buying bad paintings
   (B) A joke targeted at the art criticism of the day
   (C) A scholar making some surprisingly good art
   (D) Racism in the art world in the 1920s

2) What are some of the things Paul Jordan-Smith did to appear more convincing?
   Choose 2 answers.
   (A) He impersonated an art critic and praised his own work.
   (B) He made up a school of art that he claimed to have founded.
   (C) He learned a different language so that he could appear more exotic.
   (D) He submitted a photo of himself making a strange expression.

3) Listen to **Track 47**.
   Why does the professor say this?
   (A) To argue that Smith's child was the actual painter
   (B) To imply that Smith's painting had a fresh and new look
   (C) To criticize Smith for copying other painters' styles
   (D) To explain why Smith's art might have fooled critics

4) How does the female student feel about the paintings by "Pavel Jerdanowitch?"
   (A) They are not original or creative conceptually.
   (B) They lack three-dimensional perspective.
   (C) They display a superior attitude toward their subjects.
   (D) They are difficult to understand without the painter's explanation.

5) According to the professor, what was Smith's explanation for his "eyeball" picture?
   (A) It shows a man imagining his wife's critical eyes.
   (B) It shows what it is like to come home to a big family.
   (C) It shows a storm and the people caught in it.
   (D) It shows how many people are watching the painter.

6) What best describes Smith's attitude toward art critics?
   (A) He was respectful.
   (B) He was irreverent.
   (C) He was reverent.
   (D) He was neutral.

Take notes as you listen to the lecture on **Track 48**. Then answer the multiple-choice questions that follow.

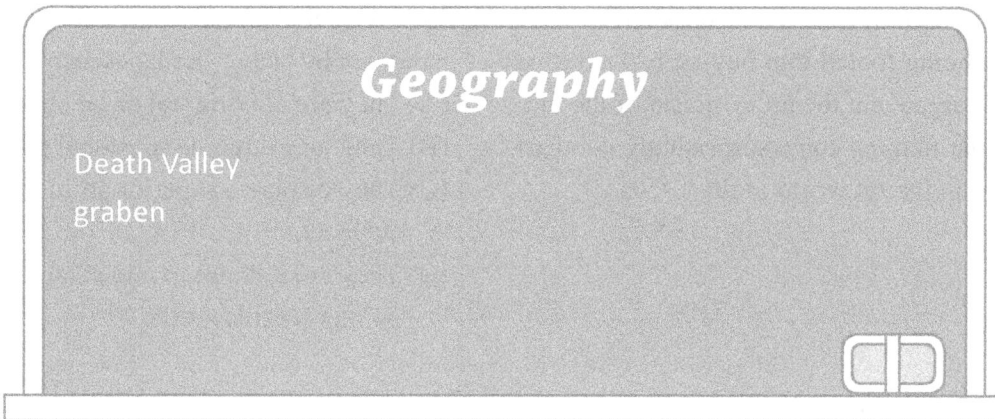

Notes

Circle the letter next to the correct answer or answers to each of the multiple-choice questions below.

1) What is the main topic of the lecture?
   (A) A scientific report about Earth's temperature based on findings at Death Valley
   (B) A geographical location in eastern California with some interesting features
   (C) An important geological mineral which requires hot, dry environments to form
   (D) An earthquake in the early twentieth century that caused a flood in Death Valley

2) Which of the following are prominent features of Death Valley that are mentioned in the lecture?
   Choose 2 answers.
   (A) It is the most volcanically active location in the world.
   (B) It contains more mineral deposits than any other location.
   (C) It is the hottest location in the Western Hemisphere.
   (D) It is located nearly 100 meters below sea level.

3) According to the professor, how did Death Valley form?
   (A) A large lake from rainfall eroded a channel in between two mountain ranges.
   (B) A series of earthquakes dropped a block of land down between two faults.
   (C) A glacier melted, causing a flood to create a valley millions of years ago.
   (D) A group of miners dug out so many minerals in the area that it became a hole.

4) In what way does the professor say Death Valley was different in ancient times?
   (A) It contained a large lake.
   (B) It had much less biological diversity.
   (C) It contained a larger prehistoric civilization.
   (D) It looked like the area near Israel's Dead Sea.

5) According to the professor, which mineral was mined most at Death Valley?
   (A) Gold
   (B) Silver
   (C) Copper
   (D) Borax

6) What does the professor imply about Death Valley?
   (A) Frequent volcanic activity changes Death Valley's landscape.
   (B) Death Valley's elevation is decreasing at an alarming rate.
   (C) Today, Death Valley contains very few human inhabitants.
   (D) Many people still travel to Death Valley in search of gold deposits.

Take notes as you listen to the conversation on **Track 49**. Then answer the multiple-choice questions that follow.

double major   literature classes
major requirements

Notes

Circle the letter next to the correct answer or answers to each of the multiple-choice questions below.

1) Why does the student visit the advisor?
   (A) To explain why he wants to graduate early
   (B) To determine when he can graduate
   (C) To complain that his major requires too many classes
   (D) To discuss what literature classes he should take

2) What are the student's majors?
   Choose 2 answers.
   (A) Language studies
   (B) Art history
   (C) Classical studies
   (D) Literature

3) Listen to **Track 50**.
   Why does the student say this?
   (A) To imply that he needs to follow his friend to class
   (B) To suggest that the advisor should repeat what she said
   (C) To show that he understands what the advisor is saying
   (D) To indicate that he will follow the advisor somewhere

4) What does the advisor say about the student's majors?
   (A) Some of his classes contribute credit to both his majors.
   (B) The advisor studied the same majors as the student.
   (C) Many students decide to pursue the same majors as the student.
   (D) The student's majors are the most difficult offered by the university.

5) What does the advisor imply about when the student will be able to graduate?
   (A) He cannot complete both of his majors before graduating.
   (B) He must improve his grade point average before he can graduate.
   (C) He must take four more classes in order to graduate.
   (D) He can graduate earlier than he expected.

Take notes as you listen to the lecture on **Track 51**. Then answer the multiple-choice questions that follow.

Biology

- "living fossil"
- lungfish
- eel-like
- gills
- vertebrates
- cocoon
- estivation
- air bladder

Notes

Circle the letter next to the correct answer or answers to each of the multiple-choice questions below.

1) What is the main topic of the discussion?
   (A) The various fish species of Africa, South America, and Australia
   (B) A special organ that allows fish to survive in muddy water
   (C) An ancient type of fish with interesting characteristics
   (D) A behavior that is only exhibited by prehistoric fish

2) According to the professor, from where does the lungfish obtain its name?
   (A) It has two small lungs that are similar to mammalian lungs.
   (B) It has an organ called an air bladder that functions like a lung.
   (C) It lives on land for most of its life and breathes air.
   (D) It is found in the lungs of larger aquatic species.

3) Listen to **Track 52**.
   Why does the professor say this?
   (A) To explain the reason for the lungfish's odd appearance
   (B) To explain why the name "lungfish" is misleading
   (C) To suggest that lungfish are more evolved than other fish species
   (D) To suggest that all fish species evolved from eels

4) Which of the following does the lungfish eat?
   Choose 2 answers.
   (A) Small birds
   (B) Snails
   (C) Seaweed
   (D) Small fish

5) According to the professor, why does the lungfish remain inactive for part of the year?
   (A) It must watch over its eggs.
   (B) It needs to save energy in order to mate.
   (C) Its habitat becomes too dry.
   (D) Its food sources migrate elsewhere.

6) Based on the information in the discussion, what is probably the proper definition of "hibernation"?
   (A) Winter breath
   (B) Winter fish
   (C) Winter swim
   (D) Winter sleep

Take notes as you listen to the lecture on **Track 53**. Then answer the multiple-choice questions that follow.

Social Psychology

Nathaniel Brandon
Carol Dweck
growth mindset
self-esteem
fixed mindset

Notes

Circle the letter next to the correct answer or answers to each of the multiple-choice questions below.

1) What is the lecture mainly about?
   (A) How important it is to let children experience failure
   (B) Why parents and teachers should reward positive social behavior
   (C) How people's attitudes toward learning can be shaped by feedback
   (D) The conditions that foster high self-esteem

2) Listen to **Track 54**.
   Why does the professor say this?
   (A) To admit in a humorous way that he likes receiving praise
   (B) To persuade the students to praise his lectures
   (C) To point out that he thinks he is the best professor at the university
   (D) To introduce the theme of how people hint that they want praise

3) According to the professor, what mistake did many parents and teachers in the U.S. make?
   (A) They put a halt to healthy yet competitive activities.
   (B) Their positive feedback overwhelmed children.
   (C) They gave unearned rewards and general praise.
   (D) They did not give their children motivation to succeed.

4) What does the controlled study by Carol Dweck conclude?
   (A) Praise should mainly take place in the classroom.
   (B) Praise should mainly emphasize specific actions, not qualities.
   (C) Children already know their skill levels and do not need praise.
   (D) Praise should only focus on what children might do in the future.

5) What is the purpose of the term "growth mindset?"
   (A) It defines a process of brain training.
   (B) It serves as a synonym for "high self-esteem."
   (C) It explains how the brain grows.
   (D) It summarizes an optimistic self-concept.

6) Why does the professor imply when he says that research is emphasizing brain plasticity?
   (A) Plastics technology allows for more accurate neurological studies.
   (B) Science has concluded that it is impossible to test intelligence.
   (C) Researchers are able to see images of brain changes over time.
   (D) It is possible that traits such as intelligence can change.

Take notes as you listen to the conversation on **Track 55**. Then answer the multiple-choice questions that follow.

group project   case study

Notes

Circle the letter next to the correct answer or answers to each of the multiple-choice questions below.

1) Why does the woman talk to the man?
   (A) To borrow some psychology books from him
   (B) To ask if she can join his group for a project
   (C) To find out if he has seen her partners for a group project
   (D) To explain why she cannot work on a project with him

2) Listen to **Track 56**.
   Why does the man say this to the woman?
   (A) To express concern
   (B) To give advice
   (C) To question her behavior
   (D) To criticize her appearance

3) What is the presentation, PowerPoint, and research paper for the group project supposed to analyze?
   (A) A medical phenomenon
   (B) The stages of childhood development
   (C) A famous case study
   (D) The psychological effects of isolation and neglect

4) Listen to **Track 57**.
   What does the woman mean when she says this?
   (A) The Power Point will address normal language development.
   (B) The man already has images of "Genie."
   (C) The presenation will explore how to get kids to talk.
   (D) The woman is particularly good at Internet searches.

5) What can be inferred about Sam and Cody, the members of the woman's previous project group?
   (A) They failed out of the psychology class.
   (B) They completed more of the group project than the woman did.
   (C) They dropped the class because they did not like working with the woman.
   (D) They put little effort into completing the group project.

Take notes as you listen to the lecture on **Track 58**. Then answer the multiple-choice questions that follow.

Art History

pop art
abstract expressionism
Andy Warhol
Roy Lichtenstein
Claes Oldenburg

Notes

Circle the letter next to the correct answer or answers to each of the multiple-choice questions below.

1) What is the main topic of the lecture?
   (A) Three of the professor's favorite modern artists
   (B) The influence of modern art on advertising and popular culture
   (C) A style of art which emerged during the mid-twentieth century
   (D) Why abstract expressionism became unpopular during the 1950s

2) According to the professor, when was pop art at the height of its popularity?
   (A) The 1920s
   (B) The 1930s
   (C) The 1940s
   (D) The 1950s

3) Listen to **Track 59**.
   What does the professor suggest when she says this?
   (A) Works of pop art were confusing to most viewers.
   (B) Pop artists wanted to redefine what was considered "art."
   (C) Pop art was usually created by trained and well respected artists.
   (D) Pop artists only created artwork for financial gain.

4) According to the professor, what led to the creation of the pop art style?
   Choose 2 answers.
   (A) A need to represent abstract ideas in concrete form
   (B) A plea from the public for simpler, more understandable art
   (C) A reaction to the strict standards of past artistic styles
   (D) A desire to incorporate popular culture into art

5) Why does the professor mention abstract expressionism?
   (A) To mention an artistic movement that influenced pop art
   (B) To imply that pop artists stole their ideas from other artists
   (C) To describe an art movement that was more successful than pop art
   (D) To argue that pop art influenced many other artistic movements

6) What is implied about the three artists mentioned by the professor?
   (A) They had very different styles but are still considered pop artists.
   (B) They influenced one another, but no one realized it until recently.
   (C) They immigrated to the U.S. primarily to seek financial success.
   (D) They hated advertising, but used it frequently in their works.

Take notes as you listen to the lecture on **Track 60**. Then answer the multiple-choice questions that follow.

Geology

continental drift　　　lithosphere
Alfred Wegener　　　asthenosphere

Notes

Circle the letter next to the correct answer or answers to each of the multiple-choice questions below.

1) What is the main topic of the lecture?
   (A) The discovery of a large landmass in the Arctic
   (B) The role of fossil discoveries in proving continental drift
   (C) A revolutionary scientist whose methods have shaped modern research
   (D) A controversial scientific theory that slowly gained acceptance

2) What factors led Wegener to believe that the continents were once joined?
   Choose 2 answers.
   (A) Evidence of an ancient land bridge
   (B) A document of a fossil discovery
   (C) The observation that the continents seem to fit together
   (D) The discovery of mid-ocean ridges and deep sea trenches

3) Why does the professor compare the continents to puzzle pieces?
   (A) To explain the relationship between the mid-ocean ranges and the asthenosphere
   (B) To provide evidence for the existence of the lithosphere
   (C) To explain an observation that led to the idea of continental drift
   (D) To provide evidence for the existence of ancient land bridges

4) Listen to **Track 61**.
   Why does the professor say this?
   (A) To clarify that Wegener was building on the assertions of previous scientists
   (B) To suggest that Wegener received too much credit for his accomplishments
   (C) To explain why scientists initially rejected Wegener's theory of continental drift
   (D) To transition to a discussion of other 20th century scientists

5) Which of the following best describes the scientific community's initial attitude toward Wegener's proposal of continental drift?
   (A) Accepting
   (B) Skeptical
   (C) Hopeful
   (D) Oblivious

6) According to the professor, what causes the movement of the lithosphere?
   (A) The gravitational pull of the Moon
   (B) The forces created by the rotation of the Earth
   (C) Heat currents from deep within the Earth
   (D) Repelling forces created by mid-ocean ridges

Take notes as you listen to the conversation on **Track 62**. Then answer the multiple-choice questions that follow.

- resident assistant (RA)
- application process
- responsibilities
- downsides

Notes

Circle the letter next to the correct answer or answers to each of the multiple-choice questions below.

1) Why does the student talk to the resident assistant?
    (A) To find out if he is qualified to become a resident assistant
    (B) To complain about the responsibilities of being a resident assistant
    (C) To see if there are any open resident assistant positions
    (D) To ask about various aspects of being a resident assistant

2) What are some responsibilities or a resident assistant?

    Choose 2 answers.

    (A) Make sure that students remain safe.
    (B) Ensure that students keep up with their schoolwork.
    (C) Enforce university rules in the dorm buildings.
    (D) Provide students with psychological counseling and medical assistance.

3) Listen to **Track 63**.
    What does the resident assistant imply when she says this?
    (A) Most professors used to be resident assistants at the university.
    (B) Most professors understand that resident assistants have busy schedules.
    (C) Most professors give resident assistants very long and difficult assignments.
    (D) Most professors give resident assistants less work.

4) According to the resident assistant, what is the best part of becoming a resident assistant?
    (A) Enforcing dorm rules
    (B) Helping first-year students
    (C) Receiving a free dorm room and meal plan
    (D) Having plenty of free time to socialize with friends

5) Listen to **Track 64**.
    Why does the resident assistant say this?
    (A) To emphasize the importance of friendship in college
    (B) To explain why she enjoys interacting with first-year students
    (C) To imply that most students dislike their first year of college
    (D) To suggest that she intimidates many first-year students

Take notes as you listen to the lecture on **Track 65**. Then answer the multiple-choice questions that follow.

U.S. History

Gettysburg Address
President Abraham Lincoln
Battle of Gettysburg
cemetery

Republican Party
Democratic Party
Edward Everett
Union

Notes

Circle the letter next to the correct answer or answers to each of the multiple-choice questions below.

1) What does the professor mainly discuss in the lecture?
   (A) Why the city of Gettysburg, Pennsylvania, was important in the Civil War
   (B) Five little known secrets about the pre-presidential life of Abraham Lincoln
   (C) How President Lincoln motivated the North to win the Civil War
   (D) Some background information about a famous American speech

2) Listen to **Track 66**.
   What does the professor suggest when he says this?
   (A) Every American should memorize the speech in full.
   (B) The speech resonated with Americans even after the Civil War had ended.
   (C) America was the first nation to promote equality for all people.
   (D) The speech caused Americans to demand immediate territorial expansion.

3) Which written version of the Gettysburg Address did Lincoln use when he gave the speech?
   (A) The first version
   (B) The second version
   (C) The third version
   (D) The fifth version

4) Why did Lincoln probably add the phrase "under God" after the word "nation" to his spoken version of the Gettysburg Address?
   (A) To convey sentiments that could unite the entire country
   (B) To please a religious friend who was listening in the audience
   (C) To make the speech longer in order to compete with Edward Everett
   (D) To surprise the audience with something unexpected and different

5) According to the professor, what is a "false story" that is often told about the Gettysburg Address?
   (A) It was not given at Gettysburg but in a city further south.
   (B) It was actually written by a noted orator and not President Lincoln.
   (C) It was made to convince all Americans to become Republicans.
   (D) It was widely disliked and viewed as a failure at the time he gave it.

6) Why did Edward Everett write a letter to President Lincoln?
   (A) To ask Lincoln to speak with him again in the future
   (B) To state that some people in the South liked the Gettysburg Address
   (C) To praise the speech Lincoln made at Gettysburg
   (D) To say the speech Lincoln made at Gettysburg was too long

Take notes as you listen to the lecture on **Track 67**. Then answer the multiple-choice questions that follow.

Environmental Studies

- ozone
- stratosphere
- ultraviolet radiation
- chlorofluorocarbons (CFCs)
- Montreal Protocol
- melanoma

Notes

Circle the letter next to the correct answer or answers to each of the multiple-choice questions below.

1) What is the main topic of the lecture?
   (A) The permanent damage that has been done to the ozone layer
   (B) The correlation between ozone layer decay and hurricane activity
   (C) The effects of the international bans on some chemical compounds
   (D) The efforts to stop both global warming and ozone layer decay

2) What point does the professor make when he mentions harmful ultraviolet radiation?
   (A) Many industrial products are powered by this radiation.
   (B) The U.S. is exposed to more of this radiation than other nations.
   (C) The ozone layer protects Earth's surface from this radiation.
   (D) Products that release CFCs produce this radiation.

3) Why were the chlorofluorocarbon compounds (CFCs) so popular with chemists designing products?
   (A) They are easy to extract and refine from mines.
   (B) They are very valuable in making batteries for electric cars.
   (C) They are available in many colors.
   (D) They are inexpensive, inflammable, and non-toxic.

4) Which nations were first to ban chemicals that damaged the ozone layer?
   Choose 2 answers.
   (A) Canada
   (B) The Netherlands
   (C) The United States
   (D) Israel

5) Why does the professor point out that the United States began to act against ozone pollution without the support of other countries?
   (A) To imply that other countries are not interested in protecting the environment
   (B) To suggest that the U.S. wants to claim the ozone layer as part of its territory
   (C) To show that the U.S. did not communicate with other nations
   (D) To show that individual countries can take initiative on global issues

6) What is the professor's attitude toward the international efforts to repair the ozone layer?
   (A) Skeptical
   (B) Optimistic
   (C) Apathetic
   (D) Disappointed

ACTUAL PRACTICE 13

Take notes as you listen to the conversation on **Track 68**. Then answer the multiple-choice questions that follow.

- food-service job
- hair net
- apron
- scheduling
- lunch shift
- brunch shift
- dinner shift

Notes

Circle the letter next to the correct answer or answers to each of the multiple-choice questions below.

1) Why does the student visit the manager?
   (A) To apply for an on-campus job
   (B) To receive training for a new job
   (C) To ask the manager how to pronounce his name
   (D) To complain about being given a bad work schedule

2) Listen to **Track 69**.
   What does the manager mean when he says this?
   (A) The student should have included more information on her resume.
   (B) The student should have been given a higher-paying position.
   (C) The student seems very qualified for her new job.
   (D) The student needs certain credentials before she can begin working.

3) Why does the manager talk about singing the song "Happy Birthday"?
   (A) To compare the excitement of a new job to celebrating a birthday
   (B) To inform the student that it is her coworker's birthday
   (C) To explain to the student that employees do not work on their birthdays
   (D) To tell the student about hand-washing policies for employees

4) How does the manager assign the students their work schedules?
   Choose 2 answers.
   (A) He works around their school schedule and other commitments.
   (B) He lets the students who have worked the longest choose the hours they want.
   (C) He assigns students their work shifts by alphabetical order.
   (D) He gives the best shifts to the students he likes the most.

5) What does the manager imply about working on weekends?
   (A) It is often much easier than working on weeknights.
   (B) It is very boring because few students visit the dining hall.
   (C) It is much less fun than working on weeknights.
   (D) It is very difficult because the dining hall is understaffed.

Take notes as you listen to the lecture on **Track 70**. Then answer the multiple-choice questions that follow.

Archaeology

Vesuvius
Pompeii
intact skeletons
cremate

Herculaneum
ash and debris
pyroclastic surge

Notes

Circle the letter next to the correct answer or answers to each of the multiple-choice questions below.

1) What is the main topic of the lecture?
   (A) An overview of the excavations of two ancient Greek cities
   (B) The cultural and artistic discoveries made at Herculaneum and Pompeii
   (C) A volcanic eruption and its effects on nearby Roman cities
   (D) The geological factors that lead to a volcanic eruption

2) Why does the professor mention the Italian city of Naples?
   (A) To give an example of a city that was affected by the eruption of Vesuvius
   (B) To help explain the geographical location of Vesuvius
   (C) To name the city built atop the ruins of Pompeii
   (D) To point out where refugees from Pompeii fled after the eruption of Vesuvius

3) According to the professor, why did people build Pompeii and Herculaneum so close to Vesuvius, an active volcano?
   (A) They believed that the locations had special religious significance.
   (B) The locations provided strategic military advantages for the Romans.
   (C) The locations provided access to large mineral deposits
   (D) They did not realize that Vesuvius was an active volcano.

4) Listen to **Track 71**.
   What does the professor suggest when she says this?
   (A) They did not realize that Vesuvius had erupted.
   (B) They did not realize how much danger they were in.
   (C) They were unwilling to leave their homes behind.
   (D) They did the right thing by waiting at Herculaneum's port.

5) Based on the information in the lecture, why did the excavations of Herculaneum probably begin so much later than the excavations of Pompeii?
   (A) Herculaneum was buried under more debris than Pompeii was.
   (B) Herculaneum contained little of interest to archaeologists.
   (C) Another city had been build atop Herculaneum, delaying excavation efforts.
   (D) Archaeologists hoped to find survivors of the eruption in Pompeii.

6) Why was the discovery of skeletons in Herculaneum's port so important to archaeologists?
   (A) Few Roman skeletons have ever been discovered due to the Roman's practice of cremation.
   (B) Discovering the age of the skeletons allowed researchers to determine when Vesuvius erupted.
   (C) Estimates of Herculaneum's population are based on the number of skeletons found in the city's port.
   (D) The discovery of skeletons has led many to believe that the city is haunted.

Take notes as you listen to the lecture on **Track 72**. Then answer the multiple-choice questions that follow.

Economics

transit tariffs
export tariffs
consumer
foreign

import tariffs
consumption
domestic

Notes

Circle the letter next to the correct answer or answers to each of the multiple-choice questions below.

1) What is the main topic of the discussion?
   (A) The history and purposes of different types of tariffs
   (B) The reasons that countries no longer use any tariffs
   (C) The way tariffs affect industries within a country
   (D) The way that the free trade movement is destroying tariffs

2) According to the professor, what are the main reasons that countries impose tariffs?

   Choose 2 answers.

   (A) To raise the quality of their own products
   (B) To encourage their own citizens to invest in stocks
   (C) To raise money for their own governments
   (D) To protect their own domestic industries

3) Why does the male student mention the stock market at the end of the discussion?
   (A) To discuss a personal experience that he has had with import taxes
   (B) To imply that import taxes are a great way for individuals to make money
   (C) To talk about one of the main purposes of import taxes today
   (D) To create an analogy that helps him to understand import tariffs

4) Listen to **Track 73**.
   What does the student mean when she says this?
   (A) She wants the professor to draw a picture illustrating his point.
   (B) She has never understood the different between export and import tariffs.
   (C) She believes that import tariffs are better than export tariffs.
   (D) She thinks that import tariffs started when export tariffs ended.

5) Match the letter of each description with the appropriate type of tariff.
   Note: There are two answers for each box.

Match each description with its corresponding term.		
Transit tariffs	**Export tariffs**	**Import tariffs**

   (A) Most popular from the 17th to 19th century, during the time of colonialism.
   (B) Most popular during the Industrial Revolution, at a time when capitalism was developing.
   (C) Most popular in the modern world, during the 20th and 21st centuries.
   (D) Taxes that are levied on things coming into a country.
   (E) Taxes used to discourage sales to outside countries.
   (F) Taxes on things that originate in one country, pass through a second country, and arrive in a third country.

Take notes as you listen to the conversation on **Track 74**. Then answer the multiple-choice questions that follow.

- research project
- pine trees
- encyclopedia
- field guide
- pine needles
- pine cones

Notes

Circle the letter next to the correct answer or answers to each of the multiple-choice questions below.

1) Why does the student talk to the librarian?
   (A) To ask for help with finding specific information for a project
   (B) To ask her to explain the instructions for an upcoming project
   (C) To ask her to identify a certain species of tree located on campus
   (D) To ask for directions to the library's encyclopedias

2) What does the librarian say about printed resources?
   (A) They are always much better than digital ones.
   (B) They are no longer helpful for research.
   (C) They should be part of any research project.
   (D) They are simple to use and trustworthy.

3) What is the librarian's attitude toward the student's assignment?
   (A) Enthusiastic
   (B) Confused
   (C) Critical
   (D) Bored

4) Why does the librarian mention an "app" for identifying birds?
   (A) To recommend the app for the student's project
   (B) To suggest that there may be a similar app for identifying trees
   (C) To describe an interesting problem that she helped to solve
   (D) To explain why a cell phone is necessary for the project

5) Listen to **Track 75**.
   Why does the student say this?
   (A) To explain that he will check out a particular book
   (B) To convince the librarian to help him find a particular book
   (C) To imply that he will purchase the bird-identification app
   (D) To express appreciation for the librarian's efforts

Take notes as you listen to the lecture on **Track 76**. Then answer the multiple-choice questions that follow.

American Studies

Kurt Weill
The Three-Penny Opera
Langston Hughes

Bertolt Brecht
"Mack the Knife"

Notes

Circle the letter next to the correct answer or answers to each of the multiple-choice questions below.

1) What is the main purpose of the lecture?
   (A) To explore the history surrounding World War II
   (B) To explain something about the roots of jazz
   (C) To discuss the significance of American opera
   (D) To describe a unique contribution to American culture

2) What can be inferred from the lecture about the city of Berlin during the 1920s?
   (A) The city was home to a large number of outlaws and beggars.
   (B) It offered many opportunities for musical composers to find work.
   (C) The city's residents preferred opera performances more than jazz.
   (D) Musical composers faced overwhelming competition for jobs.

3) Why does the professor call Weill's music in *The Three-Penny Opera* "ironic?"
   (A) The value of the musical score is much higher than three pennies.
   (B) German audiences did not like it even though it was composed by a German.
   (C) The music is melancholy even though the characters are cheerful.
   (D) Its mood is upbeat when its characters are acting despicably.

4) According to the professor, why did Weill's work in the early 1930s anger the Nazis?
   (A) It drew large crowds of opponents together in one place.
   (B) It inspired negative attitudes toward capitalist society.
   (C) It indirectly criticized Nazi goals and practices.
   (D) It employed a jazz style that Nazis condemned.

5) What was Weill's professional goal in America?
   (A) To focus his work exclusively on jazz and blues
   (B) To combine classical opera, jazz, and naturalistic spoken word
   (C) To inspire more interest in European opera among Americans
   (D) To change American society via music

6) Why does the professor share a quote from poet Langston Hughes?
   (A) To assert Weill's open attitudes and musical skill
   (B) To describe Weill's impact on Hughes' career
   (C) To explain how Weill had inspired Hughes' interest in opera
   (D) To make use of a public metaphor

Take notes as you listen to the lecture on **Track 77**. Then answer the multiple-choice questions that follow.

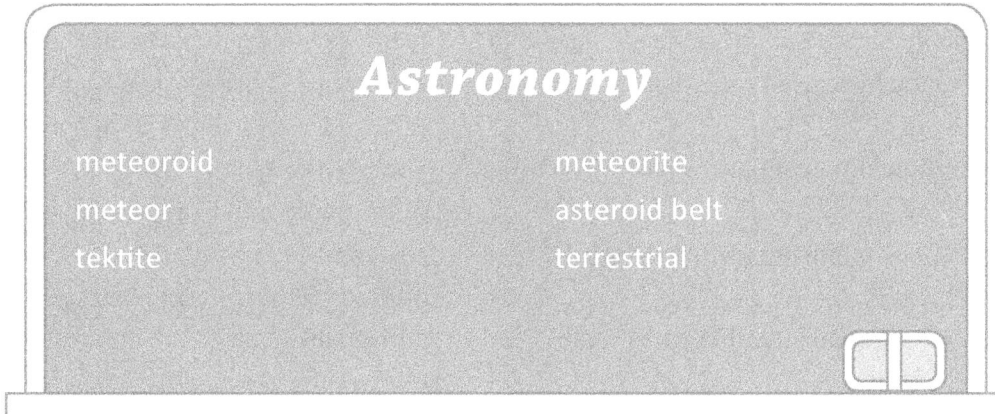

Notes

Circle the letter next to the correct answer or answers to each of the multiple-choice questions below.

1) What is the main topic of the discussion?
   (A) The locations of some famous meteorite discoveries
   (B) The characteristics and classification of meteoroids
   (C) The use of meteoroids in understanding the origins of the solar system
   (D) The contents of a television program about meteors and tektites

2) According to the professor, how are meteors, meteoroids, and meteorites distinguished from one another?
   (A) Their relationship in location to Earth's atmosphere
   (B) Their physical size, shape, and compositional material
   (C) Their value to the astronomical community
   (D) Their planet of origin in our solar system

3) Why does the professor mention the asteroid belt in the discussion?
   (A) To tell students about the formation of the solar system
   (B) To point out a poorly understood category of meteor
   (C) To explain where most meteors originate
   (D) To contrast tektites with meteors

4) What materials comprise the cores of most planets?

   Choose 2 answers.

   (A) Silicon
   (B) Nickel
   (C) Oxygen
   (D) Iron

5) According to the professor, where do tektites come from?
   (A) The asteroid belt
   (B) The moon
   (C) Earth
   (D) Jupiter

6) Listen to **Track 78**.
   Why does the professor say this?
   (A) To emphasize the confusion about tektites
   (B) To acknowledge other explanations for tektites
   (C) To refute a commonly held belief about tektites
   (D) To explain the origins of stony and metal meteorites

ACTUAL PRACTICE 15

Take notes as you listen to the conversation on **Track 79**. Then answer the multiple-choice questions that follow.

- string quartet concert
- Tree Frog Café
- a temporary pass
- Student Lot 8
- a parking sticker

Notes

Circle the letter next to the correct answer or answers to each of the multiple-choice questions below.

1) Why does the student talk to the clerk?
   (A) To ask for an on-campus parking permit
   (B) To ask about upcoming concerts on campus
   (C) To ask about on-campus parking for an upcoming event
   (D) To ask for directions to the university's main concert hall

2) Why does the student text her friend?
   (A) To find out when an event starts
   (B) To find out the location of an event
   (C) To find out where to park for an event
   (D) To find out the cost of admission for an event

3) Listen to **Track 80**.
   Why does the student say this?
   (A) To explain why she needs directions to the café
   (B) To show that she is a university student
   (C) To suggest that she will miss her friend's performance
   (D) To complain that the university is too large

4) What does the student purchase from the clerk?
   (A) A detailed map of campus
   (B) A year-long parking permit
   (C) A ticket to her friend's performance
   (D) A temporary parking pass

5) What does the clerk suggest about on-campus parking?
   (A) It needs to be expanded.
   (B) It is extremely expensive.
   (C) It frequently causes confusion.
   (D) It is used very infrequently.

Take notes as you listen to the lecture on **Track 81**. Then answer the multiple-choice questions that follow.

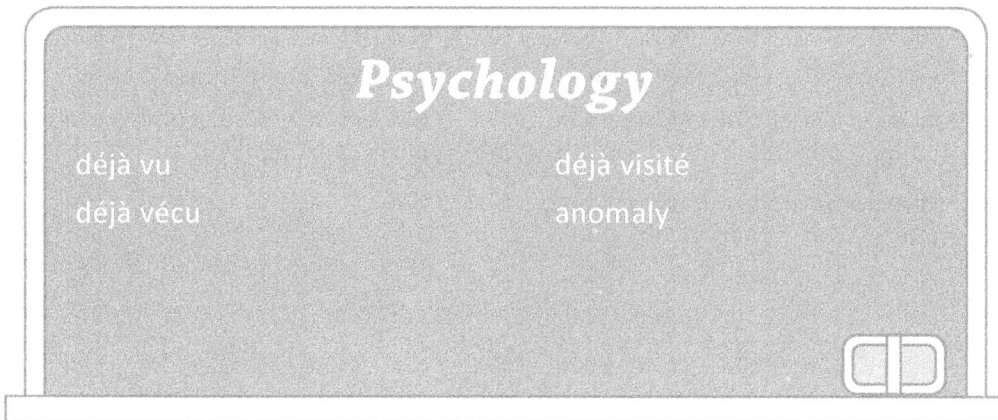

Notes

Circle the letter next to the correct answer or answers to each of the multiple-choice questions below.

1) What is the main topic of the lecture?
   (A) A French theory of human memory that is very mystical
   (B) A strange experience related to memory that many people have
   (C) A special treatment for people with a rare type of brain damage
   (D) A personal experience that changed the professor's life and outlook

2) According to the professor, which of the following are true of the déjà vu experience?
   Choose 2 answers.
   (A) It has been experienced by a majority of people.
   (B) It is difficult to document in formal scientific experiments.
   (C) It is most often experienced by people over the age of 50.
   (D) It causes people to take risks and endanger their lives.

3) Listen to **Track 82**.
   What does the professor mean when he says this?
   (A) Dickens had many déjà vécu experiences himself.
   (B) Dickens describes déjà vécu in a painterly-like way.
   (C) Dickens was an excellent painter as well as writer.
   (D) Dickens' description of déjà vécu is very accurate.

4) Why does the professor talk about visiting a museum for the first time?
   (A) To tell students where to find information on déjà vu
   (B) To argue that déjà vu is a supernatural phenomenon
   (C) To introduce an example of deja visité
   (D) To show that ancient people experienced deja visité

5) According to the professor, how do scientists explain déjà vu?
   (A) It is a mysterious event similar to precognition or prophecy.
   (B) It is the creation of a false memory by misfiring brain cells.
   (C) It is a real experience that has been rearranged by the brain.
   (D) It is a personal experience to which only individuals can give meaning.

6) What does the professor imply about déjà vu experiences in the lecture?
   (A) Many aspects of déjà vu experiences remain poorly understood.
   (B) Déjà vu experiences have become more common in recent decades.
   (C) Charles Dickens was the first person to have a déjà vu experience.
   (D) Déjà vu experiences are among the most studied psychological phenomenon.

Take notes as you listen to the lecture on **Track 83**. Then answer the multiple-choice questions that follow.

Economics

get-rich-quick scheme
investment seminar
initial investment

employment scam
startup fee
testimonials

Notes

Circle the letter next to the correct answer or answers to each of the multiple-choice questions below.

1) What is the main topic of the discussion?
   (A) Strategies for investing money
   (B) How to accumulate wealth quickly
   (C) How to find a job in sales
   (D) Scams about getting rich

2) What does the professor imply about investment seminars?
   (A) Investment seminars are a cheap way to learn how to predict the stock market.
   (B) Almost no one really makes money from the strategies outlined in the seminars.
   (C) Attending investment seminars helped her to become wealthy.
   (D) Most investment seminars are useful, but they can be expensive.

3) According to the professor, which group of people are commonly victims of employment scams?
   (A) Young people
   (B) Old people
   (C) Immigrants
   (D) Americans

4) What are some typical features of fake jobs offered by employment scammers?
   Choose 2 answers.
   (A) They allow the employee to work from home.
   (B) They require several years of experience.
   (C) They don't pay very well.
   (D) They require an initial investment.

5) Why does the professor mention Microsoft and Apple?
   (A) To mention stocks recommended to her in an investment seminar
   (B) To give an example of companies that utilize employment scams
   (C) To give examples of high risk investments that succeeded
   (D) To offer her students advice about investing

6) What does the professor suggest about investing in risky stock?
   (A) Risky stocks have the potential to produce high returns.
   (B) Risky stocks always fail.
   (C) Risky stocks can be bought and sold easily.
   (D) Risky stocks are guaranteed to succeed.

Take notes as you listen to the conversation on **Track 84**. Then answer the multiple-choice questions that follow.

> Computer Programming class
> teaching assistant (TA)
> coding

Notes

Circle the letter next to the correct answer or answers to each of the multiple-choice questions below.

1) Why does the student visit the professor?
   (A) To ask for help on an upcoming assignment
   (B) To explain why she has been missing class
   (C) To complain about her grade on the midterm exam
   (D) To request an extension on her assignment

2) Why have so many students been to see the professor today?
   (A) They have questions about a difficult homework assignment.
   (B) They need letters of recommendation for graduate school.
   (C) They are upset with their low midterm grades.
   (D) The professor is giving extra credit for visiting his office during office hours.

3) Why does the professor mention the class website?
   (A) To tell the student where she can see her midterm grade
   (B) To tell the student how to contact a teaching assistant
   (C) To tell the student where to find good programming tips
   (D) To tell the student where to turn in her assignment

4) Listen to **Track 85**.
   Why does the professor say this?
   (A) To encourage the student to keep working on her assignment
   (B) To differentiate between "bad" and "good" computer programs
   (C) To explain why he decided to become a computer programmer
   (D) To argue that computer programming requires more patience than intelligence

5) What do the student and the professor imply about computer programmers?
   (A) They are usually very forgetful.
   (B) They are often extremely committed to their work.
   (C) They usually become addicted to illegal substances.
   (D) They are required to work extremely long hours.

Take notes as you listen to the lecture on **Track 86**. Then answer the multiple-choice questions that follow.

American Literature

Gary Soto
Mexican American
border patrol

Philip Levine
"Oranges"

Notes

Circle the letter next to the correct answer or answers to each of the multiple-choice questions below.

1) What does the professor mainly discuss?
   (A) The imagery used by many Mexican-American poets
   (B) The ways in which Latino writers have influenced other poets
   (C) Styles that students can use when they write poetry
   (D) The background and artistry of an American poet

2) What can be inferred from the lecture about the artistic influence of Philip Levine?
   (A) Levine inspired Soto to write about nature in a realistic way.
   (B) Levine required his university students to write about their childhoods.
   (C) Levine set an example with meaningful poetry about ordinary events.
   (D) Levine crafted beautiful language about even boring landscapes.

3) Listen to **Track 87**.
   Why does the professor provide this information?
   (A) To explain what life is like for Mexican immigrants to the U.S.
   (B) To suggest connections between Soto's life and his writing
   (C) To show why Soto's poetry tends to be sad and bitter
   (D) To illustrate the challenges Soto faced in getting an education

4) In Soto's poem "Oranges," what surprising event occurs?
   (A) A store clerk infers a boy's dilemma and helps him.
   (B) A successful poet describes having been poor as an adolescent.
   (C) Merchants in a small town begin accepting oranges as currency.
   (D) An adolescent boy asks a girl to walk with him, and she does.

5) Why does the professor quote Gary Soto about "not being a cheerleader"?
   (A) To offer the opinion that cheerleading is unnecessary
   (B) To state Soto's reluctance to represent his community
   (C) To explain why Soto does not depict Mexican Americans as being perfect
   (D) To suggest that there are not enough Latinos represented in poetry and literature

6) What best describes the professor's attitude toward Soto's poem, "Mexican Begin Jogging"?
   (A) Disappointed
   (B) Offended
   (C) Amazed
   (D) Admiring

Take notes as you listen to the lecture on **Track 88**. Then answer the multiple-choice questions that follow.

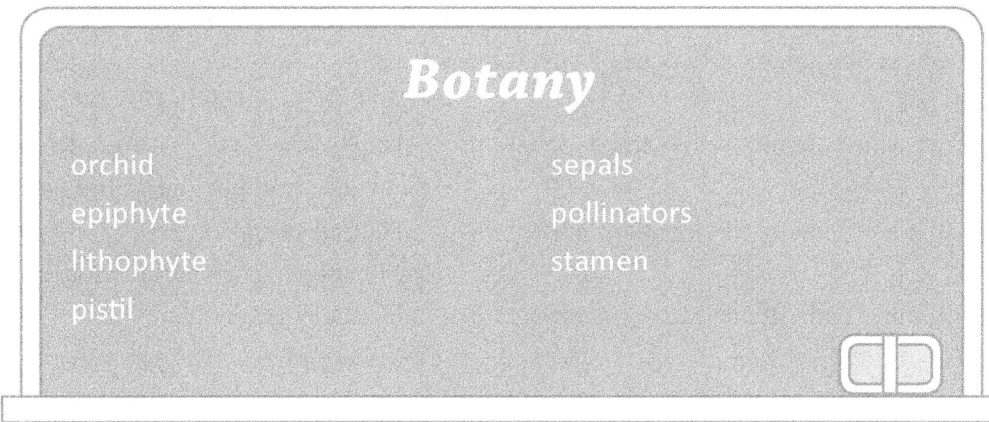

Notes

Circle the letter next to the correct answer or answers to each of the multiple-choice questions below.

1) What is the main topic of the lecture?
   (A) The process of orchid domestication
   (B) The evolution of orchids from a single species into multiple species
   (C) Physical and botanical characteristics of orchids
   (D) Reasons that orchids can grow in some environments but not others

2) Listen to **Track 89**.
   Why does the professor say this?
   (A) To imply that all students should care for flowers
   (B) To encourage students to purchase orchids
   (C) To point out that orchids grow well indoors
   (D) To emphasize the popularity of orchids

3) According to the professor, which of the following characteristics make orchids popular as houseplants and for scientific study?
   Choose 2 answers.
   (A) They grow well in every type of soil.
   (B) They can survive in many different environments.
   (C) They are available in many different scents and colors.
   (D) They tend to remain small no matter where they are grown.

4) Why does the professor mention diamonds and ivory?
   (A) To give examples of materials which have been traded for orchids
   (B) To refer to the harmful collection of other natural products
   (C) To talk about some surfaces on which orchids have the ability to grow
   (D) To explain where the scientific names of some orchids originated

5) According to the professor, how do most orchids get their nourishment?
   (A) They have long roots that absorb water and food from the air.
   (B) They draw nourishment from nearby plants to survive.
   (C) They convert the minerals in rocks into food using their roots.
   (D) They consume their own roots, which contain all the nourishment that they need.

6) What are two of the mechanisms orchids use for pollination?
   Choose 2 answers.
   (A) They disguise their lip as a female insect to attract male insects.
   (B) They produce pollen that can be smelled from hundreds of miles away.
   (C) They make high-pitched noises that attract keen-eared birds and bats.
   (D) They expel nectar onto an insect's wings and make insects crawl past pollen.

Take notes as you listen to the conversation on **Track 90**. Then answer the multiple-choice questions that follow.

- rhetoric
- burning plastic
- neighborhood video footage
- incinerating
- public policy

Notes

Circle the letter next to the correct answer or answers to each of the multiple-choice questions below.

1) Why does the student visit the professor?
   (A) To seek advice on his final project
   (B) To complain about his classmates
   (C) To change his major from biochemistry to rhetoric
   (D) To ask the professor about her grading policy

2) What reason does the student give for taking a class in public speaking?
   (A) He wants to impress his parents.
   (B) He wants to be a politician and give good speeches.
   (C) He wants to overcome his fear of giving speeches.
   (D) He wants to be on television after he graduates from university.

3) Listen to **Track 91**.
   What does the professor imply when she says this?
   (A) The student has a very soothing voice.
   (B) The student should rest before beginning his project.
   (C) The student's presentation may bore his classmates.
   (D) The student should do his final project on sleep cycles.

4) What advice does the professor give the student about his final video project?
   Choose 2 answers.
   (A) Change his topic from the effects of burning plastic to plastic recycling.
   (B) Use information from his own neighborhood's experience with an incinerator.
   (C) Include an opposing viewpoint in his video presentation.
   (D) Support his argument by naming chemicals and presenting statistics.

5) Why does the student talk about his childhood?
   (A) To explain why he decided to study at the university
   (B) To explain how he became interested in biochemistry
   (C) To explain how he developed his public speaking skills
   (D) To explain how he got the idea for his project's topic

Take notes as you listen to the lecture on **Track 92**. Then answer the multiple-choice questions that follow.

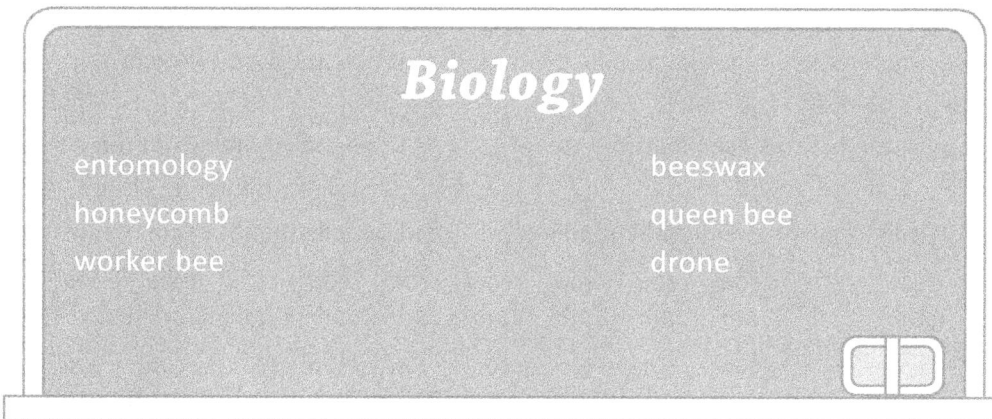

Notes

Circle the letter next to the correct answer or answers to each of the multiple-choice questions below.

1) What is the main topic of the lecture?
   (A) The specialized traits that distinguish a queen bee
   (B) The mating habits of African bumblebees
   (C) The skills necessary for beekeeping
   (D) The lifecycle and habits of honeybees

2) According to the professor, what do worker bees spend most of their time doing?
   (A) Cleaning the hive
   (B) Looking for food
   (C) Laying eggs
   (D) Looking for mates

3) What does the professor imply about queen bees?
   (A) Queen bees are smaller than workers.
   (B) Queen bees rarely leave the hive.
   (C) Queen bees are genetically identical to workers.
   (D) Queen bees guard the hive by themselves.

4) Listen to **Track 93**.
   Why does the professor say this?
   (A) To express her opinion of male honeybees
   (B) To criticize the actions of female honeybees
   (C) To emphasize the insignificance of drones
   (D) To clarify the relationship between drones and queens

5) Which of the following are behaviors of young worker bees?
   Choose 2 answers.
   (A) Laying eggs
   (B) Feeding larvae
   (C) Mating with drones
   (D) Guarding the hive

Take notes as you listen to the lecture on **Track 94**. Then answer the multiple-choice questions that follow.

Notes

Circle the letter next to the correct answer or answers to each of the multiple-choice questions below.

1) What is the main topic of the discussion?
   (A) A large protest that positively impacted the American legal system
   (B) An American legal case that caused a great deal of strife and agitation
   (C) An American immigration policy that affected Italians and anarchists
   (D) A horrible crime that caused Americans to pass a series of harsh laws

2) Why does the female student mention her high school history textbook?
   (A) To indicate where she first learned of the Sacco and Vanzetti case
   (B) To criticize its presentation of the Sacco and Vanzetti case
   (C) To criticize it for excluding the Sacco and Vanzetti case
   (D) To indicate that the she already knows everything about the case

3) Why does the professor mention Sacco and Vanzetti's anarchist, anti-war beliefs?
   (A) To argue that views towards anarchism have not changed
   (B) To argue that Sacco and Vanzetti were rightfully persecuted
   (C) To explain why so few Americans enlisted to fight in World War I
   (D) To explain why many Americans distrusted Sacco and Vanzetti

4) What does the professor suggest about Judge Thayer?
   (A) He paid the jury to find Sacco and Vanzetti guilty of murder.
   (B) As an Italian immigrant, he sympathized with Sacco and Vanzetti.
   (C) He broke the law to ensure that Sacco and Vanzetti were found guilty.
   (D) He secretly believed that Sacco and Vanzetti were not guilty of any crime.

5) Why does the professor mention famous American and European intellectuals?
   (A) To imply that intellectuals were in favor of anarchy
   (B) To suggest that the jury was not very intelligent
   (C) To show that many people felt the trial was unjust
   (D) To imply that many people used the trial to promote themselves

6) According to the professor, what are two clear results of the Sacco and Vanzetti case?
   Choose 2 answers.
   (A) The American criminal justice system was improved.
   (B) Organizations protecting people's civil liberties were strengthened.
   (C) Fewer Italian immigrants came to the United States.
   (D) The Sacco and Vanzetti Trial became part of American history.

Take notes as you listen to the conversation on **Track 95**. Then answer the multiple-choice questions that follow.

Oxford English Dictionary (OED) etymology
Arabic library catalog

Notes

Circle the letter next to the correct answer or answers to each of the multiple-choice questions below.

1) What is the conversation mainly about?
   (A) How students work together on group projects
   (B) Greek and Latin roots of familiar English words
   (C) How to find resources to research word origins
   (D) The foreign language classes offered at the university

2) What does the student imply about her linguistics project?
   (A) She has not had much time to work on it.
   (B) She does not like working on group presentations.
   (C) She wishes that she had chosen different words to research.
   (D) She feels overwhelmed by all the information for her topic.

3) According to the librarian, why is the *Oxford English Dictionary* a good resource?
   Choose 2 answers.
   (A) It contains much valuable information on the English language.
   (B) It contains references to other resources on linguistics.
   (C) The library has a digital subscription that students can use.
   (D) It is published by a very prestigious university.

4) Other than the *Oxford English Dictionary*, what library resources does the librarian recommend?
   Choose 2 answers.
   (A) Tutors of the Arabic language
   (B) Online educational videos
   (C) Books that explain word histories
   (D) Online academic journals

5) Why does the librarian recommend that the student visit professors of the Arabic language?
   (A) To see if they are willing to be interviewed
   (B) To ask them for resources for her project
   (C) To ask them to edit and fact-check her project
   (D) To see if they are currently teaching linguistics classes

Take notes as you listen to the lecture on **Track 96**. Then answer the multiple-choice questions that follow.

Notes

Circle the letter next to the correct answer or answers to each of the multiple-choice questions below.

1) What is the main topic of the lecture?
   (A) A description of the ethical systems of two Greek philosophers
   (B) The application of Plato's ethics to modern social issues
   (C) The historical impact of Greek philosophy
   (D) The differences between ethical and unethical actions

2) Why does the female student mention Epicurus in the discussion?
   (A) To point out that not all ancient Greek philosophers were alike
   (B) To follow up with a question she had from yesterday's lecture
   (C) To try to connect Epicurus' and Plato's views on achieving happiness
   (D) To show that other Greek philosophers influenced Plato's thinking

3) According to the professor, how is Plato's system of ethics different from Christian ethics?
   (A) Plato's ethical beliefs maintain that humans do not have a soul.
   (B) Plato claimed that ethical behavior requires knowledge, not will.
   (C) Plato focused more on the physical life than on the spiritual life.
   (D) Plato was more concerned with sadness than with happiness.

4) Which of the following are similarities between the ethical systems of Plato and Aristotle?
   Choose 2 answers.
   (A) They adopted many of the teachings of Epicurus.
   (B) They believed that wisdom was the source of all other virtues.
   (C) They describe the lifestyle and behaviors of a good person.
   (D) They outlined a way that governments can enforce ethical behavior in society.

5) What is the main limitation to Plato and Aristotle's ethical systems?
   (A) They rely on faith and not reason for making moral decisions.
   (B) They praise behaviors that modern readers consider horrible.
   (C) They focus on complex choices that have no application in the modern world.
   (D) They do not explain how a person can become virtuous.

6) Listen to **Track 97**.
   Why does the student say this?
   (A) He wants the professor to clarify a point about Plate and Aristotle.
   (B) He believes Plato's system of ethics is missing an important component.
   (C) He thinks most students could learn from Plato and Aristotle.
   (D) He wants to know more about where good people come from.

Take notes as you listen to the lecture on **Track 98**. Then answer the multiple-choice questions that follow.

Neuroscience

electroencephalography (EEG)
cerebral cortex
occipital lobe
parietal lobe

Notes

Circle the letter next to the correct answer or answers to each of the multiple-choice questions below.

1) What does the professor discuss in the lecture?
   (A) The process by which electrical signals are turned into memories
   (B) An experiment that explains the connection between dreams and imagination
   (C) An experiment that attempted to differentiate areas of the brain
   (D) Research involving the flow of electrical signals in the brain

2) Why does the professor mention the University of Wisconsin?
   (A) To refer to the university where she studied neuroscience
   (B) To explain where the experiment described in the lecture took place
   (C) To point out a university that is active in neuroscience research
   (D) To discuss the university's emphasis on EEG technology

3) According to the professor, what was the goal of the experiment she describes?
   (A) To test a new algorithm that isolates flow of electric signals
   (B) To compare a new algorithm to an older method of brain research
   (C) To learn how the brain integrates sensory and imagined information
   (D) To better understand the relationship between the occipital and parietal lobes

4) According to the professor, which conclusions are supported by the research?
   Choose 2 answers.
   (A) Visual information goes from lower to higher-order processing.
   (B) Imagined images had a more horizontal pathway in the brain.
   (C) The imagination process appears to be the opposite of the sensory process.
   (D) Though processes in the brain mainly take the form of images.

5) Why does the professor mention epilepsy and schizophrenia?
   (A) To describe the goals of the researchers' next study
   (B) To list some of the neurological disorders that researchers have cured
   (C) To provide examples of neurological connectivity disorders
   (D) To illustrate the specialized role of various brain areas

6) What does the professor imply about sleep?
   (A) It cannot be studied using EEG equipment.
   (B) It is unlikely to involve a flow from higher to lower-order processing.
   (C) Sleep disorders might underlie most neurological disorders.
   (D) It remains somewhat mysterious to neurologists.

Take notes as you listen to the conversation on **Track 99**. Then answer the multiple-choice questions that follow.

summer field study program   salmon run
fish ladder

Notes

Circle the letter next to the correct answer or answers to each of the multiple-choice questions below.

1) Why does the student go to see the professor?
   (A) To apply for a special marine biology course
   (B) To complain about a grade the professor gave him in a class
   (C) To apply to become a teaching assistant in a biology class
   (D) To see if he can write a report on his upcoming camping trip

2) Which of the following are prerequisites for the marine biology summer field-study course?
   Choose 2 answers.
   (A) Students must complete a physical education course in swimming and lifesaving.
   (B) Students must complete a three course sequence in marine biology.
   (C) Students must be in good physical condition.
   (D) Students must be able to swim one mile without stopping to rest.

3) What does the student say about his physical condition?
   (A) He used to wrestle, and now he rides bikes.
   (B) He was a swimmer in high school, and now he is a lifeguard.
   (C) He is on the university's wrestling team.
   (D) He used to mountain bike, but now he races motorcycles.

4) What is the student's attitude toward working outside?
   (A) He prefers to work on mechanical equipment.
   (B) He only likes to work outside when the weather is pleasant.
   (C) He prefers working at home on his computer.
   (D) He enjoys working outside and does not mind messy work.

5) What does the professor suggest about the salmon run?
   (A) It has stopped working recently.
   (B) Its natural course has been blocked by a dam.
   (C) It is the longest salmon run in the United States.
   (D) It is extremely expensive to maintain and repair.

Take notes as you listen to the lecture on **Track 100**. Then answer the multiple-choice questions that follow.

Cultural Anthropology

Alexander Humboldt
clay
calcium

Amazon
iron

Notes

Circle the letter next to the correct answer or answers to each of the multiple-choice questions below.

1) What is the main topic of this lecture?
   (A) An eating disorder that can be treated with medication and therapy
   (B) A religious ritual that began in the Amazon River Basin
   (C) A worldwide dietary and religious practice
   (D) An overview of different types of mud, clay, and soil

2) Why do tribes in the Amazon River basin eat earth for three months each year?
   (A) It is part of a religious ritual that goes back to ancient times.
   (B) The tribes eat earth because they believe that it protects them from harm.
   (C) They have no way of getting plant foods during one season.
   (D) The flooding of the rivers keeps them from hunting or fishing for food.

3) Listen to **Track 101**.
   Why does the professor say this?
   (A) To suggest that the student should go eat some dirt
   (B) To provide a playful response to the student's question
   (C) To mock the student for asking an unrelated question
   (D) To learn about his students' dietary habits

4) What medicinal or nutritional needs does geophagy meet in many cultures?
   (A) To supplement the amount of fiber in the diet
   (B) To add flavor to meals without using salt or pepper
   (C) To supply substances not available in local foods
   (D) To provide gluten-free foods to people who are allergic to gluten

5) What is the professor's opinion of consuming earth as a dietary supplement?
   (A) It is understandable as long as the clay is cleaned and cooked.
   (B) It should only be practiced by pregnant women.
   (C) It is associated with harmful side effects such as vomiting.
   (D) It is a beneficial and sometimes necessary practice.

6) Why does the professor point out that geophagy is part of Catholic and Muslim rituals?
   (A) To suggest that members of those religions suffer from vitamin deficiencies
   (B) To emphasize how widespread the practice of geophagy is
   (C) To show that edible clay soil is available in many regions of the world
   (D) To argue that Humboldt brought the tradition of geophagy to Europe

Take notes as you listen to the lecture on **Track 102**. Then answer the multiple-choice questions that follow.

Notes

Circle the letter next to the correct answer or answers to each of the multiple-choice questions below.

1) What is the main topic of the lecture?
   (A) The obstacles that small businesses must overcome
   (B) The production techniques used in different industries
   (C) Some reasons that businesses come together to form industries
   (D) Some terms often used to describe industries

2) Why does the professor mention Proctor and Gamble?
   (A) To explain how the laundry detergent industry became so successful
   (B) To show how oligopolies often benefit consumers
   (C) To give an example of a business in a highly concentrated industry
   (D) To introduce the successful business model used by the company

3) Listen to **Track 103**.
   Why does the professor say this?
   (A) To highlight the downsides of economies of scale
   (B) To simplify a potentially confusing definition
   (C) To argue that most industries only produce large products
   (D) To imply that big companies provide high-quality products

4) What can be inferred about the laundry detergent industry in the United States?
   (A) It uses cheap overseas labor to make a larger profit.
   (B) It was once dominated by a single brand of laundry detergent.
   (C) It is connected to both the tennis shoe and media industries.
   (D) It does not have room for smaller businesses to compete.

5) According to the lecture, which of the following are "entry barriers" for new companies trying to establish themselves into an industry?
   Choose 2 answers.
   (A) The acquisition of raw materials
   (B) The expansion of large companies into foreign markets
   (C) The high costs of equipment and manufacturing space
   (D) The use of cheap labor by large businesses

6) Which of the following best describes a diversified business?
   (A) A large business that sells cars, computers, televisions, and kitchen appliances
   (B) A large business that controls the majority of production in a particular industry
   (C) A small business that produces one high-quality product
   (D) A small business that benefits from economies of scale

Take notes as you listen to the conversation on **Track 104**. Then answer the multiple-choice questions that follow.

- student loan check
- change-of-address form
- landlord
- "please forward"

Notes

Circle the letter next to the correct answer or answers to each of the multiple-choice questions below.

1) Why is the student talking to the advisor?
   (A) To tell her that he has recently moved to a new apartment
   (B) To submit an application to receive financial aid
   (C) To apply for an academic scholarship
   (D) To get help locating an important piece of mail

2) Why did the student not receive his student loan check?
   (A) His roommate lost the check.
   (B) The check was sent to his old address.
   (C) He is no longer a registered university student.
   (D) He does not qualify to receive student loans.

3) How will the student receive his student loan check?
   (A) He will wait for the post office to deliver it.
   (B) He will call the student loan center and explain his situation.
   (C) He will have the current check canceled and pick up a new one.
   (D) He will ask his roommate to pick up a new check for him.

4) What does the student imply about his old landlord?
   (A) The landlord was satisfactory.
   (B) The landlord is a university student.
   (C) The landlord stole the student's mail.
   (D) The landlord receives financial aid from the university.

5) Why did the student move recently?
   (A) To save money for tuition
   (B) To live closer to the university
   (C) To escape a mean landlord
   (D) To move away from a bad roommate

Take notes as you listen to the lecture on **Track 105**. Then answer the multiple-choice questions that follow.

American Literature

F. Scott Fitzgerald
The Great Gatsby
Daisy

Nick Carraway
Jay Gatsby
Tom Buchanan

Notes

Circle the letter next to the correct answer or answers to each of the multiple-choice questions below.

1) What is the main idea of this lecture?
   (A) Biographical information about Jay Gatsby
   (B) Symbolism in the novel *The Great Gatsby*
   (C) Reasons for Gatsby being called "great"
   (D) The novel's insight into society

2) According to the professor, how is Gatsby different from other rich characters?
   (A) They do not know him.
   (B) He lives in a different area.
   (C) He is from somewhere else.
   (D) Jazz is his favorite music.

3) What does the female student say about Gatsby's viewpoint?
   (A) He seems romantic, but values money above all else.
   (B) He wants to forget Daisy, and has tried to do so.
   (C) He is devastated to find out that she is married to someone else.
   (D) He is living in the past, believing love does not change.

4) Why does the professor mention a prince and a tower?
   (A) To argue that Gatsby always fights for what is right
   (B) To suggest that Gatsby has a naive view of the situation
   (C) To clarify that Gatsby is more like a prince than a king
   (D) To identify rescuing as a theme in the novel

5) Why does the professor say that Gatsby "seems ridiculous for his dream?"
   (A) To agree that Daisy is never going to leave Tom
   (B) To suggest that Gatsby is somewhat unintelligent
   (C) To explain the author's opinion on setting goals
   (D) To point out that Gatsby is not a serious person

6) What is the professor's opinion of *The Great Gatsby*?
   (A) It is complex, but honest.
   (B) It hopelessly confuses most readers.
   (C) It receives too much attention.
   (D) It is fun to re-read.

Take notes as you listen to the lecture on **Track 106**. Then answer the multiple-choice questions that follow.

Notes

Circle the letter next to the correct answer or answers to each of the multiple-choice questions below.

1) What is the main topic of the discussion?
   (A) Light bulb inventors who competed with one another
   (B) Problems with light bulbs which have never been solved
   (C) Some precursors of the modern light bulb
   (D) Reasons that electrical lights are better than gas lights

2) Why does the professor mention the city's gas lamps downtown?
   (A) To describe what a carbon-arc lamp looked like using a familiar example
   (B) To explain that gas lamps have always been popular and are still in use today
   (C) To criticize Thomas Edison for failing to design a brighter light bulb
   (D) To give an example of a place where carbon-arc lamps are still in use

3) What does the professor imply about kerosene lamps?
   (A) They provide more light than light bulbs.
   (B) They are less safe than light bulbs.
   (C) They are more energy-efficient than light bulbs.
   (D) They are more affordable than light bulbs.

4) According to the professor, why did people stop using carbon-arc lamps?
   Choose 2 answers.
   (A) They required too much electricity to be practical.
   (B) They allowed people to see long distances but not short distances.
   (C) They burned so hotly that they caused burns and fires.
   (D) They emitted a light that was too bright for most places.

5) Listen to **Track 107**.
   Why does the student say this?
   (A) He wants to share a story about light bulbs with the class.
   (B) He wants the professor to show a picture of a kerosene lamp.
   (C) He wants to know more about the development of light bulbs.
   (D) He wants the professor to confirm a fact he read in the textbook.

6) What will the class do next?
   (A) Discuss the problems of the early light bulb
   (B) Look at diagrams of the types of lights they have discussed
   (C) Walk downtown to see the actual gas lamps
   (D) Read a passage from their textbooks

Take notes as you listen to the conversation on **Track 108**. Then answer the multiple-choice questions that follow.

- Introduction to Anatomy
- university tutoring center
- medical school
- study groups

Notes

Circle the letter next to the correct answer or answers to each of the multiple-choice questions below.

1) Why does the student visit the professor?
   (A) To explain why he did poorly on the last quiz
   (B) To learn about the professor's grading system
   (C) To ask for advice on improving his grade in her class
   (D) To discuss the benefits of becoming a biology major

2) What does the professor imply about teaching classes that have many students?
   (A) Many students complain that they cannot hear her talk.
   (B) Many students come to visit her office hours.
   (C) It is difficult to make sure that every student gets an "A."
   (D) It is difficult to learn so many students' names.

3) Listen to **Track 109**.
   Why does the professor say this?
   (A) To explain that people become doctors through hard work
   (B) To give examples of medical terms that the student should know
   (C) To show off her extensive medical knowledge
   (D) To differentiate some important medical terms

4) What does the professor recommend that the student do to improve his grade in her class?
   Choose 2 answers.
   (A) Learn about memorization strategies at the tutoring center.
   (B) Learn how to improve confidence by talking to a university counselor.
   (C) Make flash cards and carry them around at all times.
   (D) Study with classmates to prepare for tests and quizzes.

5) Which of the following best describe the student's attitude by the end of the conversation?
   (A) Excited by the prospect of forming a study group
   (B) Appreciative of the professor's study advice
   (C) Upset because the professor is unwilling to change his grade
   (D) Anxious that he will fail the professor's class

Take notes as you listen to the lecture on **Track 110**. Then answer the multiple-choice questions that follow.

Literature

science fiction *Frankenstein*
Jules Verne H.G. Wells
time travel

Notes

Circle the letter next to the correct answer or answers to each of the multiple-choice questions below.

1) What is the main topic of the lecture?
   (A) The stylistic differences between several influential authors
   (B) The development and characteristics of a literary genre
   (C) An analysis of the novel *Frankenstein*
   (D) The ways that 20th-century literature influenced politics

2) Listen to **Track 111**.
   What does the professor mean when he says this?
   (A) Many people believe the term "science fiction" should be redefined.
   (B) Science fiction stories often include future scientific discoveries.
   (C) Most critics cannot agree on a consistent definition for the genre.
   (D) "Classic" science fiction is not well-regarded today.

3) Listen to **Track 112**.
   Why does the professor say this?
   (A) To explain why H.G. Wells wrote *The War Of The Worlds*
   (B) To give an example of a discovery that inspired a science fiction story
   (C) To illustrate how the genre was received when it first became popular
   (D) To explain the reasons for the proliferation of science fiction

4) According to the professor, which of the following are typical features of science fiction stories?
   Choose 2 answers.
   (A) Creating life from nonliving matter
   (B) Speculating about future discoveries
   (C) Explaining the unknown using science
   (D) Exploring impossible locations

5) What does the professor suggest about the novel *Frankenstein*?
   (A) Its science fiction elements often go unrecognized.
   (B) It was once made into a controversial film.
   (C) Its entertainment value is stronger than its literary value.
   (D) It should not be read in high school, but in college.

6) According to the professor, what is one frequent modern-day plot in science fiction?
   (A) Finding water on Mars
   (B) Technology hypnotizing people
   (C) Robots taking over Earth
   (D) People living for hundreds of years

ACTUAL PRACTICE 21

Take notes as you listen to the lecture on **Track 113**. Then answer the multiple-choice questions that follow.

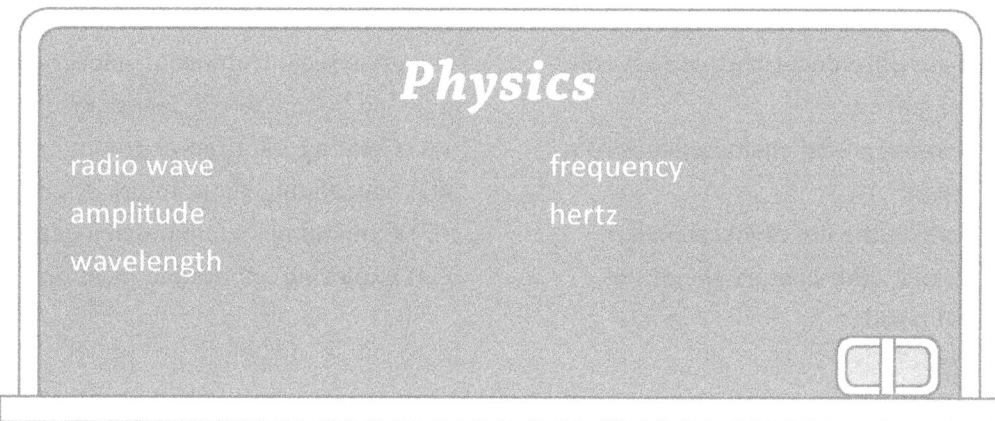

Physics

radio wave   frequency
amplitude   hertz
wavelength

Notes

Circle the letter next to the correct answer or answers to each of the multiple-choice questions below.

1) What is the main purpose of the lecture?
   (A) To put a scientific concept into historical perspective
   (B) To explain how radio waves transmit information
   (C) To teach students how to build a radio
   (D) To clarify the differences between AM and FM signals

2) What do hertz measure?
   (A) The number of seconds it takes for radio waves to travel from one location to another
   (B) The effect that a radio wave's amplitude has on its wavelength
   (C) The maximum amount of energy that a radio wave can transmit
   (D) The number of waves that pass through a given point in a second

3) Why do people use radio waves to send and receive information?
   (A) They can hold more information than other types of energy can.
   (B) They travel more quickly than other types of energy.
   (C) They can be transmitted over longer distances than other types of energy can.
   (D) They are the only form of energy that is compatible with modern technology.

4) Listen to **Track 114**.
   Why does the professor say this?
   (A) To explain why radio signals often overlap with each other
   (B) To point out some of the numerous applications of radio waves
   (C) To criticize the technology industry's over-reliance on radio waves
   (D) To name some alternatives to radio waves for transmitting information

5) Why does the professor describe the transmission and reception of an AM radio signal?
   (A) To give a practical example of a potentially confusing concept
   (B) To illustrate the development of early radio-wave technologies
   (C) To suggest that radio broadcasting is more complicated than people realize
   (D) To argue that using radio waves is outdated and unnecessary

6) Based on the information presented in the lecture, what can be inferred about a radio station called AM 425?
   (A) It broadcasts a radio signal that can travel for approximately 425 miles.
   (B) It broadcasts a radio signal at 42,500 hertz.
   (C) It broadcasts a radio signal that stores information using frequency modulation.
   (D) It broadcasts a radio signal at 425,000 hertz.

Take notes as you listen to the conversation on **Track 115**. Then answer the multiple-choice questions that follow.

career center
job listings
employment workshops

Notes

Circle the letter next to the correct answer or answers to each of the multiple-choice questions below.

1) Why does the student visit the advisor?
   (A) To schedule an appointment with a career counselor
   (B) To ask about job opportunities
   (C) To find out about upcoming volunteer opportunities
   (D) To meet with an academic tutor

2) Why does the advisor tell the student not to give certain pieces of personal information to potential employers?
   (A) To suggest that most employers are not trustworthy
   (B) To emphasize how much difficulty students have finding part-time work
   (C) To avoid having the information stolen by scammers
   (D) To point out the importance of scheduling in-person interviews

3) What information does the career center's workshop cover?
   Choose 2 answers.
   (A) How to write a resume
   (B) How to balance one's class schedule with one's work schedule
   (C) How much personal information to send to potential employers
   (D) How to do well in an interview

4) What does the advisor imply about on-campus jobs?
   (A) They are more convenient than off-campus jobs.
   (B) They are much harder to get than off-campus jobs.
   (C) They often pay much better than off-campus jobs.
   (D) They require a bigger time commitment than off-campus jobs.

5) Where are the most on-campus jobs available?
   Choose 2 answers.
   (A) The university's gym
   (B) The university's libraries
   (C) The university's food courts
   (D) The university's bookstore

Take notes as you listen to the lecture on **Track 116**. Then answer the multiple-choice questions that follow.

Evolutionary Biology

attention deficit hyperactivity disorder (ADHD)
dopamine receptor
Ariaal tribe

Notes

Circle the letter next to the correct answer or answers to each of the multiple-choice questions below.

1) What is the main purpose of the lecture?
   (A) To explain the causes of and treatments for ADHD
   (B) To point out the biological differences between farmers and hunter-gatherers
   (C) To explore the relationship between dopamine and mood regulation
   (D) To discuss how ADHD may have benefited prehistoric humans

2) What effects does dopamine have when it is absorbed by the brain?
   Choose 2 answers.
   (A) It releases chemicals that reduce fatigue.
   (B) It improves concentration.
   (C) It creates feelings of happiness.
   (D) It produces feelings of hunger.

3) What point does the professor make when she mentions the dopamine receptors of people with ADHD?
   (A) They only feel rewarded when they accomplish simple, familiar tasks.
   (B) Their brains release different chemicals than the brains of people without ADHD.
   (C) Their brain chemistry limits their attentiveness during repetitive tasks.
   (D) They are often interested in jobs related to farming and agriculture.

4) Why does the professor shift the discussion from ADHD to a hunter-gatherer lifestyle?
   (A) To link the symptoms of ADHD to human evolution
   (B) To discuss a disorder that closely resembles ADHD
   (C) To explain that prehistoric humans also had treatments for ADHD
   (D) To argue that ADHD developed as a result of hunter-gatherers' diets

5) How might the symptoms of ADHD have benefited our hunter-gatherer ancestors?
   (A) These symptoms would have improved the linguistic abilities of our ancestors.
   (B) These symptoms would have caused our ancestors to be more social and cooperative.
   (C) These symptoms may have increased the height and strength of our ancestors.
   (D) These symptoms would have made our ancestors more aware of their environments.

6) According to the lecture, what is the reason that modern society views ADHD negatively?
   (A) Most cultures place a high value on one's ability to concentrate.
   (B) Most people with ADHD are aggressive and violent.
   (C) Most cultures are trying to return to a hunter-gatherer lifestyle.
   (D) Many people believe that children with ADHD are just naughty.

Take notes as you listen to the lecture on **Track 117**. Then answer the multiple-choice questions that follow.

U.S. History

President Lyndon Baines Johnson
Civil Rights Act of 1964
Medicare
Voting Rights Act
The Vietnam War

Notes

Circle the letter next to the correct answer or answers to each of the multiple-choice questions below.

1) What is the main purpose of the lecture?
   (A) To explain why President Johnson always opposed civil rights
   (B) To blame President Johnson for the Vietnam War
   (C) To explain the reasons for President Kennedy's popularity
   (D) To argue that President Johnson was a competent leader

2) Why did Lyndon Johnson become more conservative over time?
   (A) He disagreed with many of Kennedy's view on taxation.
   (B) He disapproved of the social changes that occurred in the 1950s.
   (C) He became distrustful of the government while serving in Congress.
   (D) He wanted to appeal to voters and politicians in his home state.

3) What were President Johnson's most significant accomplishments?
   (A) Ending the Cold War and bringing down the Berlin Wall
   (B) Ending the U.S.'s involvement in the Vietnam War
   (C) Making laws to protect civil rights, voting rights, and creating Medicare
   (D) Establishing the National Park System and the National Forest System

4) Listen to **Track 118**.
   What does the professor suggest when he says this?
   (A) The Vietnam War caused many people to lose their civil rights.
   (B) Many people disagreed with Johnson's decision to join the anti-war movement.
   (C) Johnson's civil rights accomplishments were overshadowed by the Vietnam War.
   (D) The Civil Rights Movement led to the formation of the anti-war movement.

5) Why does the professor explain the history of U.S. involvement in Vietnam?
   (A) To explain how Johnson eased tensions between the U.S. and Vietnamese armies
   (B) To describe how the United States tried to contain Russia and China during the Cold War
   (C) To explain the command structure of the North Vietnamese Army
   (D) To show that President Johnson was not completely responsible for the war in Vietnam

6) What can we infer about the professor's opinion of President Johnson?
   (A) He thinks that Johnson was a weak, indecisive president.
   (B) He implies that Johnson was rigid and unchanging in his positions.
   (C) He believes that Kennedy was a better president.
   (D) He believes that Kennedy's Civil Rights plan would not have passed without Johnson.

Take notes as you listen to the conversation on **Track 119**. Then answer the multiple-choice questions that follow.

- silent movies
- *Birth of a Nation*
- NAACP
- U.S. Civil War
- American studies class
- Ku Klux Klan (KKK)
- *In Our Gates*
- backlash

Notes

Circle the letter next to the correct answer or answers to each of the multiple-choice questions below.

1) What do the professor and the student mainly discuss?
   (A) How to write about early American films
   (B) Narrowing down a research topic
   (C) Whether the film *Birth of a Nation* had an effect on society
   (D) The best way of presenting facts in a research paper

2) Listen to **Track 120**.
   Why does the professor say this?
   (A) To imply that the student has good manners
   (B) To emphasize the blandness of the film
   (C) To insist that the film's stereotypes were not so bad
   (D) To suggest that calling the KKK "dangerous" was too weak

3) What does the student say about the battle scenes in *Birth of a Nation*?
   (A) The filmmaker used real footage from the Civil War.
   (B) The filmmaker strove to make them look real.
   (C) The filmmaker created offensive views of battle.
   (D) The filmmaker used techniques from stage plays.

4) According to the professor, what is one measurable effect of the film?
   (A) It inspired some white Americans to join a violent group.
   (B) It made many Americans more thoughtful about war.
   (C) It stimulated audience demand for films instead of books.
   (D) It created prejudice against African Americans.

5) What does the professor imply about the assignment?
   (A) Students will get extra credit if they finish on time.
   (B) Student papers must include at least two sources.
   (C) Papers with factual support will earn higher grades.
   (D) Papers with broad topics will be the easiest to write.

Take notes as you listen to the lecture on **Track 121**. Then answer the multiple-choice questions that follow.

U.S. History

President Richard Nixon
National Environmental Policy Act of 1969
Environmental Impact Report (EIA)
Environmental Protection Agency
Endangered Species Act

Notes

Circle the letter next to the correct answer or answers to each of the multiple-choice questions below.

1) What is the main topic of this lecture?
   (A) The long-term impacts of the Endangered Species Act
   (B) The reasons that President Nixon is often regarded as a bad president
   (C) A comparison between the presidencies of Teddy Roosevelt and Richard Nixon
   (D) The many environmental accomplishments of President Nixon

2) Which of Nixon's achievements does the professor compare with the Magna Carta?
   (A) Nixon's resigning as President in 1973
   (B) Nixon signing the Endangered Species Act
   (C) Nixon's establishment of the National Parks System
   (D) Nixon winning the 1972 presidential election

3) Why was Richard Nixon's National Environmental Policy Act of 1969 so important?
   (A) It led to the creation of many government jobs.
   (B) It save countless endangered species from extinction.
   (C) It required Environmental Impact Reports to be written for federal projects.
   (D) It helped the United States acquire many new territories in Asia.

4) Why does the professor list so many of President Nixon's laws and executive orders on the environment?
   (A) To show that Nixon only pretended to care about the environment
   (B) To imply that Nixon cared more about the war in Vietnam
   (C) To show that Nixon cared very much about environmental issues
   (D) To suggest that Nixon was America's most important modern president

5) Why does the professor mention manufacturing and mining industries?
   (A) To suggest the sources of Nixon's political support
   (B) To explain the fierce opposition to environmental laws
   (C) To describe the environmental crises of the era
   (D) To criticize President Nixon for opposing important industries

6) Listen to **Track 122**.
   What does the professor suggest when she says this?
   (A) Historians do not like to discuss obvious facts for fear of looking uneducated.
   (B) Historians do not think to praise Nixon because he has a bad reputation.
   (C) Many historians believe that Nixon is obviously the best president.
   (D) Historians often have difficulties discussing events from the recent past.

Take notes as you listen to the lecture on **Track 123**. Then answer the multiple-choice questions that follow.

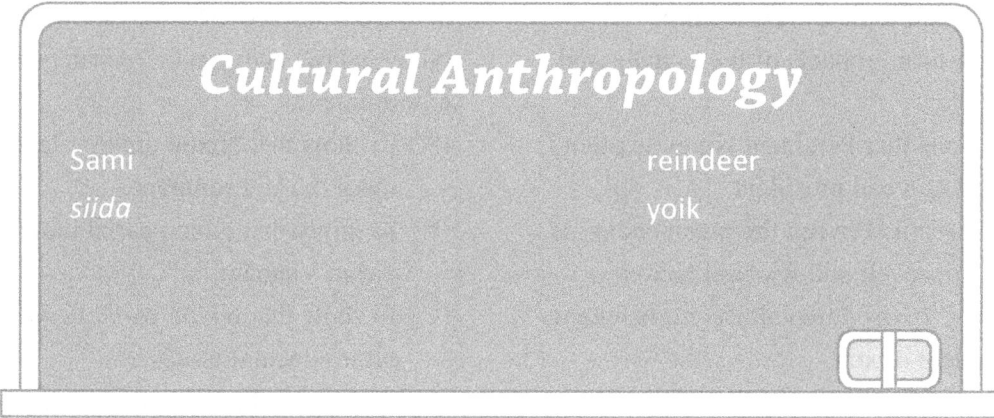

Notes

Circle the letter next to the correct answer or answers to each of the multiple-choice questions below.

1) What is the main topic of the lecture?
   (A) How cultural adaptations have helped people thrive in a challenging habitat
   (B) What the Sami people are doing to try to preserve their cultural heritage
   (C) How best to fish, hunt, and trap animals in the Arctic Circle
   (D) The story behind the myth of Santa Claus and his elves

2) Listen to **Track 124**.
   What does the professor imply with this statement?
   (A) The Santa Claus story tends to trivialize a complex culture.
   (B) The Santa Claus story has made Sami culture look better.
   (C) Animated reindeer are cuter than real reindeer.
   (D) Santa Claus was invented more recently than the student thinks.

3) Why does the professor describe Sami skis and dog breeds?
   (A) To argue that the Sami may have invented skiing
   (B) To explain why Sami people have always enjoyed their lifestyle
   (C) To describe how Sami people managed to hunt for food
   (D) To discuss how Sami people domesticated reindeer

4) What one feature of the Sami language does the professor discuss?
   (A) The frequent reference to snow as a metaphor
   (B) The belief that shamans could communicate with the spirit world
   (C) The tendency to sing words rather than them
   (D) The ability to express highly specific conditions with words for "snow"

5) According to the professor, how has yoikking benefitted the Sami?
   (A) It has brought them worldwide attention.
   (B) It has resulted in people developing good singing voices.
   (C) It has helped foster closer bonds in the community.
   (D) It is seen as a kind of sorcery or magic.

6) How does the professor organize the information in the lecture?
   (A) From oldest to most recent cultural developments
   (B) From practical to social adaptations
   (C) From winter to summer cultural practices
   (D) From the traditional roles of males to those of females

Take notes as you listen to the conversation on **Track 125**. Then answer the multiple-choice questions that follow.

prompt
writing strategies
analogy

labeling
evaluation

Notes

Circle the letter next to the correct answer or answers to each of the multiple-choice questions below.

1) What are the speakers mainly discussing?
   (A) How to write a detailed summary of an academic article
   (B) What high school subjects are most important
   (C) How to complete the student's writing assignment
   (D) What math class the student should take next year

2) The writing tutor divides the student's writing assignment into what tasks?
   Choose 2 answers.
   (A) The student must analyze the author's writing strategies.
   (B) The student must explain why the author's analysis of the situation is wrong.
   (C) The student must comment on the effectiveness of the author's writing strategies.
   (D) The student must decide whether the writing tutor has been helpful in writing this assignment.

3) What analogy is used by the author of the essay that the student is analyzing?
   (A) She compares learning algebra to learning the alphabet.
   (B) She compares learning algebra to watching a new movie.
   (C) She compares summarizing information to learning how to read.
   (D) She compares understanding variables to understanding metaphors.

4) Why does the tutor tell the student to "label" the author's writing strategies?
   (A) To give an example of a common analogy used by writers
   (B) To point out several issues with the author's argument
   (C) To criticize the student for failing to analyze the author's argument
   (D) To help the student understand how to analyze an author's writing

5) What will the student probably do to complete her writing assignment?
   (A) Ignore the tutor's advice and recommendations.
   (B) Rewrite the assignment, and then return to the tutor.
   (C) Ask her professor to give her more writing advice.
   (D) Ask her friend to proofread her assignment.

Take notes as you listen to the lecture on **Track 126**. Then answer the multiple-choice questions that follow.

Neuroscience

nerve
neuron
oligodendroglia

astroglia
glia (glial cell)

Notes

Circle the letter next to the correct answer or answers to each of the multiple-choice questions below.

1) What is the main topic of the lecture?
   (A) The similarities between the peripheral and central nervous systems
   (B) The functions of different types of cells found in the nervous system
   (C) The reasons that neurons are more important than glial cells
   (D) The process by which neurons send electrochemical signals to one another

2) What is the professor's opinion of the term "neuroscience"?
   (A) He believes that it is too difficult for students to understand.
   (B) He believes that it accurately describes the main parts of the brain.
   (C) He believes that it should be replaced by a more modern term.
   (D) He believes that it fails to include an important group of cells.

3) Listen to **Track 127**.
   What does the professor suggest when he says this?
   (A) Understanding glia requires knowledge of neurons.
   (B) The professor enjoys discussing neurons more than he does glia.
   (C) Neurons are star-shaped cells found in the brain.
   (D) There are more types of neurons than there are types of glia.

4) Listen to **Track 128**.
   Why does the professor say this?
   (A) To question the necessity of neurons in the nervous system
   (B) To argue that neurons and glia are actually quite similar
   (C) To emphasize the numerous functions of astroglia
   (D) To differentiate astroglia from other glial cells

5) What does a cell do first when sending an electrochemical signal?
   (A) It sends positive charges to nearby astroglia.
   (B) It lets sodium and potassium pass through its cell membrane.
   (C) It disconnects a cell body from its corresponding axon.
   (D) It sends oligodendroglia from the brain to the rest of the body.

6) Based on the lecture information, what is the main function of oligodendroglia?
   (A) They carry electrochemical signals from one neuron to the next.
   (B) They surround neurons, protecting them from harm.
   (C) They supply neurons with sodium and potassium.
   (D) They help axons send electrochemical signals.

Take notes as you listen to the lecture on **Track 129**. Then answer the multiple-choice questions that follow.

Physics

- atmosphere
- visible light
- Rayleigh Scattering
- electromagnetic radiation
- wavelength

Notes

Circle the letter next to the correct answer or answers to each of the multiple-choice questions below.

1) What does the class mainly discuss?
   (A) The reasons for the colors of Earth's sky
   (B) The sun and the electromagnetic spectrum
   (C) The importance of air to survival on Earth
   (D) The composition of Earth's atmosphere

2) Why does the professor mention ponds and rivers?
   (A) To describe how light travels differently through different bodies of water
   (B) To imply that light cannot penetrate fluids, such as water or air
   (C) To create an analogy that may help his students understand a difficult concept
   (D) To explain why light travels more slowly in water than it does in air

3) What color is associated with a longer wavelength of visible light?
   (A) Violet
   (B) Blue
   (C) Yellow
   (D) Red

4) Why does light scatter after interacting with gas particles in the atmosphere?
   (A) Light travels too quickly to bond to gas particles.
   (B) Light does not chemically alter gas particles.
   (C) There is too much light for the atmosphere to absorb.
   (D) Light has too much energy to stay in one place.

5) What color of light interacts most with the gases in Earth's atmosphere?
   (A) Orange
   (B) Green
   (C) Blue
   (D) Red

6) Listen to **Track 130**.
   What can be inferred from this?
   (A) Sunlight produces different colors when it interacts with different objects.
   (B) Sunlight has no natural color of it own.
   (C) Different stars create different colors of light than the sun.
   (D) Earth absorbs all the light from the sun.

Take notes as you listen to the conversation on **Track 131**. Then answer the multiple-choice questions that follow.

> grading on a curve
> water-down
> calculus class

Notes

Circle the letter next to the correct answer or answers to each of the multiple-choice questions below.

1) Why does the student visit the professor?
   (A) To retake a quiz that she did poorly on
   (B) To argue that the professor's quizzes are too difficult
   (C) To ask about the grade she received on a quiz
   (D) To report another student for cheating on a quiz

2) The student scored a 65 percent on her quiz. What letter grade did she receive for this score?
   (A) An "A"
   (B) A "B"
   (C) A "C"
   (D) A "D"

3) Listen to **Track 132**.
   Why does the professor say this?
   (A) To refute the student's claim that the class is too easy
   (B) To argue that calculus is the most difficult academic subject
   (C) To discourage the student from continuing with the class
   (D) To explain why he uses an alternative grading system

4) Listen to **Track 133**.
   Why does the student say this?
   (A) To indicate that most people in her class got similar scores
   (B) To describe a scenario that would be unfair
   (C) To acknowledge that she did not do well on the test
   (D) To imply that she considered herself an unlucky person

5) What does the professor suggest about his grading system?
   (A) It allows many students to receive better grades in his class.
   (B) It is too confusing for most students to understand.
   (C) It has been criticized by many other calculus professors.
   (D) It ensures that no student ever fails his calculus class.

Take notes as you listen to the lecture on **Track 134**. Then answer the multiple-choice questions that follow.

Economics

- income tax
- tariff
- labor union
- excise tax
- Industrial Revolution

Notes

Circle the letter next to the correct answer or answers to each of the multiple-choice questions below.

1) What is the main topic of the discussion?
   (A) How the modern income tax system evolved in the U.S.
   (B) Different forms of taxation used throughout history
   (C) A rebellion to a very unpopular tax on alcohol
   (D) How the U.S. paid off its debt after the Revolutionary War

2) According to the professor, which of the following taxes were employed prior to the collection of income taxes?
   Choose 2 answers.
   (A) Estate taxes
   (B) Tariffs
   (C) Property tax
   (D) Capital gains tax

3) According to the professor, what is one reason the U.S. implemented an income tax?
   (A) Excise taxes had become too unpopular
   (B) People began selling land to avoid property tax
   (C) To pay for public services, such as schools
   (D) To pay off its growing debt

4) What was the primary cause of the Whiskey Rebellion?
   (A) A Constitutional amendment banning whiskey
   (B) A tariff to discourage Americans from importing alcohol
   (C) A shortage of whiskey caused by excessive taxation
   (D) An excise on domestically distilled spirits

5) Why does the professor mention socialism and labor unions?
   (A) To give an example of ideas that helped shape public policy
   (B) To persuade his students to join labor unions and vote for socialist candidates
   (C) To describe the average American's political beliefs
   (D) To answer the student's question about income tax

6) What does the professor imply about public schools?
   (A) They offer a high quality education.
   (B) They are usually underfunded.
   (C) They are expensive.
   (D) They originally served only poor children.

Take notes as you listen to the lecture on **Track 135**. Then answer the multiple-choice questions that follow.

Biology

Philae lander   Stanley Miller
organic compounds   Harold Urey
abiogenesis

Notes

Circle the letter next to the correct answer or answers to each of the multiple-choice questions below.

1) What is the main topic of the lecture?
   (A) The discoveries made by the *Philae* lander
   (B) A theory for the origins of life on Earth
   (C) The differences between various organic compounds
   (D) A method for tracking the reproductive cycles of maggots and frogs

2) According to the professor, what chemical elements do all organic compounds contain?
   Choose 2 answers.
   (A) Hydrogen
   (B) Methane
   (C) Carbon
   (D) Ammonia

3) Listen to **Track 136**.
   What can be inferred from this?
   (A) People who believed in abiogenesis feared maggots and frogs.
   (B) Acceptance of abiogenesis was based on observation, not experimentation.
   (C) Many people in the past did not regard maggots and frogs as living creatures.
   (D) Mud was a valuable substance because it supposedly produced life.

4) What did the Miller-Urey experiment attempt to demonstrate?
   (A) Life on Earth originated from the process of biogenesis, not abiogenesis.
   (B) Life was transported to Earth on comets approximately 4 billion years ago.
   (C) Life on Earth originated well over 4 billion years ago.
   (D) Life on Earth originated from reactions between non-living organic compounds.

5) Listen to **Track 137**.
   What does the professor suggest when he says this?
   (A) Scientists have not yet replicated abiogenesis in their experiments.
   (B) Any combination of chemicals contained in a sterile environment will undergo abiogenesis.
   (C) Very few forms of life are composed of organic compounds.
   (D) The conditions on Earth have not changed in the past 4 billion years.

6) Why does the professor discuss the *Philae* lander throughout the lecture?
   (A) To show that life on Earth began in outer space
   (B) To introduce a theoretical connection between comets and abiogenesis.
   (C) To present evidence that disproves the theory of biogenesis
   (D) To argue that space exploration is more important than biological research

APPENDIX

Listening Scripts

CHAPTER 2

ACTUAL PRACTICE 1

PRACTICE 1 - TRACK 1

Narrator: Listen to a conversation between a student and a teaching assistant (TA).

Female Teaching Assistant (TA): So, Lucas, let's see how that first draft of your research paper looks.

Male Student (MS): Oh, was I supposed to bring my research paper to this meeting? I thought we were just going to talk about my topic.

TA: Well, going over your topic was part of what I wanted to discuss today. But the primary purpose of this meeting is for me to review what you've written so far and to give you pointers if necessary.

MS: Oh, I see. Well, to tell you the truth, I've had a bad case of writer's block lately.

TA: You haven't been able to start writing your paper yet? Uh-oh, there are only two weeks left before the paper is due. Have you at least done some research?

MS: Oh, yes, I have, I've done that. My topic is the history of the minimum wage in the United States. And, I've done a lot of reading on it. The problem is that I can't really seem to narrow anything down. I mean, I feel like I almost know too much about it now.

TA: I see. Well, sometimes that happens with these big research projects. But why didn't you come in to see me sooner? That's what I'm here for.

MS: Oh, well, I would have, but I kept thinking that I just needed to read more about the topic. I was reading and reading and reading. The time kind of slipped away from me. I did start a rough draft, but I felt like it wasn't nearly focused enough. So for the last week, I've just been trying to figure out how to start over, but I haven't had much luck.

TA: I see. Well, if you've done as much research as you say, you may not have to, you know, start over. Let's take a look at that rough draft that you worked on. Do you still have it saved on your computer?

MS: Well, yeah, I think so. Though I don't see how it can do me much good. It's basically just a summary of all the stuff I read about the minimum wage in the United States. It has no focus.

TA: Maybe you're right. But maybe there's something in that paper you can actually use. So, do you think we could meet again tomorrow and you could bring that rough draft?

MS: Oh, sure. That's no problem.

TA: Great. So, while you're here, let's talk about some of what you've learned about the minimum wage in the United States. Perhaps by talking about it, you will think of ways to focus and organize the information.

MS: Well, I guess it's worth a try. I mean, maybe we could just talk about it from when it started to now?

TA: Good idea. Let's discuss it chronologically then. Tell me about when the law was first proposed…

Narrator: Now get ready to answer the questions.

PRACTICE 1 - TRACK 2

Narrator: What is the teaching assistant's attitude when she says this?

TA: You haven't been able to start writing your paper yet? Uh-oh, there are only two weeks left before the paper is due. Have you at least done some research?

PRACTICE 2 - TRACK 3

Narrator: Now listen to a lecture in a visual arts class.

Female Professor (FP): Good morning, class. If you feel like you've just walked into preschool classroom, well, that was somewhat my intention. Sitting in front of you, on your desks, are finger paints! That's right, the very same paints that many of you used growing up!

So, in my opinion, finger painting is perhaps the simplest form of creative expression with paints. As you may be aware, finger painting began as a means of developing the imaginative and artistic powers of young children. But, over the years, finger painting has become a popular hobby for people of all ages because no artistic training is required and because there is no technique to master. Moreover, by working with one's fingertips and with one or both hands and arms, people can express basic creative instincts. And actually, that's what you guys will be doing in a few minutes, as soon as I finish giving you some background information.

So now, let's get into some history. The idea of using finger painting as a means of artistic expression is credited to a woman named Ruth Faison Shaw. Ms. Shaw ran a school for English-speaking children in Rome from 1922 to 1932. While teaching in Rome, she worked to develop new ways for children to express themselves creatively. But ultimately, the idea for finger painting came about through chance, not planning. One day, as the story goes, Ms. Shaw sent a pupil with a scratched finger to the bathroom for some iodine. Iodine, as you may know, is a dark-reddish, paint-like antiseptic used for cleaning wounds. When the pupil did not return, Ms. Shaw investigated and found him, she said, and I quote from a book she wrote about the subject: "blissfully absorbed in decorating the bathroom door with a finger dipped in iodine." And it was from this incident that Ms. Shaw got the idea of finger painting. Pretty interesting, huh?

Now then, let's get to the meat of today's class: The technique of finger painting itself. Well, the finger-painting technique used by most people is just as you might expect: whatever works, goes. But I do recommend that you follow some guidelines that seem to help those who finger paint. First, most finger painters spread their paint with sweeping movements of the hands, fingers, and arms. Second, most finger painters like to stand up when they are working because this allows the arms to move more freely than from a sitting position. And third, most finger painters like to make a variety of movements rather than just one single movement over and over, because varying one's movements yields the most interesting results.
And what about the so-called "tools of the trade" in finger painting? Well, Ms. Shaw actually developed a special paint that is harmless to the skin and clothing. It washes off easily, feels like mud to the touch, spreads smoothly, and does not dry too quickly. Her recipe for finger paints consists of liquid starch mixed with dry colored pigment or crumbled chalk. Ms. Shaw also created enlarged paper with a glazed surface to hold the paint and to give finger painters enough space for creative expression.

So, before I let you start your finger painting, let me give you just a few more tips and an explanation of all the things that you see on your desks. Well, first of all, you'll probably notice that the paint itself is stiff and lumpy. That being the case, you'll have to stir it around a bit before applying it to the paper. Also, if the paint becomes sticky or dry, sprinkle some water in it using the glasses of water I've left on all of your tables. It will soften the paint up a bit. Also, if you want to mix colors, it's best to do that on the paper itself, rather than before you apply the colors to the paper. Mixing colors on the paper allows for better shading. And when you're done with your painting, you can place it on the drying racks. Part of your grade will be based on a one-page reflection that you write about the experience; you should have a rubric for the project in your syllabus packet.

So, unless there are any questions, I'm just going to let you go and see what you can come up with.
Narrator: Now get ready to answer the questions.

PRACTICE 2 - TRACK 4

Narrator: Now listen again to part of the lecture. Then answer the question.
FP: Now then, let's get to the meat of today's class: The technique of finger painting itself. Well, the finger-painting technique used by most people is just as you might expect: whatever works, goes.
Narrator: What does the professor imply about the technique of finger painting when she says this?
FP: …whatever works, goes.

PRACTICE 3 - TRACK 5

Narrator: Now listen to a lecture in a zoology class.
Female Professor (FP): Today, I want to discuss an animal that's strongly associated with the American Southwest—the coyote. This animal, viewed as a pest by some and a legendary figure by others, is one of the most familiar on the North American continent.

So first, let me give you some background information about this animal and describe some of its physical characteristics. Actually, it's important to note that a coyote is a close relative of the wolf; in fact, they belong to the same genus, *Canis*. However, there are some crucial differences between the two types of animals. While most wolves reach heights of about 80 centimeters and weigh about 30 to 35 kilograms, most coyotes are much smaller, measuring 50 centimeters in height and 15 to 20 kilograms in weight. Moreover, both wolves and coyotes tend to have brown or grayish-black coats of fur with tints of white throughout, but the coats of wolves are quite thick while those of coyotes are often thinner. You'll notice the difference in size and coat thickness when I show you some pictures of coyotes and wolves at the end of the lecture.

Yet in other ways, wolves and coyotes share similar characteristics. For example, like the wolf, the coyote's basic social unit is the breeding pair. So among both coyotes and wolves, a male and female pair and their offspring make up a typical pack. And let me use this fact to point out one of the biggest misconceptions people have of coyotes from watching Western movies and television shows, which often show the "lone coyote" traveling across the plain. The image of the coyote as a solitary animal is more or less erroneous. Although it's true that coyotes can travel alone while looking for a mate, they typically live in packs, especially when a major food resource is easily available. When an abundance of food can support large groups of the animals, juveniles stay with their parents longer. So, in this situation, rather than leaving their family when they are old enough to mate, young adult coyotes remain with the pack, where their main responsibility is to protect younger pups from predators.

Male Student (MS): But what about situations in which forming packs is not advantageous? How do coyotes travel then?

FP: Well, as I suggested, in those situations, the primary coyote group is the male-female pair. Their pups will begin to leave within a year, traveling as far as 160 kilometers from home to find a mate of their own and settle down. This is fairly similar to the social groups maintained by wolves, as well.

Coyotes are nocturnal predators, so they usually do their hunting at night. Their diet includes mice, insects, rabbits, and other small prey. Coyotes may also group together to hunt large mammals, such as deer. To catch these animals, coyotes can reach speeds of 65 kilometers per hour. And, when they are able, coyotes will supplement their diet with fruit.

Because coyotes have such an adaptive social organization and varied diet, they can thrive in a wide variety of habitats, from mountains to forests to deserts to plains. Thus, biologists have classified 19 subspecies of coyote, which inhabit almost all of the North American continent. But they are most strongly associated with the American Southwest. And decades of increasing human population in this region has caused the coyote population to *increase*. Now, based on the ecological models we have looked at, what can you suggest about human population in an area resulting in increased coyote populations?

MS: Well, maybe we kill off whatever kills coyotes?

FP: Very good, good point. The main predators that prey on coyotes are wolves. When humans push out wolf populations, coyotes multiply. When coyote populations become too large for a wild environment, they'll exhaust their food sources, and begin trekking into nearby suburban and urban areas. So urban development results in the driving away of large predators, which then results in increased coyote populations.

Narrator: Now get ready to answer the questions.

PRACTICE 3 - TRACK 6

Narrator: What does the professor suggest when she says this?

FP: Now, based on the ecological models we have looked at, what can you suggest about human population in an area resulting in increased coyote populations?

ACTUAL PRACTICE 2

PRACTICE 1 - TRACK 7

Narrator: Listen to a conversation between a student and a professor.

Male Student (MS): Oh, excuse me, Professor Gonzalez? Do you have a minute?

Female Professor (FP): Sure, Marcus, what's up?

MS: Well, I just wanted to apologize for leaving class early over the last few weeks. I know it creates a disturbance in such a small class, where students are supposed to be listening to each other and everything.

FP: Oh, okay. Is it a scheduling problem?

MS: No, not that, it's more that I'm experiencing some… sometimes I just feel like I have to leave, you know, get out of the situation. It's just a really strong feeling, but it's not that I don't like the class or anything.

FP: Hmm, so do you think you're feeling anxiety? Is it like a nervous feeling?

MS: Yeah, I guess so. I feel sweaty, and my heart starts pounding.

FP: That sounds tough. Well, let's think of some strategies here. Could you get the notes from class discussions from another student? So you would know what we talked about when you are gone?

MS: Well, no, not really. I mean, I don't really talk to anyone in the class. I feel like they're all older, you know, like I'm the youngest one in class.

FP: I can see how that would feel a little intimidating. You are a freshman, right? So how did you end up in Advanced Spanish Conversation?

MS: Well, I took extra Spanish classes during high school. I was pretty good at it, but here I get really nervous when people are speaking it so fast.

FP: I understand. Listen, next week I'll be setting up the groups for class presentations. I'll make sure you are in a group with some of the second-year students. I think you'll feel more comfortable when you get to know some of the other students. You will get to know them at least a little by working with them on a project outside of class.

MS: Yeah, that sounds like a good idea.

FP: I think you'll be fine as long as you keep trying. Remember to keep up with the grammar assignments in the textbook, and with your required hours in the Listening Lab. You've done well on the quizzes so far, right?

MS: Oh, definitely, those things are pretty easy for me.

FP: Good, well, that should boost your confidence over time. Also, just sit near the door. If you start feeling like you have to leave, you can go. Just try to leave during a transition, not when someone is talking.

MS: Okay. Thanks for understanding. I really appreciate it.

FP: No problem. And Marcus, if you're feeling a lot of anxiety at other times, it would be a good idea to make an appointment at the campus health center. You know, talk to them about getting help with your anxiety.

MS: Yeah, maybe I will. Thanks, Professor!

Narrator: Now get ready to answer the questions.

PRACTICE 1 - TRACK 8

Narrator: Why does the professor say this?

FP: I think you'll be fine as long as you keep trying. Remember to keep up with the grammar assignments in the textbook, and with your required hours in the Listening Lab.

PRACTICE 2 - TRACK 9

Narrator: Listen to a lecture in an ecology class.

Male Professor (MP): Good morning. So I hope everyone did the reading last night on the flora of New Zealand. I won't spend much time talking about the reading because today, I want to talk about the endemic animals of New Zealand. For those of you unfamiliar with the term, "endemic" means found nowhere else on Earth. So, as a famous example, the Galapagos tortoise is *endemic* to the Galapagos Islands—that is, it's found nowhere else.

Okay, so today is all about the ecological history of New Zealand, and I'll be paying special attention to the bird species of New Zealand. So the island of New Zealand, which is located to the south of Australia, is an incredibly unique ecosystem that's filled with endemic species of plants and animals. Does anyone remember what the reading said about why there are so many unique species? (*To student*) Yes. What do you think?

Female Student (FS): Doesn't it have to do with how long New Zealand has been isolated from other major landmasses? I think the reading said that New Zealand has been isolated for, like, 65 million years.

MP: Yes, that's exactly it. So New Zealand's isolation made it inaccessible to land mammals for millions of years. In fact, before humans arrived, the only mammals that lived on the island for the previous 20 million years are a few species of bat, which were able to fly to the island. And without any mammals on the island, there were a lot of ecological niches that needed to be filled. So, because there were—(*To student*) You have a question?

Male Student (MS): Yeah. Sorry to interrupt, but what do you mean when you say there were "ecological niches that needed to be filled?"

MP: Well, every species interacts with the environment in a particular way, creating consequences that affect other species; in other words, it fills a role or niche. As a simple example, deer tend to live around meadows and to eat plants and grasses, preventing plant overgrowth. Meanwhile, deer become food for wolves. So the deers' niche is as a grass-eating prey animal near meadows. So in many habitats, mammals fill many of the niches. But, with the exception of bats, mammals couldn't get to New Zealand. So can anyone tell me how all these ecological niches were filled?

FS: Well, I'm kind of guessing here, but wouldn't most of these niches be filled by birds? Birds could easily fly to the island, and they wouldn't have to worry about being preyed upon by mammals.

MP: You got it. To a lesser extent, insects and lizards filled some niches, but without mammals, New Zealand became the island of the birds. So over millions of years, hundreds of endemic bird species evolved to fill every ecological niche imaginable. And, because they didn't have to worry about flying away from any mammalian predators, many of these bird species became flightless: they walked.

About 800 years ago, trouble wandered onto this bird paradise. Sometime around the year 1200, the Maori people, originally from Polynesia, began to inhabit New Zealand. And thus began the decimation of New Zealand's indigenous species. The Maori people hunted some of the endemic bird species to extinction. For instance, the moa, a 12-foot-tall, 500-pound flightless bird species, was hunted to extinction by 1400. Many other endemic bird species went extinct due to habitat loss. But possibly the biggest cause of extinction among New Zealand's endemic bird population was the introduction of invasive mammal species brought over by ship. Probably the most harmful invasive mammal was a species of rat that decimated bird populations by outcompeting the birds for food resources.

Now the Maori's settlement of New Zealand had a large impact on the island's ecosystem, but it doesn't even begin to compare to the damage done when European settlers arrived to the island in the 1700s. Wanting to make New Zealand look more like their home countries, European settlers reshaped the land. In doing so, they destroyed huge amounts of New Zealand's forests, and introduced countless non-native mammalian and avian species to the island. The introduction of dogs, cats, and European rats has been especially damaging to New Zealand's endemic species. By the 1990s, nearly half of New Zealand's endemic bird species were driven to extinction. So in the span of less than 1,000 years, human activities have decimated a fragile and unique ecosystem. Only recently have people been trying to reverse this damage. Now let's look at the efforts that are being undertaken to preserve the remaining endemic species of New Zealand.

Narrator: Now get ready to answer the questions.

PRACTICE 3 - TRACK 10

Narrator: Listen to a talk in a music history class.

MP: Good morning. Today we're going to talk about what has been called the only art form to originate in the United States. And I'm not talking about the art of eating hamburgers with French fries! I'm referring to jazz music. So, as many of you know, early jazz music was produced sometime in the late 1800s in New Orleans. The music grew from a combination of influences, including African-influenced rhythms and European classical music. But, when we hear the term "jazz" today, just what does it mean? After all, there have been so many different styles of jazz—"Dixieland," swing, bebop, avant-garde, etc. What makes all of these "jazz"? Well, let's get into to that right now. Does anyone want to venture a guess? (*To student*) Yes, Lisa?

Female Student (FS): Don't jazz musicians always use the same type of instruments—you know, there are some horns, a piano, and drums, right?

MP: Well, you make a good observation. A lot of early jazz styles, such as "Dixieland," swing, and bebop relied mostly on those instruments. For example, the typical bebop band had a saxophonist, a piano player, a bass player, and a drummer. But the more modern styles of jazz do not rely on those instruments. For example, many jazz-fusion bands during the 1970s and 1980s used electric guitar and electric keyboards. Some avant-garde jazz bands even use instruments like the violin and the kazoo. So, it's not exactly accurate to say instruments are a defining feature of jazz music. So does anyone else want to take a guess. What is it that makes jazz "jazz"?

Male Student (MS): I think I have a good idea. One thing that's really unique about jazz music is the rhythmic structures it uses.

MP: Good. And when you say "rhythm," can you be more specific?

MS: Um, I'm not sure how to explain it. It's like the beats are different. Like the musicians put stress on unexpected notes.

MP: Well, you're definitely on the right track. What you're describing is called "syncopation." Syncopation is a type of rhythm that shifts the accents from what is normally a strong beat to a weak beat.

For example, let's illustrate syncopation with language. In English, we accent certain syllables in normal speech. Take the first sentence from President Lincoln's Gettysburg Address: Normally, it's read with the accents like so: "FOUR-score and SE-ven YEARS a-GO." But a "jazz reading" of this sentence would put the accents on the areas that are usually unaccented: "four-SCORE and se-VEN years A-go." Does that make sense?

MS: Yeah, definitely. I guess that syncopation stuff... I guess that's what makes people want to dance and move to jazz. I mean, when you start getting all those beats in weird places, it encourages people to tap their feet and snap their fingers.

MP: Yes, that's true. In fact, it's not just the drums that do the syncopating in jazz music. All of the instruments often play using some sort of syncopation. And that's why jazz music sounds so chaotic at times. (*To student*) Lisa. You have another comment?

FS: Yeah. I think I have another idea of what constitutes an essential feature of jazz.

MP: Go ahead.

FS: Well, I'm thinking improvisation. I know that all music has parts where instrumentalists play solos, but it seems like jazz really exemplifies that. The solo is like the main part of the music.

MP: You've got it. Improvisation, the spontaneous creation of music while playing, is an essential feature of jazz. Jazz musicians often start with a basic musical framework, and develop it as they play. In fact, the same jazz piece rarely sounds exactly the same for two performances in a row.

FS: Yeah, I guess that's what I was getting at. It's like the soloing is more important than the "basic musical framework."

MP: I think you've hit on something interesting. Improvising is more important than the "basic musical framework" in jazz. So, for many jazz songs, you'll just hear a few minutes or sometimes even seconds of the core part of the song, then, for the rest of the song, each musician trades off playing solo improvisation. Let me play you a song to show you what I mean.

Narrator: Now get ready to answer the questions.

PRACTICE 3 - TRACK 11

Narrator: What does the professor suggest when he says this?

MP: Today we're going to talk about what has been called the only art form to originate in the United States. And I'm not talking about the art of eating hamburgers with French fries!

PRACTICE 3 - TRACK 12

Narrator: Why does the professor say this?

MP: ...the typical bebop band had a saxophonist, a piano player, a bass player, and a drummer. But the more modern styles of jazz do not rely on those instruments. For example, many jazz-fusion bands during the 1970s and 1980s used electric guitar and electric keyboards.

ACTUAL PRACTICE 3

PRACTICE 1 - TRACK 13

Narrator: Listen to part of a conversation between a student and a professor.

Female Student (FS): Thanks for meeting with me on such short notice, Professor Chun. I just wanted to get in here before the deadline for dropping Chemistry 201.

Male Professor (MP): Oh? My lectures are not boring you to tears, I hope?

FS: Oh, no way. It's just that, well, I don't know if I can handle the workload. I mean, the weekly lab, the textbook reading, the problem sets, and then also the requirement to write summaries of the lectures. And that's in addition to my three other classes!

MP: Yes, Sophia, it's tough—these upper-division classes are a lot of work. But this is supposed to be a demanding class. It is, after all, designed for juniors or seniors who need an advanced understanding of chemistry for their majors.

FS: Yeah, I know.

MP: Tell me, how did you do in the lower-division classes that were prerequisites for this class?

FS: Well, those classes didn't seem too hard to me at the time, and I think my grades were pretty good. I actually got "As" in Chemistry 101 and 102. And I got "Bs" in math.

MP: Well, it sounds like you did quite well in those

classes, and even those lower-division classes are no walk in the park.

FS: Yeah, but I'm not feeling very confident. I was hoping to get good enough grades to get into veterinary school. I've wanted to be a vet and work with animals ever since I was a little kid. But I mean, if I can't even keep up with the work in a chemistry class…

MP: Well, Sophia, don't be too hard on yourself. A lot of students have struggled to keep up in this class, even some that later went on to earn Ph.Ds. in chemistry.

FS: Really?

MP: Yes, it's true. Sophia, if you got "A"s and "B"s in your lower-division courses, I do indeed believe that you can excel in this class, too, especially since you seem to be so motivated to become a veterinarian.

FS: You think so?

MP: Of course. Now, I know that you feel like you're under a great deal of pressure, but what you can do is to make a homework schedule. You just get a calendar, and write down when assignments are due for each of your classes, and when you have quizzes or tests.

FS: So I can plan when to study for each one?

MP: Yes, it kind of breaks the huge tasks into smaller "chunks." You will feel like you have only one thing to do in that time period. So, for example, you could write on you calendar, 'on Tuesday night from 8:00 to 10:00, I will read the 50 pages that I need for Wednesday's chemistry lab.' Or something like, 'on Thursday morning I don't have a class, so between breakfast and lunch, I will write my English essay.' The beauty of a schedule is that you can relax and focus on one task at a time.

FS: Okay, so you're saying to plan what I will study and when, and then focus.

MP: Yes, and once you make the schedule, you need to stick to it. No slacking off, no taking phone calls, no going out for snacks… You'll need self-discipline.

FS: Whoa, you mean like, no breaks?

MP: (*Laughing*) No, of course, schedule yourself some breaks! You are the boss on this!

FS: Okay, Professor Chun, if you say so! I guess I'll stick with the class, then. Thanks for your advice.

MP: Anytime, Sophia. Glad I could be of help.

Narrator: Now get ready to answer the questions.

PRACTICE 1 - TRACK 14

Narrator: Listen to part of the conversation. Then answer the question.

FS: Well, those classes didn't seem too hard to me at the time, and I think my grades were pretty good. I actually got "As" in Chemistry 101 and 102. And I got "Bs" in math.

MP: Well, it sounds like you did quite well in those classes, and even those lower-division classes are no walk in the park.

Narrator: What does the professor mean when he says this?

Male Professor: …even those lower-division classes are no walk in the park.

PRACTICE 2 - TRACK 15

Narrator: Listen to a lecture in an education class.

Male Professor (MP): Today we're going to take a closer look at a debate within the field of education that began more than a century ago, and really continues to this day. I'm talking about the issues raised by the Progressive Education movement. This movement was a call for radical change in the classroom, a call that began gathering steam in the U.S. from the 1880s to the 1920s.

So to set the scene, what did the typical American classroom look like in the late 19th century? What were progressive educators arguing against? Well, you may have seen films or T.V. shows depicting rural one-room schoolhouses. The students often sat on benches and held slates—small chalkboards, really—on their laps. The school day would consist of students using their slates to practice penmanship, English grammar, spelling, or arithmetic. Periodically the teacher would call students up to the front of the classroom to be drilled on or to recite memorized information. The teacher was the authority on everything, and was free to hit the students with a ruler.

It may make sense that this idea of a school came about from European settlers. After all, education in monasteries starting in the medieval period may not have looked too much different. The goal was for students to passively absorb language, information, and ideas from old, authoritative texts. Latin grammar and good handwriting were important because monks had the task of copying ancient manuscripts by hand.

So fast-forward to the 1880s: reformers were frustrated. By this time, the Industrial Revolution was in full swing and having an enormous impact on society. Factory jobs were attracting more people to cities, where their children did not have to do farm work. Kids were put to work in factories or mines, but social reformers wanted them in school instead. Cities were building more elementary schools, and for the first time, public high schools.

Meanwhile, at the purely practical level, people had access to mass-produced paper, pencils, fountain pens, newspapers, and books. I mean, imagine the effects of such materials on the typical late-19th century classroom. With reading material, paper, and pencils available, kids could write compositions. Instead of memorizing a few texts for oral recitations, they could just read, and read, and read.

This was certainly agreeable to progressive educators. They wanted to change the curriculum, the teaching methods, methods of school discipline, indeed, the whole underlying purpose of education. They associated education with democracy. They believed that a democracy required an educated public, people who could think critically.

The Progressive Education movement's goals were best articulated by the philosopher John Dewey. He wrote books and articles in which he argued that learning is interactive. So, he said students should be able to interact with teachers, fellow students, and the subject material. Instead of memorizing, students should be able to question and investigate. Learning activities should be hands-on, so that, for example, when learning about biology, students should raise tadpoles or butterflies in the classroom. Children should be engaged in learning, not forced by fear of punishment. Well, of course, all of this means that the whole idea of the student as an individual is lifted up.

Perhaps you can see how in some ways we are still debating this in American education. On the one hand we have the belief that students should learn standard information that can be demonstrated on a nationwide or statewide multiple-choice test. On the other hand, we have the "progressive idea" that students will learn more if they can explore and question. It's a classic tension. Now, let's open this up for discussion. In the classrooms that you have been observing for your final project, have you seen examples of these opposing philosophies?

Narrator: Now get ready to answer the questions.

PRACTICE 3 - TRACK 16

Narrator: Listen to a lecture in a plant biology class.

Male Professor (MP): Good morning. Today I'd like to talk about the biochemical substances known as "hormones." Now we think of hormones as belonging to the human body, but pretty much every organism produces hormones. That brings us to today's focus: the roles of hormones in plants. Now one characteristic of hormones is that they're produced in one part of an organism, but they *affect* a different part of the organism. Hormones act as "chemical messengers" to help different parts of an organism function in a coordinated way.

In fact, the word "hormone" comes from a Greek word that means "to set in motion." As you probably know, in human beings, hormones control such activities as growth, development, and reproduction. However, in plants, the only significant role of hormones is in regulating growth.

So, there are three main types of plant hormones. One type is called "auxins." Auxins are arguably the most important of all the hormones in plants. Auxins cause plants' stems and roots to lengthen. They also stimulate the growth of fruit on fruit-bearing plants and trees.

But auxins also slow some parts of plant growth, too. For example, auxins slow the growth of side branches on some plants. (*To student*) Yes, did I see a hand over there?

FS: I was wondering why does this happen? I mean, if auxins are growth hormones, why do they slow growth, too?

MP: Good question. Well, auxins slow the growth of side branches because these branches use up the energy the plant needs to grow tall and sturdy. So, it's kind of confusing, but some auxins slow the growth of small parts of the plant, resulting in greater height and overall growth. We will look at the process more carefully later in today's lecture.

FS: Okay, thank you.

MP: Great. So now let's look at a second type of plant hormone, called "cytokinin." This hormone controls cell division in plants. The primary function of cytokinin is to determine which cells of a developing plant will become root cells, which will become leaf cells, and which will become branch cells. (*To student*) Yes, did you have a comment or question?

Male Student (MS): So, do cytokinins kind of guide plant cells in a certain direction?

MP: Yeah, that's right. You can think of cytokinins like career or guidance counselors. They help show plant cells their ultimate direction or goal in life. Does that make sense?

MS: Yeah, that will help me remember them. So, without cytokinins, or if a plant has a problem generating cytokinins, the plant would, like, what, die?

MP: You know, that's an interesting question. Without properly functioning cytokinins, plants can live, but they, well, they look very abnormal—they have strange growth patterns.

Okay that is a nice transition to discussing the third type of plant hormone. These last hormones are called "gibberellins," which stimulate plants to grow larger. When used in experiments, gibberellins have made the stems of dwarf plants, abnormal plants, lengthen rapidly. (*To student*) Yes, over there?

FS: Well, I thought that was the job of the auxins—to make plants grow larger.

MP: Well, remember that all hormones in plants affect growth, to a degree. So, gibberellins, like auxins, stimulate plant growth. But, gibberellins mostly cause the seeds and flowers of plants to grow, while auxins affect mostly the stems and roots.

FS: Oh, so the two hormones affect different parts of the plant. I understand.

MP: Yeah, that's the easiest way of looking at it, though it's not completely correct. Let's take a look at the powerpoint and I can try to clarify things even better by going over some of the diagrams.

Narrator: Now get ready to answer the questions.

ACTUAL PRACTICE 4

PRACTICE 1 - TRACK 17

Narrator: Listen to part of a conversation between a student and a professor.

Male Student (MS): Hi, Professor Mew! Remember me, Joseph Kim, from your Comparative Politics class last semester?

Female Professor (FP): Oh, of course I do, Joseph! How nice to see you again!

MS: Thanks, it's nice to see you, too! I really miss being in your class. That was my favorite class ever!

FP: Yes, that's always a fun class to teach. Are you taking more political science classes this semester?

MS: Oh, I am. Right now I'm in the Modern East Asian Politics seminar. It's pretty interesting, too.

FP: Great, I'm glad to hear that you are continuing in political science. You seem to have a real passion for shaping public policy.

MS: Yeah, I do. I started out as a psychology major, but this semester I switched my major to political science. As a matter of fact, the reason I came to see you today was to ask you to write a letter of recommendation for me for a politics internship.

FP: Oh, certainly, Joseph. I'd be delighted. What kind of internship are you applying for?

MS: Well, it's kind of exciting. I've been accepted for the study abroad program in Switzerland, in Geneva…

FP: Oh, perfect!

MS: And the program includes an optional internship. So, you study for the whole school year, and then you do an internship with an international organization or agency during the following summer.

FP: Well, Geneva is certainly the place to be for that.

MS: Yep, it has all kinds of offices related to the United Nations, the World Trade Organization, all kinds of international organizations. I'm going to apply for internships at some of the nonprofit agencies that work on global environmental issues.

FP: Oh, yes, environmental work would be a perfect fit for you, wouldn't it? So, tell me, how are you preparing for this adventure?

MS: Well, I'm taking French, and so hopefully I'll at least be a little bit ready to use that there. You know, I already speak Korean… And then there is the question of how to pay for it all, so I'm getting in all my applications for scholarships and financial aid. So I think I'll pretty much be ready.

FP: Okay, sounds wonderful. So, do you want to email me with the specifics about the letter of recommendation?

MS: Okay, I'll do that. Thanks so much! Hey, by the way,

I saw in the catalog that you are going to be teaching an upper-division class having to do with the environment.

FP: That's right, Politics and the Environment in Australia and the South Pacific Region. We will look at social and political pressures regarding use of the land and seas. Lots to talk about there!

MS: I'll bet!

FP: It's a fascinating place. You should sign up for the course, that region is kind of a microcosm for other areas of the world.

MS: Okay, I'm sold! I was kind of planning to sign up for it anyway. Thanks again for agreeing about the letter, Professor. I'll get that email to you.

Narrator: Now get ready to answer the questions.

PRACTICE 1 - TRACK 18

Narrator: Listen to part of the conversation. Then answer the question.

FP: That's right, Politics and the Environment in Australia and the South Pacific Region. We will look at social and political pressures regarding use of the land and seas. Lots to talk about there!

MS: I'll bet!

Narrator: Why does the student say this?

MS: I'll bet!

PRACTICE 2 - TRACK 19

Narrator: Listen to a lecture in a botany class.

Male Professor (MP): Good morning. Today, I want to talk about a type of tree that all of you are undoubtedly familiar with. In fact, hundreds of these trees adorn our beautiful Southern California campus. By now, you've probably guessed the species of tree that I'm talking about, the eucalyptus tree. The eucalyptus is native to Australia, where hundreds of different species grow. And as you can see when walking around campus, the eucalyptus has become a popular landscaping tree in other warm parts of the world, notably California, South America, Southern Europe, and Northern Africa.

Now, like I said before, there are hundreds of species of eucalyptus. But almost all the eucalyptus found in California are from a single species called *eucalyptus globulus*, often referred to as the blue gum eucalyptus. So during today's lecture, we're going to look at the botanical characteristics and practical industrial uses of the blue gum.

First, let's look at some botanical features of the blue gum eucalyptus. This particular species of eucalyptus can grow to be over 50 meters tall. And unlike other tall trees, such as the redwood and Douglas fir, blue gums grow incredibly quickly. In fact, one blue gum was recorded to have grown about 20 meters in just 6 years! (*To student*) Yes, Jane, you have a question?

Female Student (FS): Professor, I do have a question but it's about the flowers on eucalyptus trees. Uh, I've noticed that all of the flowers on our campus eucalyptus trees are white, right? However, the flowers on the eucalyptus trees near my apartment are red. Why's that?

MP: Good question. The color of a eucalyptus' flower depends on the species. Flower coloration varies from white to yellow to red and pink. So my guess is that the eucalyptus trees planted near your house are a different species from the ones we have on campus.

FS: That makes sense. And I have one other question about eucalyptus. If you look at the leaves on eucalyptus trees closely, well, they droop down. Do you know what I mean? They hang down vertically, but the leaves on most other trees are flat in relationship to the ground.

MP: Oh, yes, I know what you're talking about. Actually, the leaves hang down because it turns them edgewise to the sun. If you think about where eucalyptus trees grow, you may have a clue as to why their leaves are turned edgewise.

FS: Hmm. Well, does it have something to do with conserving water, because they live in such dry environments?

MP: That's right. Eucalyptus trees evolved in Australia, which is mostly quite dry. As a consequence, they have leaves that contain aromatic oil—it helps conserve water, rather like hand lotion. The leaves are also positioned downward, so that they get less sunlight. The effect is to lose less moisture through evaporation, or to be more precise, transpiration.

Male Student (MS): I was wondering: Why are there so many eucalyptus trees planted on our campus?

MP: That's another good question, and it leads to the second part of today's lecture: the value of eucalyptus as a crop. Settlers started planting blue gum eucalyptus in California in the mid- to late-1800s. Some planters speculated that the trees could provide huge amounts of lumber because the trees grow so quickly. This was especially important in Southern California, which lacks easily accessible supplies of lumber because it is too dry for forests. By the 1900s, demand for lumber encouraged farmers and businessmen to plant millions of blue gums. But, soon after this eucalyptus boom, people realized that lumber from eucalyptus trees bends, warps, and cracks as it dries out. So the dream of cheap lumber from blue gums died, and many farmers replaced their blue gums with more profitable crops.

But obviously that's not the end of the story for the blue gum in California. Some farmers and developers still plant blue gums around their crops and building projects because eucalyptus trees make great wind blocks—their height and speedy growth make them perfect for blocking strong winds. And the oil within the tree is still used in some cough syrups. And finally, many people keep them around because they simply find them attractive and good-smelling.

Now, as you can tell, blue gums have proven quite useful here in California, but there are also many downsides to these trees. Some of their water-saving adaptations also make them hazardous. Let's take a look at the reasons for this...

Narrator: Now get ready to answer the questions.

PRACTICE 2 - TRACK 20

Narrator: Now listen again to part of the lecture. Then answer the question.
MP: Now, as you can tell, blue gums have proven quite useful here in California, but there are also many downsides to these trees. Some of their water-saving adaptations also make them hazardous. Let's take a look at the reasons for this...
Narrator: What does the professor mean when he says this?
MP: Some of their water-saving adaptations also make them hazardous.

PRACTICE 3 - TRACK 21

Narrator: Listen to a lecture in a paleontology class.
Male Professor (MP): Good morning. Today I want to talk about a couple of very important fossil sites that are essential to understanding our human origins. Let's start with one of the most important sites in Africa. The Laetoli fossil site—that's spelled "L—A—E—T—O—L—I"—is located in northern Tanzania. In the early 1970s, a team of paleontologists led by Mary Leakey excavated fossils of a hominid that was later named *Australopithecus afarensis*. More importantly, in 1978, scientists uncovered ancient footprints preserved in a layer of volcanic ash. The footprints, which are about 3.6 million years old, are among the oldest evidence for bipedal locomotion—or, walking upright on two legs—by a humanlike creature. Scientists consider bipedal locomotion a feature unique to the hominids. Hominids, as you know, make up the zoological family hominidae, which consists of human beings, early humanlike ancestors, and gorillas, chimpanzees and orangutans.

So the fossil footprints were preserved at the Laetoli site by a rare—but for paleontologists quite fortunate—sequence of events. About 3.6 million years ago, a volcano erupted near the site and deposited a layer of ash across the landscape. Rain fell after the eruption and dampened the ash. Many animals, including hominids, walked across the wet ash, leaving footprints in the soft material. The sun then dried the ash into cement-like hardness within a short time. Soon, the volcano erupted again and deposited a fresh layer of ash that covered and preserved the footprints. Millions of years later, erosion exposed the footprints. Hard to believe, eh?

The hominid footprints create a trail about 24 meters long. There are tracks made by two, perhaps three, hominids, and include approximately 70 footprints. Paleontologists believe that *Australopithecus afarensis* individuals, possibly walking together, made the tracks. Scientific studies of the footprints have determined that they show a pattern of upright walking similar to that of modern human beings. For example, the big toes are more in line with the other toes and less ape-like. Also, the footprints show the heels striking first and the toes pushing off for the next stride, another human characteristic we do not share with other primates. At the time of their discovery, the Laetoli footprints represented the oldest evidence for upright walking ever found. Since the 1970s, however, anthropologists have found other fossil remains that indicate pre-human ancestors were probably bipedal as early as 6 million years ago. We'll be looking at some of those other sites later today.

In 1979, Leakey and her team covered the site with sand to protect the footprints. However, scientists became worried as some of the Laetoli footprints were damaged by erosion and vandalism. In the 1990s, scientists re-excavated the site and removed vegetation that threatened the footprints. They took photographs and measurements of the footprints and the surrounding area using technologies that were unavailable to Leakey's team in the 1970s. The scientists then covered the site with a layer of earth to preserve the footprints. Greg, if you could get the lights, I'm going to prepare the slide projector in back of the class. Thanks.

Narrator: Now get ready to answer the questions.

PRACTICE 3 - TRACK 22

Narrator: What does the professor suggest when he says this?

MP: …scientists became worried as some of the Laetoli footprints were damaged by erosion and vandalism. In the 1990s, scientists re-excavated the site and removed vegetation that threatened the footprints.

ACTUAL PRACTICE 5

PRACTICE 1 - TRACK 23

Narrator: Listen to a conversation between two students.
Male Student (MS): Hey, Taylor, how is it going?
Female Student (FS): Oh, hey, Jamison. I'm good, I'm good, how are you?
MS: Hanging in there, just trying to focus on finals.
FS: Yeah, me too.
MS: But I was also wondering about trying to set up a shared rental situation for the fall semester. Are you going to try to stay on campus?
FS: Well, no, two years of living in the dormitories is enough. I need to start thinking about finding a place to rent off-campus, too. And I will be looking to share a place, too, because there is no way that I can afford to rent an apartment by myself.
MS: So, maybe we could get some other friends together and try to find a house. What do you think?
FS: Yes, that might really work out. I mean, we're both vegetarians, both nonsmokers, both math majors. Both kind of loud.
MS: That's what I was thinking. So, we might be able to find a three-bedroom house, there should be a lot of those. Then we could find another person, or maybe even two, if there's a study or a dining room that could work as a bedroom. With four people sharing costs, the overall rent and utilities would be a lot cheaper for each person.
FS: Hmm, Jamison, you must be a math major.
MS: Very funny! But we can't decide much about anything until we see what's available in town and what kinds of rent landlords are charging.
FS: True. It would be so perfect to find something near campus, so we could walk or ride our bikes. But if that is too costly, at least we should try to live near a bus route. My car is about to die, and anyway, parking permits cost so much here on campus. So what I'm saying is, we should figure transportation costs into the package, too.
MS: Why, Taylor, you sound like a math major!
FS: Ha. Ha! So, let's see, you know my friend Ashley, right? Physics major, kind of shy?
MS: Yeah, I know who you mean.
FS: Well, Ashley has been living in a house off-campus for a couple of years, but she was just telling me the other day that she has to move because all of her roommates are graduating.
MS: Maybe we could just move in when her old roommates move out?
FS: Except that she had another reason for wanting to move. Where she is now, the landlord doesn't allow any pets, and Ashley really wants to get a cat. I mean, I know, I know, having a pet usually means that you have to pay the landlord a bigger cleaning deposit.
MS: Oh, yeah, but I would like living with a cat. I like cats because they kind of act like wild animals, but they still want you to pet them and play with them.
FS: Yep, cats are always the boss of the house, right? Okay, but seriously, I will call Ashley and see what her plans are at this point. Maybe we can network and find someone who is looking for three new roommates and a cat.
MS: Who knows? Okay, and I'll go to the university's Off-Campus Housing Office website and see what is being posted so far. It's early, of course, but I've heard that a lot of landlords like to get details sorted out

before summer break.

FS: Sounds like a plan, Jamison. I'm glad we talked. Text me if you find anything.

MS: Okay, sounds good.

Narrator: Now get ready to answer the questions.

PRACTICE 1 - TRACK 24

Narrator: Listen to part of the conversation. Then answer the question.

MS: So, maybe we could get some other friends together and try to find a house. What do you think?

FS: Yes, that might really work out. I mean, we're both vegetarians, both nonsmokers, both math majors. Both kind of loud.

Narrator: What does the woman imply when she says this?

FS: Yes, that might really work out. I mean, we're both vegetarians, both nonsmokers, both math majors. Both kind of loud.

PRACTICE 2 - TRACK 25

Narrator: Listen to a lecture in a U.S. History class.

Female Professor (FP): Good morning. Today we will talk about workers in the first British colonies in America, and in particular, we will focus on indentured servants. As you know, during the 17th century, British colonies were established along the east coast of what is now the United States. What you may not know is that many of the people we think of as "early colonists" were not all British, and they were not all free. Many were indentured servants, kind of like temporary slaves. They were English, Scottish, Welsh, German, Dutch, Spanish, Portuguese, and African, and when they arrived, they were "owned" by someone else.

During the early 1600s, British colonists in Virginia were having a hard time surviving and establishing a permanent colony. They were fighting with the local tribes, the Powhatan Confederacy, and they were coping with hunger and disease. At the same time, there was an increase in demand in Europe for this "new" thing called tobacco. So, British colonists in Virginia began growing tobacco, which could return a pretty good profit. The problem that farmers faced was that they needed lots of workers; tobacco crops are very labor-intensive. Certainly, the Powhatan people did not want to sign on to work for them. So the farmers had a problem.

At first, the solution was to bring in poor people. In 1618, the colony of Virginia tried to help establish the practice by granting extra land to farmers who imported servants. So what exactly was the process? Well, indentured servants were recruited in the British Isles or elsewhere, sometimes by ship's captains. The captain would offer a contract which said that in exchange for fare to the American colony, the person agreed to work for a certain amount of time for no wages. The contract was usually for between five and seven years. When they reached the colony, the ship's captain would sell the contract to an employer, usually a farmer. Essentially, the worker was selling himself or herself to an unknown master, but both parties agreed that it would be temporary.

The practice became so common that soon, more than half of all immigrants to the British colonies arrived as indentured servants. The increasing demand for cotton in England made cotton farming profitable, and southern growers began using indentured workers to produce cotton and rice. Some southern colonies had populations that were more than 75 percent indentured servants. Seventy-five percent—can you believe that? This is something that popular portrayals of our history often leave out. "Land of the free," indeed!

Why would anyone want to come to a place that struggled with famine and disease, only to work for years with no pay? Well, some may have been excited about the adventure and new possibilities. Others may have seen it as their best option for survival. Some areas of Europe had seen an increase in population and farm technology, so there was not enough work on farms or in cities.

In other cases, the sign-ups were not what we would call "voluntary." Some people had become buried under debt, and agreed to indentured servitude instead of debtor's prison. People convicted of crimes were also sometimes allowed to become indentured servants rather than getting prison sentences. And an unknown number of people were tricked or kidnapped into servitude.

In addition, it was not widely known for some time how difficult it was to survive indentured servitude. The workers who survived the grueling journey to the colony found a tough life awaiting them. They basically had no rights, so that masters could treat them harshly, and use physical punishment such as whippings. Another form of punishment was to add time to the servants' contracts. For example, female indentured servants who became pregnant could be punished with extra years added to their contracts. So, indentured servants often did not survive to gain freedom; more than half of them died before the end of their contract, due to overwork, poor food rations, and inadequate housing.

During the 1700s, the use of indentured servants began to decline, and it had almost totally disappeared by the 1830s. One reason was that there was more shipping across the Atlantic Ocean, so that fares dropped and Europeans who wanted to come to the Americas could pay their own way, without becoming indentured. Another reason was that there was an increasing pool of laborers already living in the colonies so that employers could just hire the workers they needed. But probably the biggest reason, as you may have guessed, was that southern farmers began to rely more and more on enslaved people from Africa.

So let's take a 10-minute break, and when we come back we will discuss how the legal status of African immigrants and African Americans began to change, starting around the middle of the 17th century.

Narrator: Now get ready to answer the questions.

PRACTICE 2 - TRACK 26

Narrator: Listen to part of the lecture. Then answer the question.

FP: Some colonies had populations that were more than 75 percent indentured servants. Seventy-five percent—can you believe that? This is something that popular portrayals of our history often leave out. "Land of the free," indeed!

Narrator: What is the professor's attitude when she says this?

FP: "Land of the free," indeed!

PRACTICE 2 - TRACK 27

Narrator: Listen to part of the lecture. Then answer the question.

FP: The captain or an agent would offer a contract which said that in exchange for fare to the American colony, the person agreed to work for a certain amount of time for no wages. The contract was usually for between five and seven years. When they reached the colony, the ship's captain or other agent would sell the contract to an employer, usually a farmer. Essentially, the worker was selling himself or herself to an unknown master, but both parties agreed that it would be temporary.

Narrator: What can be inferred about indentured servants from this?

FP: Essentially, the worker was selling himself or herself to an unknown master, but both parties agreed that it would be temporary.

PRACTICE 3 - TRACK 28

Narrator: Listen to a lecture in a geology class.

Female Professor (FP): Tomorrow morning, we are going to explore the longest known cave system in the world—Kentucky's Mammoth-Flint Ridge Cave. This cave has over 550 kilometers of explored passageways. But many researchers think that this cave system may extend even further. After all, mapping out caves is a pretty new field of research, so there's a lot about caves that we have yet to uncover.

Anyway, what I'd like to do today is prepare us for our adventure by describing just how cave systems such as the ones in Mammoth-Flint are formed. So get your pens and pencils ready, because this material is going to be on next week's quiz.

Most caves, such as those in the Mammoth-Flint system, form in limestone. And these caves that form in limestone are referred to as solution caves by geologists. They form as underground water slowly dissolves the limestone rock beneath and around it. And when I say "slowly," I mean really slowly. In fact, the process of solution cave formation takes thousands of years. So just how does that—how do solution caves form? Well, it begins when surface water trickles down through tiny cracks in the limestone rock to an area that is saturated—that is, flooded or filled up—with water. The topmost level of this saturated zone is called the water table. You remember that term from our unit on water, right? Water flowing above and below the water table dissolves some of the limestone rock, forming passages and holes.

So one question you might have about all of this is, "Why do caves form in limestone?" And many people believe that the answer to this question is that limestone must be softer than other types of rock. But really, limestone is not very soft, and is only slightly soluble in water. However, the water that trickles down from the surface contains carbon dioxide. And where does this carbon dioxide come from? (*To student*) Yes, what do you think?

Male Student (MS): Doesn't the water absorb carbon dioxide from surrounding air when it's still at the surface?

FP: Yes, that's exactly it. And so when carbon dioxide combines with water, it forms a mild acid, and this acid helps dissolve the limestone rock. Limestone is particularly susceptible to dissolving with this acid-water mix.

Eventually, the water table—so where the water levels in the cave are highest—may drop below the level of the newly forming cave itself. Or the cave may be raised above the water table by a gradual uplifting of the ground. Most of the water then drains out, and air fills the cave. A surface stream may enter the cave and flow through it. The stream then continues to dissolve the rock, enlarging the cave even more. But then, how do all of these different connections from the cave to the surface develop? Well, that can happen in a couple of ways. First, connections to the surface can develop when the rock above part of the cave collapses, forming a vertical entrance called a sinkhole. Now this term should be pretty easy to remember; just think of the ground sinking into a hole, and you'll be able to remember "sinkhole." Another way that connections to the surface develop is horizontally, on a hillside or a valley slope. These are the type of cave entrances most of us are accustomed to seeing. These develop especially at a point where a spring or stream flows from the cave.

Narrator: Now get ready to answer the questions.

PRACTICE 3 - TRACK 29

Narrator: What does the professor suggest when she says this?

FP: But many researchers think that this cave system may extend even further. After all, mapping out caves is a pretty new field of research, so there's a lot about caves that we have yet to uncover.

PRACTICE 3 - TRACK 30

Narrator: Why does the professor say this?

FP: And many people believe that the answer to this question is that limestone must be softer than other types of rock. But really, limestone is not very soft, and is only slightly soluble in water.

ACTUAL PRACTICE 6

PRACTICE 1 - TRACK 31

Narrator: Listen to a conversation between a student and a professor.

Female Student (FS): Thanks for meeting with me, Professor Kustov. You must be very busy, this being the second week of classes and all.

Male Professor (MP): Oh, that's true, everyone's busy at the beginning of the quarter. But I always have time to meet with my students. Now, which class are you in, uh….

FS: My name is Eva, Eva Segreti. Actually, I am not in your class…yet. That's what I wanted to talk to you about. You see, I'd like to add your painting class, Art 209-A. I'm a studio arts major and—

MP: Whoa, hold on there a minute, Eva. You do realize that the final deadline to add classes was last Friday, don't you? I mean, you are only supposed to add classes during the first week of the quarter.

FS: I know, but what happened is, I had to have emergency surgery last week. My appendix became inflamed, and the doctors decided to remove it.

MP: Oh, Eva! You had your appendix taken out? That sounds very painful. Are you okay to come back to school so soon?

FS: Thank you. Yeah, I'm pretty much okay now, but I didn't really have time to get my schedule set up.

MP: But didn't you have your schedule set up before the quarter began?

FS: Well, yes, I did. But the problem was that your painting class was full when I tried to enroll online, so I got on the waiting list. I planned on showing up the first day, in case some students didn't show up. You know, so I could ask you if I could take their spots, and add the class to my schedule.

MP: Ah, I see. But, you were in the hospital having surgery instead?

FS: Exactly. So… is there any chance I could still get into the class?

MP: Unfortunately, the class is completely full. There were a couple of extra students who asked me if they could add the class last week.

FS: Oh, shoot.

MP: I know it seems unfair, but with a studio art classes, it's not just a matter of squeezing in another desk, you know. There has to be space and materials. Now, you could check out some of the sculpture courses, or drawing. Perhaps you could find another studio art class for this semester?

FS: I understand the problem with your class being full, Professor Kustov. But I wanted to take the year-long series of painting classes, you know, Art 209-A, -B, and -C. If I don't get into 209-A, I can't take the other two.

MP: Well, Eva, you could take the series next year, couldn't you?

FS: No, because I'm graduating in the spring. This is my last chance. And I wanted to have a class with you, because all your students say that they learned so much from you.

MP: Well, that is very kind of you to say so. How about this—I'll put you at the top of the waiting list. Then, you just attend class, start a painting with us, and see what happens. Usually, at least one person drops out within the first few weeks. Then you can officially enroll. Okay?

FS: That would be great, except, if, you know, no one drops out, could we say I was doing an independent study?

MP: That might work, and still allow you to sign up for the next class in the series. Good idea. I'll talk to the dean about that. In the meantime, I will see you in class next Tuesday.

FS: Okay! I'll be there!

Narrator: Now get ready to answer the questions.

PRACTICE 1 - TRACK 32

Narrator: Listen to part of the conversation. Then answer the question.

FS: Exactly. So… is there any chance I could still get into the class?

MP: Unfortunately, the class is completely full. There were a couple of extra students who asked me if they could add the class last week.

Narrator: What is the professor's tone in this part of the conversation?

MP: Unfortunately, the class is completely full. There were a couple of extra students who asked me if they could add the class last week.

PRACTICE 2 - TRACK 33

Narrator: Listen to a lecture in an American Literature class.

Male Professor (MP): This morning I would like to attempt the impossible. I will attempt to explain what makes a work of fiction "postmodern." You have probably heard people calling this era that we live in the "Postmodern Age," and that is referring to a cultural shift in expression. From about the middle of the 20th century, we can see a move toward postmodern characteristics in novels, stories, plays, and films.

One reason it is impossible to define post-modernism is that not everyone agrees what it is. But one way to describe it is a move away from categorizing. Thus, it is more mixed-up, participatory, playful, multi-ethnic. It's about a unique moment rather than a universal truth.

But I think I can illustrate the idea by talking a bit about television programming. Okay, so using the TV metaphor, in the 1960s, there were only three major networks in the U.S. They offered nightly news, weekly comedies and dramas, game shows, talk shows, and variety shows. All that programming could be contained in a weekly magazine called *TV Guide*. The whole experience was limited and mediated. Now, can anyone explain what I mean by "mediated?"

Female Student (FS): Uh, okay, I think you mean that there is always someone in charge, making decisions.

MP: Exactly. That's right. For example, in a talk show, such as the legendary Ed Sullivan Show, someone has decided who should be invited to be on the show, and there is a familiar host who kind of guides everyone along.

Male Student (MS): Like there is an omniscient narrator?

MP: Yes, a narrator who knows everything, decides the best way to tell it, and tells everything exactly as it is.

FS: So that's not really postmodern, is it? I mean, because in postmodernism, there is no way for one person to tell everything exactly as it is, because, uh, truth is subjective. Each person sees a situation differently.

MP: Yes, postmodernism embraces the notion that people construct their own truth, as they experience life. No one can say what is "real" for everyone. That's why it's interesting, to get back to our television metaphor here, to take a look at MTV.

"MTV" stands for "Music Television," and the cable channel began in 1981as just that—kind of a visual radio station. Most programming was videos of music bands or solo artists performing songs. Compared to what people were used to seeing, MTV seemed random. Viewers did not know which music videos would be aired when. As for the videos, they tended toward an incoherent mix of images, sort of suggesting a story, but not explaining it, more like a dream. So here we see a move away from order and toward a more random, chaotic expression. More like a montage of images. The viewer has to interpret the meaning for himself or herself.

Another postmodern characteristic in MTV was its increasing diversity of styles. At first, it featured very few nonwhite performers, but it did gradually become more inclusive. The channel premiered Michael Jackson's pop music video "Thriller" in 1983. Today, many critics regard "Thriller" as the greatest music video of all time. The video itself contained elements of postmodernism. For one thing, the viewer cannot be sure what is "real" in the video. The two main characters might be in a "real" situation, or they might be watching that situation in a movie, or they might be in a dream, or a dream within a dream. As the video unfolds, the viewer becomes delightfully confused.

That sense of playfulness is also present in some of the music videos by the undisputed queen of MTV, Madonna. For example, in her 1990 video "Vogue," Madonna urges the audience to cope with heartache on the dance floor by mimicking movie stars, with fragmented, mock-serious dress-up scenes and posing as though for a camera. It is confusing, because of course, Madonna is on camera.

Next came the rise of the Internet, and websites such as YouTube. So here we have a more complete shift against mediated programming. Viewers can choose to watch whatever they want whenever they want, and what's more, viewers can participate by uploading their own videos. YouTube represents a chaos, a vast diversity of expression. Viewers will see different things, participate differently, and create their own experiences; which is pretty much a perfect metaphor for postmodernism.

Narrator: Now get ready to answer the questions.

PRACTICE 3 - TRACK 34

Narrator: Listen to a lecture in an ecology class.

Male Professor (MP): So today, we're going to continue our unit on parasites. We've already discussed endo and ectoparasites, so now I'd like to introduce epiparasites, also called hyperparasites. Epiparasites are parasites that prey upon other, larger parasites, or sometimes on each other.

Female Student (FS): Professor, I thought parasites had to infect another plant or animal? Are you saying that some parasites can actually feed on their own species, like cannibals?

MP: Yes, Emily, that's correct. If you recall our discussion on mistletoe last week, you'll remember there are hundreds of individual species of mistletoe. And some of these have evolved to grow on other varieties of mistletoe, or even on a plant of the same species.

Most epiparasites, however, don't infest their own species. After all, such an adaptation would inevitably result in the decline of a population, because its members would constantly be eating each other. So, the vast majority of epiparasites feed on organisms that are much larger than they are, just like traditional parasites. A classic example of this type of parasitism is the infestation of a flea by a small protozoan. The protozoan lives in the digestive tract of the flea and exploits the resources gathered by the flea; likewise, the flea lives in a cat's fur and consumes energy acquired by the host.

FS: What would be the benefit of infesting a parasite? I mean, most parasites are already so small and have such limited access to resources. Wouldn't the epiparasite be entirely dependent upon the parasite and its host? What if the cat starves?

MP: You bring up a good point. Epiparasites thrive on their hosts for the same reason traditional parasites succeed: it fills a vacant niche in the ecological network. Parasites adapt to exploit resources from successful organisms; if the parasite becomes successful enough, a smaller organism will likely evolve to exploit resources from it.

Another way to look at it is this: all organisms get diseases. Even bacterial cells can be infected with viruses or smaller bacteria. So, even though parasites are generally small, they are still susceptible to diseases, infections, and, yes, parasites.

Male Student (MS): Professor, I know you said some parasites can infect members of the same species, so can some hyperparasites infest other hyperparasites?

MP: Absolutely, James. In fact, some biologists even recognize hyperhyperparasites, or parasites that infest a hyperparasite. Again, this infestation is a natural extension of any parasitic relationship. Once an organism begins to establish itself in a given habitat, existing life forms will adapt to its presence. Eventually, even a bacterium can be invaded by parasites that have adapted to whatever opportunity for nutrients the bacterium unwittingly offers.

And to go back to your question, Emily, of course these miniature parasites have no awareness that their host is a parasite itself. Like any organism, these individuals adapt to exploit an empty ecological niche. From their perspective, it is entirely coincidental that this niche happens to be a parasite already.

Let me give you an example to help clarify. Butterflies and moths are extremely successful, evolutionarily speaking. The order they comprise, Lepidoptera, is so successful, in fact, that butterflies and moths have attracted the attention of numerous infectious diseases and parasites. Because of the success of Lepidoptera species, their parasites are also successful.

One of these parasites is a braconid wasp. This wasp lays eggs inside the caterpillar, the larval stage of a moth or butterfly. The braconid larvae hatch and consume the caterpillar's blood and nonvital organs. Before the caterpillar builds its own cocoon, the braconid larvae chew their way out. Then, they can build cocoons on the dead or dying caterpillar.

Now, the braconid has had such enduring success—thanks to the moths and butterflies it infests—that it has developed pathogens of its own. Specifically, a smaller, unrelated family of wasps infests the braconids' cocoons. This hyperparasite, a chalcid wasp, is able to utilize resources from the braconid because of the evolutionary success of the braconid and its host, Lepidoptera.

The small, chalcid wasp is entirely dependent upon both the braconid and the moths and butterflies upon which the braconid preys. Although this is true, you can see, with the abundance of Lepidoptera species in the world, neither parasite should ever go hungry. In fact, I wouldn't be surprised to learn that the chalcid wasp has its own problems with unwanted invaders.

Now, before we look at specializations in epiparasite digestion, does anyone have any questions on what we just discussed?

Narrator: Now get ready to answer the questions.

ACTUAL PRACTICE 7

PRACTICE 1 - TRACK 35

Narrator: Listen to a conversation between a student and a teaching assistant (TA).

Male Teaching Assistant (TA): Hi, have a seat. What can I do for you today?

Female Student (FS): Hi, Benjamin, I'm Mia Wilson, I'm in your discussion section for History 115.

TA: Yeah, I recognize you, Mia. How are you doing?

FS: Well, I just need to tell you that, unfortunately, I'm going to have to miss a couple of weeks of lectures and sections. I'm worried about my grade in this class.

TA: Oh, man, two weeks? You realize that there are only 10 weeks in a quarter, right?

FS: Yeah, I'm sorry, I know it's a lot. But it's because my mom hurt her back, and she needs help for a bit while she recuperates.

TA: Ah, that sounds like a tough situation, Mia. I'm really sorry to hear that. I hope your mother is okay.

FS: Thanks, yeah, it's been hard for her, but she's going to be getting physical therapy and everything. I think she'll just need me around for a little while to help her with meals and errands and anything that involves bending or reaching, you know.

TA: Well, I can see why you want to be there. So look, there are several ways you can keep up with the class while you're gone. Be sure to look at the syllabus for all assignment information and, you know, keep up with the reading. That's really important.

FS: Okay, definitely. I will do that.

TA: So I believe the next two weeks will be on different aspects of the colonial empire of Portugal in the early 16th century. Like, Portuguese sailing technology, Portuguese goals regarding the spice trade in Asia, Portugal's explorations of the Americas and Greenland, Portuguese relations with the Dutch and the Spanish, and the effects of the Portuguese empire on the people who were colonized.

FS: Portugal, got it.

TA: So, you know that the professor's PowerPoints for her lectures should be on the class website, of course. You can email me if you have any questions.

FS: Okay, thanks. I will look at those PowerPoints.

TA: Now, in the syllabus you can find all the details for the paper that's due on the 15th. That will be right before you get back. So just attach it to an email and send it to me by then, okay?

FS: Uh, okay. How many pages does it have to be?

TA: Well, you'll see the details about it when you check the syllabus, or on the class website. But basically, it needs to be at least 10 pages. You have to analyze the reasons that Portuguese colonists planted sugar cane in Brazil and elsewhere, and the short-term and long-term effects of the sugar cane crops.

FS: Sugar cane? A whole paper just on sugar cane, are you sure?

TA: Trust me, there will be more than enough information to analyze in 10 pages. Even in 500!

FS: Oh, no, 500 pages!

TA: (*laughing*) No, no, please *don't* write 500 pages. I have to read it, remember. Ten pages will be plenty. Just stick to the main points.

FS: Great, thanks so much. I feel better. I have to keep my grades up because I'm going to be applying to law schools.

TA: Oh, you're pre-law? Well, then, I'll be expecting a strong argument in your paper.

FS: Thanks, I'll do my best, Benjamin!

Narrator: Now get ready to answer the questions.

PRACTICE 1 - TRACK 36

Narrator: Why does the teaching assistant say this?

TA: Oh, man, two weeks? You realize that there are only 10 weeks in a quarter, right?

PRACTICE 2 - TRACK 37

Narrator: Listen to a lecture in an Environmental Studies class.

Female Professor (FP): So today I would like to continue our focus on groundwater by looking at the impacts of agriculture. Now of course, applying water to crops, irrigating them, is necessary in any region where crops need more water than they can get from rainfall.

The simplest irrigation technique is to flood the field. You use pipes or ditches to divert water from a river, a lake, or a well to the crop land, and then just let it disperse over the land. With flood irrigation, farmers usually build up low retaining walls around the fields, to hold in the water and submerge the entire field. Farmers might divide their fields into sections this way, and flood each field individually by opening and closing channels of water flow. Nick, you have your hand up?

Male Student (MS): Yeah, it seems like they do that in the rice fields east of campus. I went on a bird-watching hike there for another class.

FP: Yes, the rice growers there divert water from the river and the marshes that you hiked around. And flood irrigation works best for grass-like crops, such as rice or alfalfa. From the viewpoint of the farmer, the benefits of flooding the soil include the flushing out of excess salts, which can harm plant roots; and, if water is already abundant, it is probably the least expensive method. However, under many conditions, flood irrigation does not make sense. Any ideas what those conditions might be? Yes, Alyssa?

Female Student (FS): Well, what happens to all that water if the soil becomes completely saturated? Like, if the soil is heavier and more clay-like, not all sandy, it might just kind of drown the plants.

FP: Yes, that is quite true. In heavier soils with less drainage, flood irrigation can cause anaerobic conditions around plant roots, which can kill the plant off. Most plant roots need to be able to absorb oxygen from tiny air pockets in the soil.

FS: And wouldn't it be wasteful? It seems like a lot of water would just go deeper down into the soil. I mean, especially in a dry place.

FP: That's right. About half the water evaporates, runs off, and, as you say, percolates deep into the soil. So farmers who have to buy water would see it as inefficient.

The second basic method of irrigation is sprinklers: forcing pressurized water through sprinklers in order to mimic rainfall. Sprinkler irrigation became much more tenable in the 1950s with the invention of sprinklers attached to field-length pipes that are elevated and mounted on huge wheels. These can be wheeled back and forth in the field as watering is needed.

When it is time to plow or harvest, the pipes can be wheeled out of the way.

Sprinkler irrigation gives farmers more control than flood irrigation does. In general, it uses water more efficiently, depending on the dryness of the air. But obviously, it is only an option in places with pressurized water, which requires a power source and a network of delivery pipes. So it is not feasible in many places.

The third basic method of irrigation is to water from the bottom up. Subirrigation applies water under the surface of the soil so that it is within reach of the plants' roots. Now how do you do this? One way is to lay porous pipes under the soil before planting. Then when the plants need water, you just turn on the spigot, sending water through the pipes straight to the roots. Another way is to control the water table, or the natural level of groundwater.

MS: Controlling the water table? That doesn't seem possible.

FP: You're right, it is only possible in locations that already have a fairly high water table, so that any water you add is just kind of like a topping. Or, instead of a high water table, there could be some kind of impermeable layer of granite or something not far from the surface. So, in these situations, you can dig shallow ditches or trenches about every 15 to 30 meters, and fill them with water. The water sinks down just a bit and seeps horizontally underground to the roots of the plants.

MS: What if you just elevate the rows of plants a few inches, like for strawberries, and then just apply water in the trenches between rows? Isn't that kind of the same idea?

FP: Yes, I see what you mean, because you are not applying water to the top of the plant, but rather letting it seep in to the roots from the sides. So now let's discuss the effects of irrigation on the environment…

Narrator: Now get ready to answer the questions.

PRACTICE 3 - TRACK 38

Narrator: Now listen to a lecture in a business class.

Female Professor (FP): We've been talking about different types of businesses all week. Today, I want to discuss the origins of the American fast food industry; specifically, the restaurant concept created by two brothers, Richard and Maurice McDonald, who started in Southern California in the 1930s. I want to fill in any holes in the history of the company for you. The McDonald brothers' first food venture was a hotdog stand in Arcadia, California, about 40 miles east of Los Angeles, which opened in 1937. The hotdog stand was successful, but the brothers wanted to open something bigger, so they used the profits from the hotdog stand to open their first restaurant, the McDonald Brothers Burger Bar, in San Bernardino, California, in 1940.

This restaurant was a barbecue drive-in, with various types of barbecued meats. Customers could order food from their cars, and waiters would serve the food to them in their cars. Eating in your car was a new phenomenon in the United States. It was not, however, what made McDonald's unique.

The brothers soon realized that hamburgers were responsible for almost all their profits at McDonald Brothers Burger Bar. They decided to concentrate on making just hamburgers, and greatly reduced their menu, eliminating chicken, pork, and beef ribs. In 1948, inspired by the assembly line of Henry Ford, the McDonald brothers closed their restaurant for several months, and cut service back to the essentials. When they reopened in 1949, renamed simply "McDonald's," the McDonald brothers offered a simple menu of hamburgers, French fries, and milkshakes, produced on a continuous basis (rather than made to order, as all restaurants had done) and with no substitutions offered.

Because of this assembly-line-style service, food could be served almost immediately, which was a new idea that Richard McDonald called "fast food." Most historians agree that Richard McDonald was one of the first people to use this term. At the time, the McDonald brothers also referred to their food preparation method as the "Speedee Service System." Oh, and the food at McDonald's was not only served quickly, it was priced cheaply—a hamburger at the original 1949 McDonald's cost 15 cents, half of what it cost at similar restaurants.

And in addition to the limited menu, the fast preparation, and the low cost of the food, the restaurant was also changed in other important ways. The waiters were gone. Customers now walked up to a single window to place and receive their orders. And, McDonalds made the kitchen area visible to the customers, to show how clean it was. They also eliminated all China plates and silver utensils, serving everything in paper bags and cups. The system worked well because parents would drive up and send their children up to the window to place the orders, still in full sight of the parents. The employees were instructed—in what would become a motto in the fast food industry—to "Treat Every Customer with Respect" and so children were made to feel special when they ordered. This was not a bad idea during a time period that has been called the "Baby Boom."

But, how did this one small McDonald's become the biggest restaurant company in the world? That's the story of Ray Kroc, a milkshake machine salesman who was a big fan of the McDonald brothers' fast food restaurant concept. Although the McDonald brothers had invented the "Speedee Service System," it was Kroc who recognized the enormous potential of the business model. He persuaded the brothers to put him in charge of franchising, and founded McDonald's Corporation with the opening of his first franchise, a McDonald's in Des Plaines, Illinois, in 1955. As you may guess, Kroc's enthusiasm for the company was strong. In his first year with McDonald's, he unsuccessfully tried to convince Walt Disney, a personal acquaintance, to let him open a restaurant in the forthcoming Disneyland.

Then, in 1961, Kroc bought the company from the McDonald brothers for 2.7 million dollars. After that, the relationship soured. Kroc denied them the rights to the McDonald's name for their original restaurant. He even opened a new McDonald's nearby to force the original restaurant out of business. And Kroc rewrote McDonald's history to show himself as the founder of McDonald's, barely mentioning the role the McDonald brothers played. Kroc's first restaurant inaccurately claimed to be "McDonald's #1" (it was actually the 9th McDonald's restaurant).

So let's stop for a moment and talk about some of this information. What factors would you suggest that led to the global success of the fast-food model? What was it that Ray Kroc saw?

Narrator: Now get ready to answer the questions.

PRACTICE 3 - TRACK 39

Narrator: Now listen again to part of the lecture. Then answer the question.

FP: I want to fill in any holes in the history of the company for you. The McDonald brothers' first food venture was a hotdog stand in Arcadia, California, about 40 miles east of Los Angeles, which opened in 1937.

Narrator: What does the professor mean when she says this?

FP: I want to fill in any holes...

ACTUAL PRACTICE 8

PRACTICE 1 - TRACK 40

Narrator: Listen to a conversation between a student and an advisor.

Male Advisor (MA): Good afternoon, Eliza. How can I help you today?

Female Student (FS): Well, I would like to change my major.

MA: Okay, let me bring you up on the student database. What's your ID number?

FS: 17890.

MA: (*typing*) Okay, Eliza, it looks like you're currently studying English Literature, is that right?

FS: Yes, that's correct, and I'd like to change my major to Chinese Studies.

MA: Okay. Unfortunately, none of your English Literature credits will count toward your new major. Have you taken any Chinese history, language or culture courses yet?

FS: I've taken Introductory Mandarin and I'm currently enrolled in Intermediate Mandarin. Oh, and I should have taken some of my Chinese history classes. I took two Chinese history classes for my general education requirement during my freshman year.

MA: Let's see here. Yeah, both of those classes will count toward the Chinese Studies major. Okay, so to complete the major, you would need to take Advanced Mandarin, Conversational Mandarin, Modern Chinese Culture, three upper division Chinese culture class, and one upper division Chinese history class.

FS: Okay, and what about my general education requirements?

MA: Let me see. It looks like all you need is one social sciences credit and one laboratory science credit.

FS: I thought I took a science class last year, during my second semester. The course was called Consumer Chemistry: Exploring Common Chemicals.

MA: Oh, well the problem is that Consumer Chemistry doesn't count toward your general education requirement. The university guidelines require that all students take a laboratory science course. So you'll have to take something like General Chemistry, or Intro to Physics, that includes a laboratory session.

FS: I wish they would have made it clear on the course description that Consumer Chemistry does not fulfill that requirement.

MA: Yes, that's a good point. I'll be sure to forward your complaint to the department chair. Anyway, that about covers it for general graduation requirements. Now, Eliza, this is your third year at the university, is that correct?

FS: Yes, that's right. I know it's not a good time to switch majors, but studying Chinese just makes more sense for my future career plans.

MA: You know, you might want to consider finishing your English Literature major and just adding Chinese as a minor. Since you've already taken those Chinese history courses, you would only need to take Advanced Mandarin and Modern Chinese Culture to complete the minor.

FS: You know I hadn't considered that before. But, to be honest, I really wasn't sure what I wanted to study when I declared my major. Actually, I'm just now taking my first upper division literature course this semester. At this point, I think I've made as much progress toward the Chinese Studies major as I have toward the English Literature major.

MA: Well, why don't you just think about it and I'll give you two forms. The first is to change majors and the second is to declare a minor. When you make a decision, fill out the top half of one of the forms. Make sure you get the appropriate signatures on the bottom half, then bring it back here and we'll make it official.

FS: Okay, sounds good.

MA: One more thing, Eliza. You might want to visit the registrar and change your courses for next semester.

FS: Yes, I think I'll do that. Thank you.

Narrator: Now get ready to answer the questions.

PRACTICE 1 - TRACK 41

Narrator: Listen to part of the conversation. Then answer the question.

FS: I thought I took a science class last year, during my second semester. The course was called Consumer Chemistry: Exploring Common Chemicals.

MA: Oh, well the problem is that Consumer Chemistry doesn't count toward your general education requirement. The university guidelines require that all students take a laboratory science course. So you'll have to take something like General Chemistry, or Intro to Physics, that includes a laboratory session.

FS: I wish they would have made it clear on the course description that Consumer Chemistry does not fulfill that requirement.

Narrator: Why does the student say this?

FS: I wish they would have made it clear on the course description that Consumer Chemistry does not fulfill that requirement.

PRACTICE 2 - TRACK 42

Narrator: Now listen to a lecture in a geography class.

Female Professor (FP): Good morning. All month we've been talking about seas. And to review, seas are landlocked bodies of saltwater that typically cover areas larger than lakes, but smaller than oceans. During the last class, we talked about the Black Sea. Before that, we discussed the Red Sea. Today, I want to talk about what is known by geologists and laypeople alike as the Dead Sea.

The Dead Sea is a giant saltwater body of water located at the mouth of the Jordan River and forming part of the border between Israel and Jordan. Its shore lies about 416 meters below sea level, so it is the lowest place on the surface of Earth. It is even lower than Death Valley, the lowest point in North America, which lies 82 meters below sea level. In addition to being the lowest place on the surface of Earth, the Dead Sea is also one of the saltiest bodies of water in the world. According to scientists, the Dead Sea is about nine times saltier than any of the world's oceans. Because of its high salt content, any person or animal that enters the Dead Sea will float naturally on its surface without any effort. Pretty cool, huh?

Now, in addition to salt, the Dead Sea also has large quantities of other minerals, including bromine, calcium chloride, and potassium chloride. Companies take minerals from the water to make such products as table salt, plant fertilizer, and pharmaceutical drugs. And there are many people who believe that the high mineral content of the Dead Sea can impart health benefits to those who swim in it. So to capitalize on this belief, several health resorts are located around the Dead Sea. These resorts provide facilities for bathers.

And, as you've probably guessed by now, the body is called the "Dead Sea" because few plants and no fish other than brine shrimp can survive in such a harsh, mineral-rich environment. In fact, the Dead Sea is so harsh that almost no plant life grows even on its shores. Rocky and barren land surrounds the sea itself, and steep, brightly colored cliffs rise above its shore—the coloration of the cliffs coming from the water's high mineral content.

In terms of its physical geography, the Dead Sea is much smaller than the two other seas we've recently discussed, the Red Sea and the Black Sea. The Dead Sea is only about 18 kilometers wide at its widest point and 80 kilometers long. That puts its total area at 1,040 square kilometers, which doesn't even come close to touching the 400,000 plus square kilometer areas of the Red and Black Seas. There's also a large peninsula near the middle of the Dead Sea that basically divides it in half.

Something of recent concern to scientists regarding the Dead Sea is that, since the early 1900s, the water level of this body of water has been slowly falling. Now what are some reasons for that—well, the area is a desert habitat, receiving less than 100 millimeters of rain annually, so such a development could be anticipated and expected, at least somewhat. However, the Jordan River also pours a relatively constant stream of fresh water into the sea. But in recent years, extreme heat in the area is causing more evaporation than is being replaced by its constant freshwater source. Scientists suspect that global warming is the culprit here, as it is in many other areas on the planet.

So, then, how did the Dead Sea originally form? Well, geologists and geographers don't have a definite answer to this question yet. The Dead Sea was probably formed 2- to 7-million years ago, when the Arabian Peninsula and the African continent shifted during the formation of the Great Rift Valley. The Great Rift Valley is the longest split in Earth's crust, extending from Jordan to northern Africa. Volcanoes accompanied this formation and there's still some earthquake activity in the Dead Sea area.

The name "Dead Sea" first appeared in Greek texts from 323 BCE. Ancient biblical names for it include "Salt Sea" and "Sea of the Plain." In the biblical book of Genesis, the cities of Sodom and Gomorrah were described as standing near the shores of the sea. There is an interesting connection here; Genesis describes Lot and Lot's wife fleeing the city of Sodom as it burned, but Lot's wife turned back to look, which God had forbidden, so she turned into a pillar of salt. As you can see from this slide, there are actually many salt columns around the sea, giving us an idea of the story's origin.

Narrator: Now get ready to answer the questions.

PRACTICE 3 - TRACK 43

Narrator: Listen to a lecture in a world history class.

Male Professor (MP): This century we've had global problems with Avian Flu, SARS, and Ebola. It helps to look back to the previous century to see what a catastrophic epidemic—that is, a pandemic—really looks like. The Influenza Pandemic of 1918 was possibly the worst natural disaster in recorded history. The Spanish Flu, as it was called, killed more people in six months than AIDS has in 25 years. More people died of the Spanish flu in one year than died of Bubonic Plague—an outbreak commonly referred to as the Black Death—in 100 years.

The Spanish Flu was an influenza virus. Antiviral medicines and vaccines hadn't been invented yet, so there was no treatment for the virus. The influenza strains that affect humans first appear in birds and are then transmitted to humans. Or the virus may pass through pigs. Although it's unclear where the Spanish Flu originated, doctors now believe that the virus mutated and successfully crossed from birds to men at a military base in France, during World War I.

At the base, there was a hospital for wounded soldiers, large numbers of English and American troops moving through, and pigs and chickens being raised for food. This would optimize the opportunity for the virus to move between three host populations, changing along the way.

Female Student (FS): When you say "changing," do you mean mutating?

MP: Yes, exactly. The virus was mutating. Most likely, the virus infected soldiers heading back to the United States from France. The virus, related to the same H1N1 strain that surfaced in 2009, probably originated in China around 1917. Or it may have appeared before that in Europe. What we do know is that in March, 1918, soldiers at Fort Riley, Kansas, began developing symptoms. In one week the virus had reached New York. By May it was already back in France, bringing illness and death to soldiers of all armies.

Now, what really made the virus unique was who it killed. Usually, influenza is most dangerous to the very young and the very old. The Spanish Flu, however, was most deadly to the healthiest, most robust patients. People between the ages of 20 and 40 died at much higher rates than older or younger patients. This is because the virus provoked an overreaction from the immune system, called a cytokine storm. Young people in the prime of life, with strong, well-developed immune systems, were most vulnerable.

The virus spread throughout Europe to Russia, India, China, and Africa. It was very contagious, but this first wave was not the deadliest. And by the end of July, 1918, the virus appeared to die out.

It came roaring back in August, exploding in three busy port cities: Boston, Massachusetts; Brest, France; and Freetown, Sierra Leone. Victims were turning blue from cyanosis, tearing muscles from coughing, and foaming bloody mucus from mouth and nose. Some people died within hours of their first symptom. The disease ravaged around the world, destroying entire villages in Africa and Alaska, and wasting populations in Tahiti and Samoa.

Then, after several months, the virus seemed to die out. A third wave was triggered, by peace! The Armistice of November 11, 1918, put tens of thousands of men on the move home, and countless thousands of refugees as well. Families flocked to greet the returning soldiers and displaced persons, and the virus made a final, fatal run around the world. When the year was finally over, the mortality was staggering: approximately 25 million dead in 25 weeks. One of every three people in the world was infected. Overall, the total loss of life was estimated at between 50 and 100 million people, as much as 5 percent of the world's population.

And, the virus left us with so many questions: Why did it attack young and healthy people? Why did it spread so easily? Finally, where did it go, and can it come back?

Several factors contributed to the wide and rapid spread of the virus. First, the Spanish Flu was the first pandemic moved around by modern transportation. Steam locomotives and steam ships seem antique to us, but in 1918 these modes of transportation were much faster than a horse and wagon or a wooden sailing ship. Faster transportation moved the virus around faster, too. Second, medical science was not up to the challenge. Virology, the study of viruses, had just begun. And the kind of care that could have slowed transmission or saved a patient from dying of a secondary illness was not well developed, either. But the fact remains, it was the world's biggest modern pandemic, and we still don't really know why!

Narrator: Now get ready to answer the questions.

PRACTICE 3 - TRACK 44

Narrator: Why does the professor say this?
MP: More people died of the Spanish flu in one year than died of Bubonic Plague—an outbreak commonly referred to as the Black Death—in 100 years.

ACTUAL PRACTICE 9

PRACTICE 1 - TRACK 45

Narrator: Listen to a conversation between a student and a university employee.
Female Student (FS): Excuse me; are you the person to talk to about rec department trips for spring break?
Male University Employee (UE): Well, I'm the administrative assistant for the recreation department, so you can talk to me about a lot of things! What do you need to know about the Spring Break trips?
FS: Well, my roommate and I heard someone talking about these trips in the bookstore, and they sounded fun. We asked the person where to go to learn about these trips, and they told us about your office. They also said that, because the university sets them up, the trips are safe, and we don't have to worry about the company cancel-

ling or anything.

UE: Well, it's true. All the companies we work with are very good, and we've been doing business with all of them for a long, long time. We're a big school, you know, and the companies that run these tours and trips want to stay on our good side. What kind of trip are you interested in?

FS: A trip to some place that's warm! So no cold mountains or rainy forests.

UE: (*Laughing*) You know, I hear that a lot around here. I guess it makes sense to want to relax on a sunny beach during your Spring Break. But for most students, really, the most important variable is money. All of our trips are affordable, but some are, well, more affordable than others.

FS: I think we want cheap!

UE: Say no more. All our least expensive trips are in the United States. For about 500 dollars, you can fly to Florida and stay in a dorm on a college campus in Miami. The fee covers your plane ticket, a bed in a shared room, and a meal plan with two meals a day for 5 days. Or, for about 300 dollars, you can go by charter bus to the coast of North Carolina. The students stay in a forestry camp with a dining hall. There's the beach, hiking trails, that kind of stuff.

FS: Sounds like the Miami one would be a bit more lively?

UE: Well, there's not a lot of night life on the barrier islands of North Carolina, if that's what you mean. On the other hand, there's not a lot of fishing or birdwatching in Miami!

FS: Is there anything in between?

UE: Well, for 400 dollars there's a program in Southern California. You stay at three different dorms over five days, and you have two beach days, trips to Sea World and Disneyland, and an optional trip to Tijuana.

FS: That sounds great. Can I use a credit card to make a deposit?

UE: Sure. I just need to see your student ID, and the student ID of your friend, too.

FS: Oh, I'll have to come back with that. I don't want to miss the chance to sign up before these trips get full, though.

UE: Well, you're the first one to ask this year, so I think you're safe waiting until Monday.

FS: Good! And, just for curiosity's sake, can you give me an idea of your overseas trips? Maybe there's one that we could afford.

UE: Our overseas trips go from about a thousand dollars, for a trip to Belize or Costa Rica, to five thousand for trips to Paris or Greece. Mind you, it's possible for a couple days in Europe to cost 2,000 dollars.

FS: Wow, that's a lot of money to spend for just a couple of days! Do people really do that?

UE: Yes. Usually, it's students who have traveled overseas before. That cuts down on a lot of other expenses that might pop up.

FS: Like what?

UE: Well, passports, or if you travel to Thailand, for example, you need to get some inoculations. People who travel a lot already have that sort of thing!

FS: Wow, not me!

UE: Me neither! Actually, most students sign up for the trips I just told you about.

FS: Great! Then that's what we'll do, too!

Narrator: Now get ready to answer the questions.

PRACTICE 2 - TRACK 46

Narrator: Listen to a lecture in an Art History class.

Male Professor (MP): Now we have been talking for a couple of weeks about the Post-Impressionist painters. Now, recall from your reading that artists such as Paul Gauguin and Pablo Picasso experimented with more abstract, flat images. They were not concerned with photo-like realism, nor were they concerned with capturing the natural look of light or color. Gauguin had his orange water and pink beaches, and Picasso had his cubes and triangles.

But not everyone in the viewing public understood. At first, the Post-Impressionists received much the same reaction as their predecessors, the Impressionists; that their work was childish, that they had no real skill. Art critics who praised the work were looked upon as being phony, as not really knowing what they were talking about. Well, that was the attitude behind a famous art hoax in the 1920s.

In 1924, a writer by the name of Ellen Bixby Smith submitted some paintings to an art show, and the exhibition jury criticized her paintings as being too "old-school" and too conventional. Now, Smith's husband, a literary scholar named Paul Jordan-Smith, felt that his wife had suffered at the hands of fools. He already disliked Modern art and its enthusiastic supporters.

So Smith, who had never painted before, made a painting as a joke. Then he decided to try submitting it to an art exhibition in New York. He signed it "Pavel Jerdanowitch," the founder of the "Disumbrationist" art movement. He figured—and rightly so, it now appears—that exotic-sounding but phony names would impress the critics. The painting was accepted for exhibition.

As you can see from the projection here, the painting was a blurry, definitely unskilled depiction of a woman who appears to be on a South Seas island, waving a banana peel over her head. And in truth, the painting does look like it was painted by a Post-Impressionist child. Smith titled his banana-peel painting *Exaltation*.

A critic at a French art journal saw it and wrote to Smith, asking for more information. Smith, pretending to be Jerdanowitch, replied with a description of his tragic (and phony) life. He even had a mock-serious photo taken of himself with comically raised eyebrows. As for his interpretation of his painting *Exaltation*, he explained that women were not allowed to eat bananas on that island, but the woman in the picture had just taken a bite of a banana and was waving it over her head because she feels exaltation. The French critic was fooled, and wrote gushing praise.

In 1925, Smith submitted another painting to an unjuried exhibition in Chicago. The childish painting depicts an African-American woman washing clothes in a wash tub outdoors. She is looking up at a rooster standing on a laundry-line pole. Smith titled the work *Aspiration*. Again, the work attracted positive reviews from art critics. It was even included in a book on Modern art.

Female Student (FS): It seems like these paintings, both of them, they're kind of racist and sexist, I think. I mean it's almost like he's making fun of the women.

MP: Yes, that's impossible to ignore, isn't it? In *Exaltation*, the woman seems to be part of a backward culture, a quote-unquote "savage," and she is a bit frightening looking. In *Aspiration*, the woman is presented as a more American stereotype, and perhaps as someone who aspires to be a rooster. So yes, the paintings are sexist and racist. But we have to question whether that was part of Smith's purpose, part of his effort to call out the art judges and critics of his time for favoring quote-unquote "exotic" or "primitive" depictions.

Now the great and nonexistent artist Pavel Jerdanowitch did not paint only black women. This abstract painting, as you can see, is comprised mainly of eyes looking out from a dark background streaked with zig-zags. When asked, the artist "Jerdanowitch" called it *Illumination*, and he explained in writing: "It is midnight and the drunken man stumbles home, anticipating a storm from his indignant wife; he sees her eyes and the lightning of her wrath. It is conscience at work."

Male Student (MS): That one actually looks kind of cool. The eyeball one. So, I'm thinking maybe the guy really could paint?

MP (*laughing*): Well, yes, the eyeballs could make a nice design on socks or something. But soon, Paul Jordan-Smith got tired of this joke and confessed it to the *Los Angeles Times* newspaper. Smith later wrote that he got more publicity from the hoax than he did for any of the serious writing he ever did.

Narrator: Now get ready to answer the questions.

PRACTICE 2 - TRACK 47

Narrator: Why does the professor say this?

MP: And in truth, the painting does look like it was painted by a Post-Impressionist child. Smith titled his banana-peel painting *Exaltation*.

PRACTICE 3 - TRACK 48

Narrator: Now listen to a lecture in a geography class.

Male Professor (MP): As you know, we've been experiencing some really hot temperatures lately in southern California, and water supplies are at their lowest in quite some time. Many researchers argue that this is the most extreme drought California has endured in centuries. And with that in mind, I want to spend some time today talking about the hottest place in California. In fact, this place, which is located in the central part of California, is known as the hottest, driest, and lowest place in the Western Hemisphere.

It was named by a group of European American pioneers for its desolate, desert environment after they crossed the place in 1849 searching for gold. Does anyone want to guess where I'm talking about? No? Well, today that location is known as Death Valley.

So physically, Death Valley is a deep channel—about 209 kilometers long and up to 23 kilometers wide. And as I said before, Death Valley contains the lowest point in the Western Hemisphere; parts of it lie about 86 meters below sea level. In fact, this is one of the lowest places located on the surface of the Earth, second only to the Dead Sea, in Israel. But ironically, Death Valley is surrounded by mountains: the Panamint Mountains stand west of the valley, and the Amargosa Mountains are located to the east. As a result, the highest point in Death Valley is Telescope Peak, which is over 3,000 meters tall and is a part of the Panamint Mountains.

And, interestingly enough, Death Valley isn't really a valley at all, at least not in geographic terms. If you'll recall from one of our earlier units, most valleys are formed either by rivers or by melting glaciers. But Death Valley wasn't formed by either of these processes. It was actually formed by earthquakes, and because of its unusual formation, it has a special name. Death Valley is technically a "graben." A graben is a block in Earth's surface that's dropped down by faults that form around the walls of that surface. Essentially, the channel part of Death Valley is like a large block that dropped down when two earthquakes occurred along its sides. After this occurred, erosion of the steep cliffs formed beautiful canyons. And in the northern and southern parts of the graben there are even small volcanoes with occasional lava flows.

What about the climate and weather in Death Valley? Well, if you'll recall, a few years ago, Death Valley got more rain than it had in an entire century. As such, a large part of the channel turned into a giant lake. In fact, during the last Ice Age—so 10,000 to 20,000 years ago—a large lake occupied Death Valley. But today, rainfall averages only about 5 centimeters a year. As such, Death Valley is normally very dry. Likewise, as I mentioned earlier, the highest temperature ever recorded in the United States, about 57 degrees Celsius, was recorded in Death Valley on July 10, 1913. Summer temperatures of 52 degrees Celsius are common in Death Valley. Because of the area's desert-like climate, plants there include those found in California deserts, such as creosote bush, desert holly, and mesquite. Wildlife there is also similar to that found in California deserts, including bobcats, coyotes, foxes, reptiles, and squirrels. What about gold? Did the early pioneers ever find any of that substance there? Well, they did, but only in small amounts, and it was mixed with lead, copper and silver in nearby mountains. However, the real "goldmine discovery," if you will, was borax deposits. Discovered in 1873, borax is a mineral that was once considered useful for making cleaning agents and antiseptics. After the discovery of borax, mining towns sprang up, with colorful names such as Bullfrog, Greenwater, and Skidoo. The towns died when the ores were exhausted. Today only cluttered debris remains.

So let me stop now and show you some slides of Death Valley. I think you'll be amazed to see some of the changes that have occurred there over time. If you have any questions after seeing the slides, I'd be happy to answer them.

Narrator: Now get ready to answer the questions.

ACTUAL PRACTICE 10

PRACTICE 1 - TRACK 49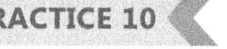

Narrator: Listen to a conversation between a student and an academic advisor.

Female Advisor (FA): Good morning, Thomas. So what can I help you with.

Male Student (MS): Morning. Well, I'm just beginning my third year at the university, and I wanted to make sure that I'm on-track with graduation. You know, I want to make sure I'm taking the right number of classes each quarter and everything.

FA: Absolutely. So first, please give me your student ID number. I need to enter into the computer so I can bring up your transcript.

MS: Oh, sure. My student ID is 2470931.

FA: (*Typing information into computer*) Okay, I see your transcript here. Let's see... (*reviewing transcript information*) so you're pursuing a double major, in literature and classical studies. Is that right?

MS: Yes, that's correct.

FA: Excellent. So classical studies is part of the history department, correct?

MS: Yes, it's a subdivision of the history department. But, for the classical studies major, I take history classes, language classes, and literature classes.

FA: Yes, I can see that on your transcript. Art history, ancient Greek, Roman literature… you've taken quite the assortment of classes. Now before we talk about how many classes you have to take before you graduate, I want to let you in on a little secret.

MS: Oh, okay. How exciting.

FA: Now not many students pursue a double major in literature and classical studies. And, as you hinted at earlier, the classical studies major is very interdisciplinary—it draws from many different areas of study. Including literature.

MS: Okay. I follow you so far.

FA: Which means you take literature classes for both your majors. And, lucky you, many of your literature classes count toward both majors.

MS: So you mean that some of the literature classes I've taken contribute toward my literature major and my classical studies major?

FA: Yes, that's exactly what I mean. So you're actually much closer to graduating than I think you realize. In fact, four of your literature classes fulfill major requirements for both your literature major and your classical studies major.

MS: Great, so that's four less classes for me to take, right?

FA: Exactly. But the university has put a limit on the number of classes that can simultaneously count toward two majors, and that number is four. So you've reached your limit with the number of literature classes that can count toward both majors.

MS: Well, that's okay, considering I didn't know about any of this until now. So how does this affect when I can graduate?

FA: Good question. Let me take a look. (*Reads student's transcript*) It looks like you'll be able to graduate two quarters early, as long as you keep taking an average course load each quarter.

MS: Two quarters! Wow, that's great news.

FA: Glad I was able to brighten your day.

MS: You really were. Thanks for telling me about the fact that my literature classes have been helping me out in both my majors. I never would've figured it out on my own.

FA: You're very welcome. That's my job, after all.

Narrator: Now get ready to answer the questions.

PRACTICE 1 - TRACK 50

Narrator: Now listen again to part of the conversation. Then answer the question.

FA: And, as you hinted at earlier, the classical studies major is very interdisciplinary—it draws from many different areas of study. Including literature.

MS: Okay. I follow you so far.

FA: Which means you take literature classes for both your majors.

Narrator: Why does the student say this?

MS: Okay. I follow you so far.

PRACTICE 2 - TRACK 51

Narrator: Listen to part of a talk in a biology class.

Male Professor (MP): Good afternoon. Today, I want to talk about a species that is considered a "living fossil"—that is, a very ancient living species that closely resembles an extinct species, and that usually has no living, related species. So "living fossils" are the last species of their kind, which makes them invaluable to paleontologists and biologists trying to understand how ancient species survived.

So the "living fossils" we'll look at today are found on the continents of Africa, South America, and Australia, and they're called lungfish. Now, the first question that probably comes to mind is, "Why is this fish called a lungfish? Does it have lungs or something?" But actually, the "lung" part of the name "lungfish" comes from the fact that it can breathe out of water. However, this fish doesn't have actual lungs, like mammals do. The lungfish breathes air by means of a lung-like organ called an air bladder. (*To female student*) Oh, yes. What's your question?

Female Student (FS): So you're saying that the lungfish is a fish that lives outside of the water? But I thought for an animal to be a fish, it had to live in the water.

MP: Well, what you point out is true. And the lungfish does live in the water, most of the time. However, lungfish live in shallow, muddy marshes, swamps and rivers. These bodies of water are low in oxygen, and lungfish make up for this lack of oxygen by breathing through their gills when in water and through their air bladders when they need to come to the surface and get a little extra oxygen from the air. (*To female student*) Does that make sense?

FS: Yeah, I think I get the picture now. So basically, lungfish are kind of like half in and half out of water due to the shallow water and lack of oxygen in their environment.

MP: Exactly.

FS: And, well, I'm sorry to keep interrupting, but why is it important that the lungfish is one of these "living fossils." I didn't quite understand what you were saying there.

MP: Well, for one thing, lungfish are among the oldest known groups of fish alive today. They date from about 400 million years ago, and they don't have any other close living relatives. And, as you know from our units on evolution, many paleontologists believe that land-dwelling vertebrates—animals with backbones—evolved from creatures like the lungfish, making the lungfish of great interest to evolutionary biologists.

Now let's briefly discuss the appearance and anatomy of this peculiar fish. As you can see, it doesn't exactly look like a typical "fish." The lungfish looks more like the eel-like animals from which it is probably evolved. For example, the body of the lungfish is long and narrow, kind of like a snake, and most species of lungfish don't have any real "fins." Instead, they have two pairs of long, threadlike materials that hang from their faces, which, incidentally, also appear eyeless.

And, as if these eyeless, eel-like creatures weren't already terrifying enough, lungfish can also grow up to two and a half meters long. (*To male student*) Yes, I see another question in the back.

Male Student (MS): How do such large creatures find enough to eat in their shallow, low-oxygen habitats?

MP: Ah, good question. Well, lungfish eat mainly small fish, frogs, and snails. They are basically large scavengers that also prey on small swamp-dwelling creatures.

MS: Oh, okay. And then, I have one other question: Can lungfish survive out of water for long periods of time? I mean, do they come out of their swamps and crawl around on land?

MP: That's an excellent question. Actually, lungfish don't really come onto land to "crawl around," as you suggest. But they do have an interesting behavior that allows them to survive land-like environments during the summer months, when the swamps and marshes where they live dry up. So during those times, lungfish tunnel into the wet mud and remain inactive for months at a time, until rain returns. They live off protein stored in their muscle tissues, staying inside a cocoon of mud and a slimy substance given off by their bodies. Of course, during that time they breathe using their air sacks. (*To male student*) Yes, you have another question?

MS: So basically the lungfish uses its air sack mostly during hibernation.

MP: Well, sort of. When an animal undergoes a period of little to no activity during the winter, it's called hibernation. However, when the behavior happens during the summer, it's called "estivation," which means "summer sleep."

Narrator: Now get ready to answer the questions.

PRACTICE 2 - TRACK 52

Narrator: Now listen again to part of the lecture. Then answer the question.

MP: Now let's briefly discuss the appearance and anatomy of this peculiar fish. As you can see, it doesn't exactly look like a typical "fish." The lungfish looks more like the eel-like animals from which it is probably evolved.

Narrator: Why does the professor say this?

MP: The lungfish looks more like the eel-like animals from which it probably evolved.

PRACTICE 3 - TRACK 53

Narrator: Listen to a lecture in a Social Psychology class.

Male Professor (MP): Now, we have been talking about the many ways that society shapes people's thoughts and attitudes. Now let's narrow this topic down to look at something that differs between cultures: praising others. How does praise shape an individual's thinking? We all love to get praise, right? We love to get an "A+." We love for someone to say that we are attractive. Nice. Good at things. The best lecturer ever, hint hint. (laughter) We love to get approval and compliments. Praise is fairly ubiquitous in American culture.

In 1969 a psychologist named Nathaniel Brandon published a highly influential paper about self-esteem. Brandon suggested that people who feel good about themselves are more likely to succeed.

So, with the best of intentions, parents and teachers across the U.S. began trying to give children higher self-esteem. The oversimplified thinking was, if you tell children they are good, they will feel good about themselves. Some schools began teaching "self-esteem" lessons, starting with "I Am Special" projects. Some junior sports organizations gave every player on every team a trophy at the end of a tournament, saying, "You are all winners!" Some people worried that children were not being allowed to fail at anything, that even grades at school were being inflated because parents would not accept that their children could ever experience failure.

From the 1980s on, thousands of studies tried to measure the positive effects of high self-esteem. But in the early 2000s, when researchers began really looking at all the studies, they found no clear support for the hypothesis that higher self-esteem motivates people to succeed. In fact, many criminals were found to have high self-esteem.

Male Student (MS): So, if high self-esteem does not necessarily lead to success, are you saying that people can hate themselves and still succeed?

MP: Hmm, well, not exactly. That's also an oversimplification. Uh, let's turn to more recent research. So, a psychologist at Stanford University, Carol Dweck, published some truly eye-opening research about praise. She set up controlled classroom studies showing that how teachers praised students made a dramatic difference in students' learning.

Dweck said that if students were told that they were intelligent, talented, got all the answers right, and so on, they actually learned less as measured by test scores. They developed what she called a "fixed mindset," a belief that their qualities were carved in stone, so to speak. One problem with that mindset or attitude is that it can create a fear of failure. For example, a student may think, "I may be smart, but if I can't answer this problem, it seems that I am not smart enough. I'd better avoid it."

However, students learned significantly more when they were praised for the learning process. If students were praised specifically for instances of effort and focus, for using effective strategies, or for making progress, the result was that they scored much higher on tests. Why was this? Well, Dweck said that they worked at learning for a longer period of time. If they complained that something was too hard, they were told, "Oh, that is just the feeling of the brain growing." They were reminded that they were learning the concept step by step, even if they did not understand it yet.

"Not yet" is the key idea here. Dweck maintains that the ideal "growth mindset" does not see failure, but rather achievements that have not been made yet. So you see, the question becomes not whether people see themselves as good or bad, but whether a person can see himself or herself an ongoing project, a work-in-progress. Yes, do you have a question over there?

Female Student (FS): Yeah, so, um, does that mean that we shouldn't really talk about people's IQ, or like, whether they are "gifted" or not?

MP: That does seem to be where this research is pointing. The emphasis is on brain plasticity, rather than fixed traits and abilities. So the research indicates that it's best to praise children for specific actions. For example, instead of saying, "You're so smart," a parent might say, "I like the way you worked so hard on that question." And it may also help to notice other kinds of praiseworthy actions, such as, "That was kind of you to make room next to you for another student." These kinds of compliments help students develop a growth-mindset socially as well as academically.

Narrator: Now get ready to answer the questions.

PRACTICE 3 - TRACK 54

Narrator: Listen to part of the lecture. Then answer the question.

MP: We all love to get praise, right? We love to get an "A+." We love for someone to say that we are attractive. Nice. Good at things. The best lecturer ever, hint hint. (laughter) We love to get approval and compliments. Praise is fairly ubiquitous in American culture.

Narrator: Why does the professor say this?

MP: The best lecturer ever, hint hint.

ACTUAL PRACTICE 11

PRACTICE 1 - TRACK 55

Narrator: Listen to a conversation between two students.

Female Student (FS): Hey, Mario. Do you have a minute?

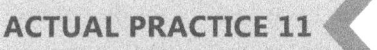

Male Student (MS): Sure, Ella. What's up? You look a little flustered.

FS: Yeah, maybe a little. Well, you know how Sam and Cody recently dropped the psychology class we're all in together.

MS: I didn't know that. I was wondering why I hadn't seen them in class lately.

FS: Well, they were both in my group for the group project. You know, for the oral presentation, PowerPoint, and research paper that all analyze a famous case study.

MS: That's terrible. I'm sorry to hear that. So I'm guessing you're the only one left in your group.

FS: That's right. I guess you really couldn't call it a group any more. Anyway, I talked to the professor, and he said I could join another group. So I was wondering…

MS: You want to join my group?

FS: Yes. I mean, to be honest, you're the only other person I know in the class, so I don't really feel comfortable approaching anyone else.

MS: I understand. You're in a tough situation. I mean, I'll ask the rest of my group, but I don't see why you can't join us. After all, there's still two weeks before the project is due.

FS: Great! Thanks so much. Do you want to see if my joining is okay with the rest of your group? Or do you think it will be okay, as long as I really contribute?

MS: I'm sure the rest of my group will be okay with you joining. So my group is analyzing the case study of "Genie," the girl who was called the "Wild Child" in the 1970s. Have you heard of her case?

FS: Yeah, isn't that the little girl who was completely isolated and neglected until she was a teenager? Psychologists studied her to better understand childhood development, right?

MS: That's basically it. I'm working on the PowerPoint portion of the project, but I haven't finished doing all the research yet. So maybe you could start by helping me research.

FS: Sounds good to me. Just let me know what you want me to research.

MS: Okay. Well, I was looking for diagrams of the brain and images of kids talking. Maybe you could look online and email me anything you find on language development, you know, especially images for the PowerPoint.

FS: That sounds great. It seems like you're way more prepared for this project than Sam and Cody were.

MS: Well, I'm glad to hear that. They seemed like nice guys, but I wouldn't exactly call them the hardest workers. Hopefully, we'll get this PowerPoint project done in no time. Then, once the PowerPoint is done, we can see if the other members of my group need any help with their portions of the project.

FS: Sounds good. Can I get your email address then?

MS: Yeah, good idea. Let's text each other our email addresses.

Narrator: Now get ready to answer the questions.

PRACTICE 1 - TRACK 56

Narrator: Listen to part of the conversation. Then answer the question.

FS: Hey, Mario. Do you have a minute?

MS: Sure, Ella. What's up? You look a little flustered.

FS: Yeah, maybe a little.

Narrator: Why does the man say this to the woman?

MS: You look a little flustered.

PRACTICE 1 - TRACK 57

Narrator: What does the man suggest when he says this?

MS: Well, I was looking for diagrams of the brain and images of kids talking.

PRACTICE 2 - TRACK 58

Narrator: Listen to a lecture in an art history class.

Female Professor (FP): Good morning. So although the images I've hung all around the class today look like advertisements, they are actually examples of a style of art known as pop art. This style of art flourished mostly during the 1950s and 1960s. So the term "pop art" was coined by an art critic during the height of the trend, in 1956. As you can see from looking at the examples I have hanging around the classroom, the name captures what artists of this style incorporated into their work: elements of popular culture and consumerism.

So first, let's talk about the origins of pop art. Let's look at how pop artists get the idea to fill their works with advertising symbols, comic strip imagery, and Hollywood movie icons. Well, like most artistic movements, pop artists were reacting to what came before them in the art world. Mostly, pop artists were rejecting the long-held, elitist idea that true "art" had to come from formally trained artists, who had to create art inspired by certain "proper" themes and subjects. Of course, images from advertising and popular culture were not included in these "proper" subjects, so advertising and popular culture were exactly what these rebellious pop artists focused on. They wanted to reject distinctions of good and bad taste, and make use of commonplace objects.

But pop art wasn't the first artistic movement to reject "proper" artistic subjects and focus instead on nontraditional subjects. In fact, this idea was popularized by an artistic movement known as abstract expressionism, which greatly influenced pop art. Abstract expressionism was popular during the 1930s and 1940s, so at about the same time as World War II. Artists who painted in the abstract expressionist style mostly depicted non-representational shapes, lines, and colors. For example, a typical abstract expressionist painting could consist of a series of circles drawn in different colors. Now, in contrast to this, pop art incorporated sharp visual imagery with photographic-like techniques into its creations.

So, one of the main philosophies of pop art was the idea that anyone can make pop art. As a result, there was no "right" or "wrong" way to create pop art. Essentially, each pop artist created his or her own style. And when you look around the classroom at the various examples of pop art, this idea—that pop art meant creating your own style—should become pretty clear. So as examples, let's look at a few pieces of pop art created by Andy Warhol, one of the best-known pop artists. Warhol's most famous pieces take images from advertising or popular culture and reproduce them over and over on a single canvas. These images are sometimes enlarged and tinted in various colors. Warhol's most famous "subjects" using this style include Campbell's soup cans, Coke soft drink bottles, the movie star Marylyn Monroe, and the Chinese leader Mao Zedong.

For another example, take a look at this piece by Roy Lichtenstein. It looks like an image from a giant comic strip, doesn't it? Well, that is exactly the style Lichtenstein used to create most of his images. So Lichtenstein used this medium to depict everyday life in an ironic, overly dramatic way. You'll also notice that Lichtenstein's huge, comic-strip-like images are made up of the same colored dots that make up the image in most pictures printed in comic books. Lichtenstein simulated and enlarged these dots to further emphasize the "pop art," the anti-elitist, aspect of his work.

And finally, take this sculpture of a giant hamburger, by Claes Oldenburg. Oldenburg is known for his exaggerated, oversized sculptures that represent such familiar objects as ice cream cones, electric outlets, lipstick tubes, and fast food items. Using these objects as the subjects of his works, Oldenburg wished to show that there was beauty in all aspects of American consumer life. Another interesting aspect of Oldenburg's sculptures is that they are made out of soft material, and can be picked up, manipulated and even thrown, unlike other more formal forms of sculpture.

Narrator: Now get ready to answer the questions.

PRACTICE 2 - TRACK 59

Narrator: What does the professor suggest when she says this?

FP: Mostly, pop artists were rejecting the long-held, elitist idea that true "art" had to come from formally trained artists, who had to create art inspired by certain "proper" themes and subjects.

PRACTICE 3 - TRACK 60

Narrator: Listen to a lecture in a geology class.

Male Professor (MP): Since the late 1500s, so shortly after all seven continents were mapped out by cartographers, people have noted that the continents appear to fit together like puzzle pieces. For example, the outline of the Eastern coasts of South America, Central America, and Mexico line up almost perfectly with Africa's Western coast. This observation led to early proposals of continental drift—in other words, the idea that the continents were once all connected, but were torn apart by some force or forces.

But in science, an idea cannot gain acceptance until it's supported by a sufficient amount of evidence, and it would take a lot of evidence to convince the scientific community that landmasses as massive as the continents move.

Today, I want to talk about the man who provided

some of the most compelling evidence for continental drift. That man is 20th-century scientist Alfred Wegener. Now Wegener was an interdisciplinary scientist; he studied astronomy, meteorology, paleontology, and geology. And it was his interest in such diverse fields that led him to his theory of continental drift.

In 1911, Wegener found a scientific paper stating that fossils of the same plant species were found on continents on either side of the Atlantic Ocean. At that time—though there was no real evidence to support this idea—most scientists guessed that fossils of the same species could be found on distant continents because land bridges once connected the continents. But Wegener, like some of his predecessors, noticed that the continents appeared to fit together, leading him to suspect that they were once all one large landmass. But, like I said before, this was a *huge* assumption to make, and Wegener knew he would need a lot of evidence to convince anyone of continental drift.

So he searched for more fossil evidence to support his case. For instance, he discovered tropical plant fossils on the Arctic island of Spitsbergen. Obviously, these fossils could not survive in a cold, Arctic environment, so Wegener proposed that the Arctic island was once much closer to the equator, and that it had traveled to its present position over millions of years.

Wegener also used geographical evidence to support his case. He noted that Brazil and parts of Western Africa have almost identical, but very unique, rock formations, leading him to suspect that South America and Africa were once the same landmass. He also noticed that the Appalachian Mountain range in North America lines up perfectly with the Scottish Highlands, even though thousands of miles of ocean separate the two mountain ranges. Thus, he proposed that North America and Scotland were once connected.

In 1915, after gathering evidence to support his case for continental drift, Wegener published *The Origins of Continents and Oceans*. Here, he claims that about 300 million years ago, all the continents were connected, forming one massive landmass he called Pangea. Since then, the continents slowly drifted apart. Now keep in mind, Wegener wasn't the first person to suggest this; he was the first person to support this idea with so much—and such varied—evidence.

And when the scientific community read about his idea of continental drift, they absolutely hated it. And not without good reason. Wegener provided a lot of evidence supporting the idea that the continents moved, but he had no convincing explanation for *how* the continents moved. Without that crucial piece of information, only a few people had accepted his hypothesis of continental drift by the time he died in 1930.

In fact, it wasn't until the 1950s and the 1960s, when researchers started extensively mapping the bottom of the oceans, that Wegener was vindicated. At this time, researchers noticed that, in certain places, the Earth's crust—which is called the lithosphere by geologists—splits apart, allowing for magma from the asthenosphere—that is, the mantle—to spill into the ocean. This magma cools, forming huge, underwater mountain ranges. These are called mid-ocean ridges. Similarly, researchers noticed that parts of the Earth's crust run into each other under water, causing one to fall beneath the other. This creates huge trenches. Appropriately, these are called deep-sea trenches.

Now these ocean ridges and trenches show that the Earth's crust is divided into huge chunks called tectonic plates. And these tectonic plates are slowly, but constantly, moving toward or away from each other, forming underwater trenches or mountain ranges. The tectonic plates are able to move because the Earth's crust—that is, its lithosphere—sits atop the asthenosphere, which is made up of liquid rock that's constantly being moved around by heat currents from below.

So in the end, Wegener was right about his theory of continental drift, and the continents were, in fact, once one large landmass. Unfortunately for him, he was able to explain what continental drift was, but not *how* it occurred.

Narrator: Now get ready to answer the questions.

PRACTICE 3 - TRACK 61

Narrator: Listen to part of the lecture. Then answer the question.
MP: Now keep in mind, Wegener wasn't the first person to suggest this; he was the first person to support this idea with so much—and such varied—evidence.
Narrator: Why does the professor say this?
MP: Now keep in mind, Wegener wasn't the first person to

suggest this…

ACTUAL PRACTICE 12

PRACTICE 1 - TRACK 62

Narrator: Listen to a conversation between a student and a resident assistant (RA).

Male Student (MS): Hey, Grace. I was wondering if you had a few minutes to talk.

Female Resident Assistant (RA): Sure, David. What's on your mind?

MS: Well, you've been an RA—you know, a resident assistant—at the university for a couple of years now, right?

RA: Yes, that's right.

MS: I want to apply for a resident assistant position for next year. So I was wondering if you could tell me a little bit about being an RA.

RA: I think I can help you there. What do you want to know?

MS: Well, first of all, how did you get the position?

RA: Let's see… that was a while ago. Well, I filled out an application with the housing office. Then they interviewed me. And then I think they had me respond to some questions. I don't remember the application process being that bad, actually.

MS: Oh, good. I was worried it'd be a really time-consuming process. And just so I know what I'm getting into when I apply to be an RA, I wanted to know: What, exactly, do you do as an RA?

RA: Well, our number one goal is to ensure the students' safety. Mostly, that means looking out for illegal drug use in the dorms. Obviously, doing drugs in the dorms is both unsafe and illegal, so we have to watch out for it. We're also supposed to enforce dorm rules—you know, make sure no one's playing loud music late at night, make sure people aren't fighting in the hallways, stuff like that. And we're here to make sure students in the dorms are comfortable and happy, so we're kind of student guidance counselors, too.

MS: Wow, it sounds like you guys are pretty busy. Does all that responsibility get in the way of your schoolwork?

RA: Sometimes. But not as often as you might think. And in my experience, professors will give you an extension on an assignment if you couldn't get it done because of RA duties.

MS: Oh, that's good to know. So, in your opinion, what are the biggest benefits of becoming an RA?

RA: Well, it may sound selfish, but the free dorm room and meal plan are the best part of being an RA. It saves me thousands of dollars every year, and living in the dorms means I'm close to my classes.

MS: I didn't realize that RAs got free housing. That sounds great.

RA: It's certainly a big incentive to become an RA. Another benefit of being an RA is getting to know the first-year students. You know, I get to be a friend and a mentor to many of the first-year students. It makes me feel like I'm making their first year of college less intimidating and confusing.

MS: Now that you mention it, I do remember the RA in my dorm building being really supportive. Okay, so now that I know the positive aspects of being an RA, I have to ask: What are the downsides?

RA: Well, like I hinted at earlier, it's a time-consuming job. Sometimes, it gets in the way of schoolwork. And sometimes it keeps me from hanging out with my friends. I mean, RAs even have to keep an eye on things on the weekends. So once you become an RA, your social life changes.

MS: Yeah, that's what I figured.

RA: But don't get me wrong. Being an RA is great. I mean, this is my second year doing it, so obviously I enjoyed it enough to come back for more!

MS: (*Laughs*) That's true. Well, thanks for all the information. I think I'll go fill out one of those applications you mentioned.

RA: Good luck.

Narrator: Now get ready to answer the questions.

PRACTICE 1 - TRACK 63

Narrator: What does the resident assistant imply when she says this?

RA: And in my experience, professors will give you an extension on an assignment if you couldn't get it done because of RA duties.

PRACTICE 1 - TRACK 64

Narrator: Why does the resident assistant say this?

RA: You know, I get to be a friend and a mentor to many of the first-year students. It makes me feel like I'm making their first year of college less intimidating and confusing.

PRACTICE 2 - TRACK 65

Narrator: Listen to a lecture in a U.S. history class.

Male Professor (MP): "Four score and seven years ago our fathers brought forth on this continent, a new nation, conceived in Liberty, and dedicated to the proposition that all men are created equal."

Does anyone recognize those words? It's the first sentence in the Gettysburg Address, a short speech that President Abraham Lincoln delivered during the American Civil War at the site of the Battle of Gettysburg in Pennsylvania. He delivered the address on November 19, 1863, at ceremonies to dedicate part of the battlefield as a cemetery for those who had lost their lives in the battle. Lincoln wrote the address to help ensure that the battle would be seen as a great Union triumph and to give the people of the North a renewed sense of purpose to fight in the war. Some historians think his simple words, which are among the best remembered in American history, reshaped the nation by defining it as one people dedicated to one principle—that of equality.

Here's something you may not know: Lincoln wrote five different versions of the speech. He wrote most of the first version in Washington, D.C., and probably completed it at Gettysburg. He probably wrote the second version at Gettysburg on the evening before he delivered his address. He held this second version in his hand during the address. But he made several changes as he spoke. The most important change was to add the phrase "under God" after the word "nation" in the last sentence. That part of the sentence reads: "We here highly resolve that these dead shall not have died in vain—that this nation, under God, shall have a new birth of freedom." Lincoln also added that phrase to the three versions of the address that he wrote after the ceremonies at Gettysburg.

Lincoln wrote the final version of the address—the fifth written version—in 1864. This version also differed somewhat from the speech he actually gave, but it was the only copy he signed. If you've ever been to Washington D.C., this version is carved on a stone plaque in the Lincoln Memorial.

Many false stories have grown up about this famous speech. One story says that the people of Lincoln's time did not like the speech. But the reaction of the nation's newspapers largely followed party lines. Most of the newspapers that backed the Republican Party, the party to which Lincoln belonged, liked the speech. The majority of the newspapers that supported the Democratic Party, who opposed Lincoln and some of whom were sympathetic to the South, did not. Here's something else you probably weren't aware of: President Lincoln was not even the main speaker at Gettysburg on that day. The main speaker was Edward Everett, a noted orator. Everett spoke for two solid hours. Afterward, Lincoln was supposed to make a few appropriate remarks. In a little less than three minutes, he finished his address. Edward Everett later wrote to Lincoln: "I should be glad if I could flatter myself that I came as near to the central idea of the occasion in two hours as you did in two minutes." Now, turn to page two hundred in your textbooks and let's go through the speech together.

Narrator: Now get ready to answer the questions.

PRACTICE 2 - TRACK 66

Narrator: What does the professor suggest when he says this?

MP: Some historians think his simple words, which are among the best remembered in American history, reshaped the nation by defining it as one people dedicated to one principle—that of equality.

PRACTICE 3 - TRACK 67

Narrator: Listen to a lecture in an environmental studies class.

Male Professor (MP): Ozone occurs naturally in the Earth's atmosphere, in different densities at different levels. It's a form of oxygen, but is very rare. There are only three molecules of ozone in every ten million molecules of atmosphere. In contrast, the diatomic oxygen we need to breathe makes up 21 percent of the Earth's atmosphere.

Ozone in the lower atmosphere, closer to the Earth's surface, is often referred to as "bad" ozone. This ozone combines with carbon dioxide and makes smog. But ozone in the ozone layer is vital for Earth's health because it blocks harmful radiation from the sun. This ozone has been badly damaged for many years. It's a wonderful surprise, then, that human effort has begun reversing this damage. We're allowing the ozone layer to repair itself.

The ozone layer, where the "good" ozone is, is in a narrow layer in the stratosphere, which is a layer of the atmosphere beginning 5 to 10 miles above the Earth's surface and extending as much as 30 miles above the Earth. Here, ozone plays the significant role of absorbing and preventing ultraviolet radiation from the Sun from reaching the surface of the Earth. The Sun's ultraviolet radiation is divided into three types by wavelength: UV-a, UV-b, and UV-c. UV-a passes through the ozone layer and reaches the Earth, but doesn't cause sunburn or direct genetic damage. UV-c is completely blocked by the stratosphere. UV-b is the wavelength that causes the greatest damage when it reaches the Earth, including causing skin diseases in humans. Normally the ozone layer is essential for blocking UV-b rays.

We don't know for how many millions of years the ozone layer blocked these rays. We do know that, by the 1970s, human pollution was making the ozone layer thinner and thinner. The cause was a family of chemicals known as chlorofluorocarbons, or CFCs for short, which are found in aerosol propellants, refrigeration units, and plastics. The use of spray cans and refrigerators was reducing the thickness of the ozone layer.

For many years, business and consumers had thought CFCs were a perfect chemical product: inexpensive, inflammable, and non-toxic. Then, scientists began noticing the thinning of the ozone layer, and a corresponding increase in the number of melanomas, skin cancers, and other diseases linked to increased radiation from the sun. Other scientists had theorized about where released CFCs would wind up in the atmosphere. It turns out that the compound floats to the stratosphere, degrades over time, and releases chlorine in amounts that damage the ozone layer.

Female Student (FS): Didn't the United States make laws about spray cans? My mom said something about that once, about window cleaners or something.

MP: Yes, the U.S. acted and it also began an important movement to change international attitudes toward CFCs. In 1978, the U.S. banned the use of CFCs in all aerosol spray cans. In 1983 Canada did the same, and Europe finally did so as well in 1995. The next steps were more difficult. To expand the ban against CFCs meant to limit the use of the compound in refrigeration. That included the cooling systems of cars, businesses, homes, food and medical refrigerators.

The ozone layer in the stratosphere literally contracted. A hole appeared each summer over Antarctica. Finally, concerned nations agreed to meet in Montreal, Canada. In the summer of 1987, the United States and 22 other countries signed the Montreal Protocol, agreeing to reduce the use of CFCs.

The U.S. began acting to meet the terms of the Montreal Protocol. In 1989, an excise tax was levied on the sale of CFCs. In 1992, the Environmental Protection Agency (EPA) ordered that all CFCs in automobile air conditioners must be recycled.

Male Student (MS): But, didn't problems with the ozone layer get even worse?

MP: They did. As scientists predicted, even though the amount of new CFCs being produced and used was greatly reduced, CFCs already in the system were being released into the environment and the situation became worse. But scientists knew this would happen, and they advised world leaders to continue the bans.

In fact, a Japan Meteorological Agency study, published in 2000, showed that the hole in the ozone layer over Antarctica was the largest ever, twice the size of the continent itself.

But the countries joined under the Montreal Protocol persevered, and in 2014 the United Nations Environmental Program and the World Meteorological Organization announced that the ozone layer was showing early signs of becoming thicker, reversing fifty years of recorded thinning.

International leaders and scientists from around the world praised the news as positive evidence that human action can solve an environmental crisis. In fact, the United Nations announced that two-million cases of melanoma will be prevented annually by the year 2030.

Narrator: Now get ready to answer the questions.

ACTUAL PRACTICE 13

PRACTICE 1 - TRACK 68

Narrator: Listen to a conversation between a student and a manager in a university dining hall office.

Male Manager (MM): Ahh, come on in. You must be Beza? Pleased to meet you.

Female Student (FS): Pleased to meet you too, Mr. Rideaux.

MM: Ah, you pronounced it right! So many people say "Rih dix."

FS: Well, I had a teacher once whose name was also "Mr. Rideaux."

MM: Ah, another one from Louisiana, was he? What do you know? Well, Beza, everyone around here calls me "Rideaux," forget the "Mr."

FS: Okay… Rideaux. Uh, I don't really have a nickname.

MM: Oh, well then, "Beza" it is. So, it's your first day, and I'm to train you as a server, is that it?

FS: I'm not sure, but I guess so. They didn't tell me what I'd be doing. They just told me to show up an hour early for training.

MM: There's not much to it, really. Have you worked in food service before?

FS: Kind of. I helped out in my aunt's Ethiopian restaurant when I was in middle school and high school. All my family worked there at different times. So, I started out just, you know, bussing tables, and then prep cooking or waiting tables. Whatever needed doing.

MM: Awesome! With those kinds of credentials, maybe you should be training me!

FS: (*Jokingly*) Okay, Rideaux: First, wash your hands.

MM: Very good, that's exactly where we begin! Here is a hairnet and an apron, and there's a sink that's only for washing hands. Remember, even though you'll be wearing plastic gloves, you must first wash your hands for at least as long as it takes you to sing "Happy Birthday."

FS: Oh, no! Does everyone have to sing?

MM: I'm joking. No, that's just a way to remember to wash for 30 seconds. The Health Department requires it. Not the singing, of course. Now when you're all ready, meet me out front and I'll show you the procedures for serving on the line. Do you have any questions for me so far?

FS: Well, I was wondering about shifts… are you the person who makes the schedules for this dining hall?

MM: Yes, I'm the one to talk to about that. I have you scheduled to work the lunch shift on Mondays, Wednesdays, and Fridays, and brunch shift on Saturdays and Sundays. That should give you 20 hours a week. Is there a problem with that?

FS: No, that's okay. That should work perfectly with my class schedule this semester.

MM: Good, I'm glad that works. That's why we have you put your class schedule and other commitments on your job application.

FS: I mean, of course I'd rather have weekends off, but… maybe in the future?

MM: Well, students who have worked here longer have the opportunity to pick and choose their hours first. Most of them want to work weeknights dinner shifts so that they can have every weekend off.

FS: Okay, I understand. After I've worked here awhile, I'll probably request those weeknight dinner shifts, too!

MM: Be careful what you wish for! Those weeknight shifts, especially at the beginning and end of the semester, can be really hard. When half the students are just finishing up a full day of classes, and the other half are rushing to night classes, it can get hectic around here. Weekends, on the other hand, can be positively quiet. Especially so a Sunday brunch when everyone was out late the night before, or close to the end of the term.

FS: That seems so far away now. I'm just worried about getting through the week.

MM: Well, one thing you don't have to worry about anymore is where your next meal is coming from. Remember, you get a full half hour and a fifteen minute break every shift, and you're welcome to eat anything you want!

Narrator: Now get ready to answer the questions.

PRACTICE 1 - TRACK 69

Narrator: Listen to part of the conversation. Then answer the question.

FS: Kind of. I helped out in my aunt's Ethiopian restaurant when I was in middle school and high school. All my family worked there at different times. So, I started out just, you know, bussing tables, and then prep cooking or waiting tables. Whatever needed doing.

MM: Awesome! With those kinds of credentials, maybe you should be training me!

Narrator: What does the manager mean when he says this?

MM: With those kinds of credentials, maybe you should be training me!

PRACTICE 2 - TRACK 70

Narrator: Listen to a lecture in an archaeology class.

Female Professor (FP): Philosopher Friedrich Nietzsche once said, "Live in danger. Build your cities on the slopes of Vesuvius." Now can anybody give this quote some context?

Male Student (MS): Well, Vesuvius is a volcano in Italy. And in Roman times, so like a couple thousand years ago, Vesuvius erupted and destroyed a nearby city—Pompeii, I think.

FP: Yes, that's a pretty good overview. But one important correction I'll make to your summary is that Pompeii was not exactly "destroyed" by the volcanic eruption—it was preserved. And I'll explain that in greater detail in just a minute. But first, some background on Vesuvius. Vesuvius is located on Italy's western coast, very close to the present-day city of Naples. And in 79 CE, the volcano erupted, covering two nearby cities in volcanic rock and ash, and killing as many as 16,000 people in the process. Yet this past tragedy has really helped modern archaeologists because the sheets of ash and volcanic debris have preserved these two cities. Thus, archaeologists study the ruins surrounding Vesuvius to better understand Roman architecture, art, and daily life.

Now, like I said, the eruption of Vesuvius buried two Roman cities: the commercial and trading city of Pompeii and the wealthy, luxurious resort town called Herculaneum. Pompeii is located just to the southeast of Vesuvius, and Herculaneum is located just to the west of the volcano. And the different locations of the cities relative to the volcano made a huge difference in how the cities were affected by the eruption.

So now let's move onto the event of the eruption. (*To male student*) Actually, I see you have a question. Go ahead.

Male Student (MS): Why did they build these cities so close to the volcano? Didn't these people realize that they were, like Nietzsche said, "living in danger"?

FP: Actually, they didn't. Before it erupted in 79 CE, Vesuvius had been completely inactive for 800 years, which is over two centuries longer than either Pompeii or Herculaneum existed. In fact, as far as we can tell, the inhabitants didn't even realize Vesuvius was a volcano.

Now, like I was saying, let's look at what happened the day of the eruption. On the afternoon of August 24, 79 CE, Vesuvius spewed volcanic ash thousands of feet into the air. As the ash settled, it was swept up by wind currents that were moving predominantly southeast. These wind currents carried the ash straight toward Pompeii, and the city became engulfed in ash and debris. The weight of the ash collapsed roofs and smothered citizens, many of whom died as they tried to flee the city.

Herculaneum, which is located to the west of Vesuvius, was only covered by a few inches of ash, and most residents had time to flee the city after seeing the plume of volcanic debris rise into the sky. Those who didn't flee Herculaneum right away went to the city's port, where they waited for ships to come and rescue them. But had they known what was coming, they would've fled the city, too.

That night—the night of August 24, that is—Vesuvius emitted the first of six pyroclastic surges; these are large amounts of rock and hot gases that get shot from an erupting volcano. And this first pyroclastic surge sped down the mountain toward Herculaneum and swept through the city at speeds of up to 100 miles per hour. The estimated 300 Romans waiting for rescue ships in Herculaneum's port likely never even saw the pyroclastic surge, as they were killed by the nearly 1,000 degree heat that preceded it.

The continued volcanic activity completely buried the city of Herculaneum, some areas being covered with nearly 75 feet of volcanic ash. But the heat and speed of the volcanic activity managed to almost perfectly preserve the city, providing an airtight cover over Herculaneum for nearly 1,700 years.

By the late 1500s, small segments of the buried city of Pompeii started to be excavated, and similar excavations of Herculaneum began about 150 years later. The gradual excavations of both cities has unearthed countless sculptures, mosaics, and other priceless works of art, many well preserved by the volcanic ash. Then, beginning in 1981, the port of Herculaneum began to be excavated, revealing 55 intact skeletons. These have proven invaluable to paleontologists hoping to learn more about Romans because Romans traditionally cremated their dead, meaning Roman skeletons are very rare.

So before I talk more about the excavations of Pompeii and Herculaneum, I want you guys to turn to page 340 in your readers and look at the illustrations by Karl Weber, who directed some of the first excavation efforts for both Pompeii and Herculaneum.

Narrator: Now get ready to answer the questions.

PRACTICE 2 - TRACK 71

Narrator: Listen to part of the lecture. Then answer the question.

FP: …most residents had time to flee the city after seeing the plume of volcanic debris rise into the sky. Those who didn't flee Herculaneum right away went to the city's port, where they waited for ships to come and rescue them. But had they known what was coming, they would've fled the city, too.

Narrator: What does the professor suggest about those who waited in Herculaneum's port when she says this?

FP: But had they known what was coming, they would've fled the city, too.

PRACTICE 3 - TRACK 72

Narrator: Listen to a lecture in an economics class.

Male Professor (MP): Good morning. Today, I'd like to talk about tariffs. A tariff, as some of you may know, is a tax placed on products when they are brought across a national border. You'll hear tariffs brought up a lot whenever there are trade talks among nations, such as the passing of NAFTA, the North American Free Trade Agreement, in the early 1990s. One primary purpose of tariffs is to raise money for the governments that impose them. But tariffs may also be used to protect domestic industries. Historically, there have been three types of tariffs: transit tariffs, export tariffs, and import tariffs. That's going to be the topic of today's class.

So if everyone is ready, let's start by talking about transit tariffs. Transit tariffs—for those of you who have never heard of them, and I assume that is a great many of you—are taxes placed on things that originate in one country, pass through a second country, and arrive in a third. They are, as their name suggests, taxes imposed by the second country as goods transit it, or make their way through it. Transit tariffs are no longer in use, but from the 16th century until the middle of the 19th century, they played a huge role in directing trade and controlling certain transportation routes.

Male Student (MS): Professor, did that have something to do with colonialism? I mean, the way colonies traded with one another and such?

MP: Absolutely. It also had to do with the fact that most things traded among countries had to be carried over land and sea routes, and those routes often involved crossing other countries. So, as you can imagine…

MS: …these countries wanted to get a piece of the pie, that makes a lot of sense. So, what, transit tariffs stopped due to the invention of the airplane? It sounds like that is what you are suggesting.

MP: Well, yes, in essence, the use of more advanced transportation methods is one reason that transit tariffs ended. However, many countries eventually came to view transit tariffs as a kind of "highway robbery" because they were forced to pay them for no apparent purpose.

MS: Oh, I see.

MP: So another type of tariff that has basically become outdated are the so-called export tariffs. Export tariffs, now rarely used, were very common during the early stages of the Industrial Revolution and the growth of modern capitalism. Their primary purpose was to keep goods from leaving a country in order to safeguard home production and consumption.

Female Student (FS): Why would a country do that? I mean, usually governments want to encourage exports. Why would it tax products to prevent them from leaving the country?

MP: Well, the tariffs were meant to discourage farmers from selling crops to richer countries, for example, and leaving fellow countrymen without food. Export tariffs encourage sellers to meet local demands. But you can imagine how unpopular that would be to sellers, who just want to get the highest price they can. So, in England in particular, as free trade doctrines began to develop, export laws faded. And, as such, by 1842, England had abolished its export taxes. By the early 20th century, export taxes had pretty much been killed off.

FS: Right, that makes sense. I mean, that's where import tariffs come into the picture, right?

MP: Well, sort of. I mean, import tariffs are the most commonly used trade tariffs today. They tax goods coming into a country. Import tariffs raise money for governments. They also protect domestic agriculture and industries because they make foreign products more expensive than domestic ones. They are more politically acceptable. However, as a government revenue source, import tariffs are unreliable because it's difficult to adjust the amounts received by tariffs to current budgetary needs.

MS: I don't get it, professor. What do you mean?

MP: Well, think about it for a minute. A country's trade needs aren't really directly connected to the federal government's budget. They are more so driven by consumer demand. So, it's hard for the governments to predict just how much money import tariffs will bring in. As consumer demand shifts, government income may be greatly impacted. Therefore, relying on tariffs as a consistent source of income can be problematic.

Narrator: Now get ready to answer the questions.

PRACTICE 3 - TRACK 73

Narrator: Now listen to part of the lecture. Then answer the question.

MP: By the early 20th century, export taxes had pretty much been killed off.

FS: Right, that makes sense. I mean, that's where import tariffs come into the picture, right?

Narrator: What does the student mean when she says this?

FS: Right, that makes sense. I mean, that's where import tariffs come into the picture, right?

ACTUAL PRACTICE 14

PRACTICE 1 - TRACK 74

Narrator: Listen to a conversation between a librarian and a student.

Male Student (MS): Excuse me. I was wondering if you could help me locate some information for a research project I'm doing.

Female Librarian (FL): Hmm… What kind of information do you need?

MS: Well, I'm trying to find some general information about pine trees. I looked in the library's online catalog, but the catalog lists, like, 400 books and journals having to do with research on pine trees. Now I have no idea where to start my research.

FL: Oh, I think I see what you mean. Well, have you tried any of our encyclopedias on the shelf here? You know, your generation doesn't usually use print encyclopedias for basic, general information, because you're all used to using the Internet. But I still recommend paper-and-print encyclopedias sometimes. After all, they are very reliable sources, and easy to use.

MS: I haven't looked at any of those yet.

FL: Well, let's give that a go then. Let's see here. Oh, here we go. "Pine trees." It looks we've got a couple of pages here. There's information on pinecones, the evolution of pines, and the different uses of pine wood.

MS: Hmmm… that sounds…. Actually, I guess I kind of need a guide book or something? Like a book that people take along when they hike, you know? With pictures and descriptions, so they can figure out which species that they are looking at.

FL: Oh, yes, you're talking about a "field guide," sometimes called a "pocket field guide" because you can put them in your pocket when you go out into the field. We may have some field guides to trees on the shelves.

MS: Yeah, what I need to do is to identify different kinds of pine trees found on campus. I think our professor said there were about 25 different species so….

FL: Oh, how interesting! That sounds like a fascinating project. I didn't realize that. Just on this campus, 25 different species of pine trees? Well, you have your work cut out for you, don't you?

MS: Yeah, we're supposed to list the location of a tree, describe the pine needles and pine cones, describe the height and shape of the tree, and make a little drawing.

FL: Hmm, this changes things. I know I was just talking about how reliable print sources are, but for your purposes, I'm thinking about the opposite.

MS: The opposite? You mean using the Internet?

FL: Well, yes, I was wondering if there's some kind of application that you could download to your cell phone. You know, then you would have a *digital* field guide, and that may be more convenient.

MS: Oh, of course! An app *would* be very convenient.

FL: Well, yes. I recently helped a student find an app for identifying birds. The program we found for her was very helpful. It gives you a short menu of differences in one characteristic, and you select, and then it asks you to select again, and it just gets more and more specific until it tells you exactly what species you're seeing.

MS: That kind of thing sounds perfect. I'll definitely check that out!

FL: Okay, and if that doesn't work, come on back and just look for a printed field guide to trees. Or, another idea is to take photos or draw the characteristics of the tree while you're walking around, and then come in and use our botany reference books to identify the species.

MS: You're right, those are all great ideas. I'm so relieved. Thanks for heading me in the right direction.

Narrator: Now get ready to answer the questions.

PRACTICE 1 - TRACK 75

Narrator: Listen to part of the conversation. Then answer the question.

FL: Well, yes. I recently helped a student find an app for identifying birds. The program we found for her was very helpful. It gives you a short menu of differences in one characteristic, and you select, and then it asks you to select again, and it just gets more and more specific until it tells you exactly what species you're seeing.

MS: That kind of thing sounds perfect. I'll definitely check that out!

Narrator: Why does the student say this?

MS: That kind of thing sounds perfect. I'll definitely check that out!

PRACTICE 2 - TRACK 76

Narrator: Listen to a lecture in an American Studies class.

Female Professor (FP): In the early 1930s, many German Jewish intellectuals were forced to leave Germany, because the rise of the Nazi Party made life dangerous for them. Those Jewish refugees who immigrated to the United States had a profound effect on American arts and sciences. One such person was Kurt Weill, who became a non-American composer of "American" music.

Kurt Weill was born in 1900 in the German town of Dessau. His family was Jewish, as I mentioned, and his father was a cantor at the local synagogue, meaning he led the congregation in prayer and song. Weill was therefore steeped in music from an early age. Weill was only 14 when World War I started; as he was too young to fight in the war, he filled in as a substitute accompanist at the local opera house.

By the time that Weill was in his 20s, World War I was over, he had studied music with a famous composer in Berlin, he had supported himself with a number of music-related jobs, and he had composed some well-received classical pieces.

Now, it just so happens that Berlin was a fabulous place to be in the 1920s, especially if you were a budding composer. Berlin at the time was a music and art hotspot. People crammed into theaters and cabarets at night to see plays and hear music, including American jazz. Weill ended up collaborating in musical theater with Bertolt Brecht, a playwright known for his criticisms of society.

In 1928, Brecht and Weill created *The Three-Penny Opera*, an opera about outlaws and beggars. In the opera, Weill's cheery, jazzy tunes add to the irony of various criminal characters. They pretend to be good while they betray and cheat each other. Brecht's message was basically that in a capitalistic society, people who think they are morally good should think again. This play features the song "Mack the Knife," which later became an American jazz standard. *The Three-Penny Opera* also shows how, from early in his career, Weill embraced stories about the poor and the powerless.

In 1931, with the Nazi Party rising in power, Weill wrote the music for an opera, *The Pledge*, in which a dictator takes over a mythical land. Two years later, he worked on *The Silver Lake*. This opera ends with two main characters getting thrown out of their castle. They resolve to drown themselves in a lake. However, when they get there, the lake is frozen. As the play ends, they walk out onto the ice, unsure of where they are going.

As you can see, both plays served as allegories of the Nazis seizing power and exiling intellectuals and Jews. In fact, when the plays were performed they were interrupted by Nazi protests; Weill realized that it was time to leave Germany before he got arrested.

Weill went to France and England for a short while, but in 1935 he moved to New York. He lived only 15 more years, but for the rest of his life, he devoted himself to writing music for Broadway theater and for films. Weill wanted to synthesize a new American sound; he combined his orchestral and operatic training with a love of jazz and the blues. He also wanted to combine the intense emotion of European opera with more natural spoken dialogue.

One of Weill's projects was to set to music an earlier hit play by Elmer Rice. The play, *Street Scene*, depicts two days in front of one New York tenement. In 1946, Weill and Rice agreed ask the poet Langston Hughes to write the lyrics to the new songs. Now this was an extraordinary thing to do in 1946: Langston Hughes was African-American, and nobody asked black writers to write the words for black characters, let alone for white characters. But Langston Hughes agreed. He changed some of the characters to African-Americans, and he even took Weill to some Harlem night clubs so that Weill could hear cutting-edge jazz and blues music. Weill wrote the music for the show's 21 songs, expressing a variety of the character's deepest, most poignant emotions. Theater critics were enthusiastic. In fact, a. writer for the Music Digest said, "American opera has at last been realized."

Later, Langston Hughes reportedly said that he regarded Weill as a truly universal artist -- an artist who could be claimed equally by Germany as a German, by America as an American, and by "me as a Negro."

Narrator: Now get ready to answer the questions.

PRACTICE 3 - TRACK 77

Narrator: Listen to a lecture in an astronomy class.

Female Professor (FP): Good afternoon, class. So to start today's class, I want you to imagine that you're an ancient person, living, let's say, 3,000 years ago. Occasionally, a flaming streak of light flashes across the night sky and disappears. Sometimes, a streak of light plunges toward Earth, exploding when it lands.. When you saw such displays, you probably wouldn't have known what to think. As such, you may have believed that you were seeing a star fall from the sky, and so you called the object a "shooting star" or a "falling star."

Of course, today pretty much everyone knows that these aren't stars at all. They are, in fact, small pieces of stony or metallic matter from outer space that enter the Earth's atmosphere and vaporize. Before they encounter Earth's atmosphere, these chunks of matter are called "meteoroids." Once they enter the atmosphere, they're called "meteors." Most meteors never reach Earth—they're so tiny that they vaporize completely soon after entering the atmosphere. But sometimes the particles are large enough that they remain partly intact. The large, dense objects that survive the fall to Earth are called "meteorites."

So as a quick review: meteoroids are objects before they encounter Earth's atmosphere; meteors are objects that enter Earth's atmosphere and vaporize before hitting the ground; and meteorites are the objects that actually make it to Earth. (*To male student*) Yes, Tim, you have a question?

Male Student (MS): Yes, Professor Delgado. It's about the physical composition of meteoroids. So you said that meteoroids are made of stone or metal, right? So, what elements and compounds are found in meteorites?

FP: That's a great question and something we'll spend some time discussing, actually. Meteoroids are classified by their physical composition, and for the most part, they're made of stone, metal, or a combination of the two. The composition of a meteoroid also gives astronomers clues as to its origins.

Let's start with stony meteoroids, for example. These make up the majority of all meteoroids that enter Earth's atmosphere. Using meteorite fragments found on Earth, scientists have determined that stony meteoroids are primarily made up of silicon and oxygen. Based on this information, scientists think stony meteoroids come from the asteroid belt between Mars and Jupiter; that is, the millions of rocky fragments that orbit around the sun out beyond the orbit of Mars. They may have had the potential to coalesce and form a planet at one point.

MS: Okay, I remember you talked about the asteroid belt a few weeks ago. So the stone fragments found in the asteroid belt match the compounds found in stony meteorites?

FP: That's correct. As a matter of fact, astronomers believe that metal meteoroids also originate from the asteroid belt.

MS: Are there also metal fragments in the asteroid belt?

FP: Yes, that's right. And most metallic meteoroids are made of an iron-nickel alloy, a relatively common compound found in the asteroid belt. On a side note, the composition of the asteroid belt gives astronomers clues about its origin as well. Does anyone want to guess why the two materials we've discussed support the hypothesis that the asteroid belt was once an unformed planet?.

Female Student (FS): Well, like you just said, metal meteoroids are composed of iron and nickel, right? And aren't the cores of most planets also made of iron and nickel?

FP: Yes, very good, Trish. So, naturally, scientists believe the iron and nickel in the asteroid belt once formed the core of this unfinished planet. Also, the surfaces of the solar system's inner planets are made of rocky materials, similar to the oxygen and silicon found in stony meteorites.

Okay, let's focus for a moment on the impact of meteorites. Scientists have known for a long time that impact sites are surrounded by "tektites." Some of you may have heard that tektites are similar to meteoroids, so I wanted to clarify this point. Although other theories regarding tektites exist, most astronomers believe that tektites are actually chunks of debris from Earth that are ejected during a meteorite collision.

So, let's say a meteorite makes it through the atmosphere, and pulled down by Earth's gravity, it superheats. Bam, the meteorite hits! The collision superheats some of the rock it lands on, which shatters and flies out in all directions. The flying, superheated rock pieces form a glassy surface. These objects never achieve enough velocity to escape our atmosphere, so they fall back to Earth as tektites. So tektites are terrestrial in origin; tektites are not actually a type of meteoroid, but they are evidence that a meteorite hit the Earth.

Narrator: Now get ready to answer the questions.

PRACTICE 3 - TRACK 78

Narrator: Listen to part of the lecture, then answer the question.

FP: Okay, let's focus for a moment on the impact of meteorites. Scientists have known for a long time that impact sites are surrounded by "tektites." Some of you may have heard that tektites are similar to meteoroids, so I wanted to clarify this point. Although other theories regarding tektites exist, most astronomers believe that tektites are actually chunks of debris from Earth that are ejected during a meteorite collision.

Narrator: What does the professor mean when she says this?

FP: Although other theories regarding tektites exist…

ACTUAL PRACTICE 15

PRACTICE 1 - TRACK 79

Narrator: Listen to a conversation between a student and a security officer.

Female Student (FS): Hi, I was wondering if you could help me. I'm looking for a place to park by the theater, the Tremont Theater, or something like that? My friend told me the name of the theater, but I just can't remember!

Male Clerk (MC): Well, let's see. We have several theaters on campus. Are you talking about the Bridge Theater? It's our main movie theater on campus.

FS: No, no, it's not that one. Oh, I should know this. I'm kind of new here, and I was taking the bus to campus at first, but I just got a car, and I don't know where to park or anything! I'm here to see a string quartet concert. My friend is playing cello. It's supposed to start in 10 minutes!

MC: Okay, so the name of the theater is something like "Tremont?"

FS: Yes, I think so. And, can you also please tell me the closest parking lot to the theater? I'm really running late.

MC: I'll try, but let's figure out which theater we're talking about here. Give me a minute, and I'll check the campus calendar on the computer.

FS: Okay, and I'll try texting my friend. Hopefully he's still got his phone turned on.

MC: I'm not seeing anything about a concert here. Lectures, plays… Not all the events are on the main website, you know. Some events are on the department web sites, the site for music or dance or drama. I'll try the music department.

FS: My friend isn't answering my texts, so I guess he's already warming up or something.

MC: That's too bad. Okay, well the music department performances this semester… let's see… there's a recital by the university wind ensemble. Then, there's the symphonic band; there's jazz, and there's a vocalist performing Italian arias of the

17th century. I'm sorry, I really don't see a string quartet here.

FS: Oh, wait, there he is, I mean there's his text. Ohhhh, it's not a theater! He says they're at the Tree Frog Café. I think I know where that is, but I have no idea how to get there from this side of the campus, or where to park.

MC: Okay, so that café is on the west side of campus, between the Life Sciences building and the dance theater. Your best bet would be to park in Student Lot 8, cross the street there, and walk toward the dance theater.

FS: Wait, which lot should I park in?

MC: Student Lot 8. You get there by turning left at the intersection here.

FS: And after I park, then it's just across the street?

MC: Yes.

FS: Got it. Thanks!

MC: Wait! One more thing. Did you just get a car? Do you have a parking sticker yet? Without a sticker on your car, you need to buy a temporary parking pass. Or else, you could get a ticket! A temporary pass costs two dollars. You can buy it here, or at a machine in the parking lot.

FS: Good idea. How much will a parking permit for the rest of the year cost me?

MC: That depends. There are different kinds of permits. You should come back when you have more time, but be sure to buy a temporary one every time you park on campus, until you have a permanent sticker. Enjoy the concert!

FS: Thanks! I hope my friend appreciates what I had to do to get here!

MC: Well, a lot of students have trouble understanding the on-campus parking system. Heck, sometimes I don't even understand it. And the Campus Police are always checking up on cars without parking stickers, so it was good you came here first.

Narrator: Now get ready to answer the questions.

PRACTICE 1 - TRACK 80

Narrator: Listen to part of the conversation. Then answer the question.

FS: Oh, wait, there he is, I mean there's his text. Ohhhh, it's not a theater! He says they're at the Tree Frog Café. I think I know where that is, but I have no idea how to get there from this side of the campus, or where to park.

Narrator: Why does the student say this?

FS: I think I know where that is, but I have no idea how to get there from this side of the campus, or where to park.

PRACTICE 2 - TRACK 81

Narrator: Now listen to a lecture in a psychology class.

Male Professor (MP): So, today I want to talk about the feeling of *already* having experienced an experience while you're having it. As you know, no doubt, the experience is often referred to as "déjà vu," a French term that means "already seen." So déjà vu, as I've already said, describes the sense that one has witnessed or experienced a new sensation previously, and this sensation is usually accompanied by a sense of "strangeness," or "weirdness."

Based on what little research has been done on the phenomenon, the experience of déjà vu seems to be very common. In formal studies, about 70 percent of people have reported experiencing déjà vu at least once in their lives. References to the experience of déjà vu are also found in literature of the past, indicating that it's not a new phenomenon. But in laboratory settings, it's extremely difficult to invoke the experience of déjà vu, so it remains a poorly studied topic. So the exact causes of déjà vu remain somewhat of a mystery.

Actually, before I get into what science has concluded about the experience of déjà vu, I'd like to describe some of its different forms. According to some scientists and psychologists, the term "déjà vu" really describes a broad range of experiences that can be broken down into two more specific terms. Like I said, the French term "déjà vu" means "already seen." "Seen"—that's the key word here. This term doesn't really cover the whole range of sensory experiences that people experience. You see, the most common kind of déjà vu is often labeled "déjà vécu." This is a French term that means "already experienced," or "already lived through," and it more accurately describes what most people experience when they claim to have experienced déjà vu.

So, then, what do most people experience when they have a déjà vécu? Well, the experience involves a great deal of detail. The author Charles Dickens describes the experience like this:

"We have all some experience of a feeling, that comes over us occasionally, of what we are saying and doing having been said and done before, in a remote time—of our having been surrounded, ages ago, by the same faces, objects, and circumstances—of our knowing perfectly what will be said next, as if we suddenly remember it!"

I think Dickens paints a pretty good picture of what it's like to have a déjà vécu experience, don't you?

Now that we've looked at déjà vécu, let's discuss the other type of déjà vu experience. This one is often labeled "déjà visité." Déjà visité, as the name implies, is the French term for "already visited." It describes the feeling of uncanny familiarity with a new place. For instance, say you're walking through a museum you've never been to before, but all of a sudden, you get the feeling that you've been in that exact museum before. Maybe something about the walls, or the art on display, gives you the sense that everything there is familiar to you. This experience, deja visité, is less common than deja vécu, but both experiences are commonly described as unsettling. As such, dreams, reincarnation and out-of-body experiences have been proposed as explanations to this phenomenon. And some suggest that reading a detailed account of a place can result in this feeling when the locale is later visited.

So then, just what does science have to say about these experiences, about their causes? Well, as you can imagine, the scientific explanation for déjà vu is far less glamorous and mystical than the "out there" speculative explanations given by people who experience the phenomenon. In recent years, neuro-physiological research has supported an explanation for both types of déjà vu that is quite simple: déjà vu isn't actually an act of "precognition" or "prophecy" but is more so an anomaly of memory. And by "anomaly of memory," I mean that déjà vu is a *false impression* of a recalled experience. In other words, the brain cells are firing to create the impression that you have been somewhere or done something before, when in fact you have never had these experiences. So really, the brain is making a mistake.

But why and how does this happen? What's the evidence? First of all, in most cases of déjà vu, the sense of "recollection" at the time is strong, but any circumstances of the "previous" experience—when, where and how the earlier experience occurred—are quite uncertain. Likewise, as time passes, subjects can exhibit a strong recollection of having the "unsettling" experience of déjà vu itself, but little to no recollection of the specifics of the event or circumstances they were "remembering" when they had the déjà vu experience.

Narrator: Now get ready to answer the questions.

PRACTICE 2 - TRACK 82

Narrator: What does the professor mean when he says this?

MP: I think Dickens paints a pretty good picture of what it's like to have a déjà vécu experience, don't you?

PRACTICE 3 - TRACK 83

Narrator: Listen to a lecture in an economics class.

Female Professor (FP): Good evening class. Today, I would like to talk about scams that promise participants a quick, fast, and easy method for making large amounts of money. In reality, participants are tricked out of their own money, contributing to the wealth of the scam's originator. These are often referred to as "get-rich-quick schemes" and may take many forms, but all will require participants to provide an initial investment. I'd like to focus on a couple of common types of get-rich-quick schemes for today's lecture. These are: employment scams and investment seminars.

So, the first of these schemes is an employment scam in which the scammer advertises a job vacancy. Typically, these jobs require little to no experience, pay much more than is standard for the type of work advertised, and offer the "employee" the opportunity to work from home. Now, in order for the scammer to make money, he or she must convince participants that this is a real opportunity and, more importantly, that an initial investment is required in order to be eligible for employment.

Male Student (MS): Professor, why would anyone fall for such a scam? I mean, wouldn't it be obvious that the job isn't real?

FP: Well, there are laws in many countries, including the United States, that prohibit employers from charging any fee to new employees. However, scammers are clever and employ various tactics to convince their audience. One popular technique is to advertise a job in sales that requires participants to market a product, such as a nutritional supplement, that the scammer convinces them sells easily. The scammer promises these vitamins, or other products, are in high demand and can be sold for two or even three times their cost. The unwitting victim buys these products only to find they actually have little to no real value, and are very difficult to sell. By utilizing this strategy, scammers avoid eliciting suspicion over the bogus startup fee.

These types of scams are actually quite common; if you browse online job listings, you'll be sure to find more than a few scams hidden among legitimate postings. If you know what to look for, these schemes are easy to avoid. So, scammers go after victims who are young, ignorant, or desperate, and may not consider the offer using common sense.

Okay, enough about employment scams. Let's move on to the second type of get-rich-quick scheme I wanted to talk about today, investment seminars. These seminars are often advertised on television and in magazines, newspapers, and online forums. They usually offer some "secret formula" to investing or for getting out of debt that allows the participant to make unreasonably high profits with little or no risk. The victims of these scams are required to pay for admission to "exclusive" seminars where wealthy "experts" lecture on investing. However, the advice given by these so-called experts turns out to be mediocre and certainly never produces the level of profit promised.

Female Student (FS): Professor, I think I've seen a commercial like this, late at night. They had a bunch of testimonials from previous participants who have made millions of dollars using the investment strategies outlined in the seminars.

FP: These schemes often rely on testimonials from paid actors to help convince the audience of their sincerity. In this way, participants are more likely to feel that the exorbitant fees charged to attend the seminar are justified. But really, no investment strategy can deliver what they promise. Like an employment scam, the offer is simply too good to be true.

FS: But, Professor, there has to be a way to get rich quick, right? What's your secret?

FP: (*laughing*) Very funny. Unfortunately, the only investments that have the potential to make a lot of money quickly also have the potential to lose a lot of money. A good example is playing the lottery, or investing in high-risk stocks, such as a tech start-up. Microsoft and Apple are great examples of technology companies that made record profits for shareholders. However, for every success story, there are at least a dozen companies that didn't make it. So, investing in these high-risk stocks is, well risky. You could get rich or you could lose everything.

The common theme among get-rich-quick schemes is that they purport to offer a guaranteed method of attaining wealth rapidly. But the only real methods of attaining wealth so quickly are risky; that is, they are not guaranteed. If there were a way to get rich quickly, don't you think everyone would be doing it?

Narrator: Now get ready to answer the questions.

ACTUAL PRACTICE 16

PRACTICE 1 - TRACK 84

Narrator: Listen to a conversation between a student and a professor.

Female Student (FS): Hi Professor Patel, do you have a few minutes? My name is Kay, and I'm in your Intro to Computer Programming class.

Male Professor (MP): Oh, certainly, Kay. You're upset about your grade on the midterm? I've had a lot of students in here about that today. A lot of students feel that they did quite poorly.

FS: No, no, I did okay on the midterm.

MP: Good. So, what's up?

FS: Well, I was wondering if I could get an extension on the programming assignment that's due tomorrow. I'm really having problems with it, and I'm supposed to work tonight.

MP: Oh, where do you work?

FS: Oh, I'm lucky to have an on-campus job. I work as a technician at the campus radio station. I checked, and no one else is available to cover for me tonight. I work until midnight, and by then I'll probably be exhausted. So... I was wondering if I could turn in the program on Friday instead?

MP: Sure, that'd be fine. Just submit it via the class website. You've done that before in this class, right? Be sure to write a little note at the top to remind me that we talked about you turning the assignment in late.

FS: That's great, thanks Professor. I'll do that.

MP: Now, that only gives you a day to figure out what's going on with the program you've written. What do you think the problem is?

FS: I wish I knew! I keep trying to fix it, but I can't get the program to run. You know, I understand all about functions and arrays in theory. That's why I got a good grade on the midterm, I guess. But it's really frustrating that I can't make my own program work.

MP: Well, it's probably something very small that needs tweaking—just a little change. Have you asked for help from one of the TAs for this class? They all have computer lab hours, you know.

FS: Yes, I went to one lab session and the TA was really helpful, and that got me started. But then afterward, when I was finishing it up, I guess I wrote some bad code.

MP: I'm sure you're on the right track. Just because it's not working yet doesn't mean it's bad. Coding, you know, writing programs to get computers to do something, it just requires patience. You end up trying different things, adding and deleting, and then one day it just works. And it's really thrilling. Then you can't wait to start writing code for the next project.

FS: That sounds like my friend who told me to take this class. He loves coding so much, he forgets to eat and sleep.

MP: Yeah, that's how it is for the truly addicted; I'm that way myself. So, good luck with your program, but even if it doesn't work yet by Friday, go ahead and turn it in so I can still give you a grade on it. I don't want you to get behind.

FS: I know. We have another program due next week. Thanks, Professor, I appreciate you working with me on this.

MP: No problem, Kay. Have a good night at work! What do you do as a technician at the radio station?

FS: Well, I make sure that the transmitter is working. Sometimes it goes offline, or shuts down because of a power surge or some kind of glitch. The on-air people get pretty upset if they find out that they've been broadcasting to no-one!

MP: I'll bet they do. Well, sounds like good on-the-job experience for anyone interested in computers!

Narrator: Now get ready to answer the questions.

PRACTICE 1 - TRACK 85

Narrator: Why does the professor say this?

Male Professor: …I'm sure you're on the right track. Just because it's not working yet doesn't mean it's bad. Coding, you know, writing programs to get computers to do something, it just requires patience. You end up trying different things, adding and deleting, and then one day it just works. And it's really thrilling. Then you can't wait to start writing code for the next project.

PRACTICE 2 - TRACK 86

Narrator: Listen to a lecture from an American Literature class.

Female Professor (FP): Let's continue our discussion of contemporary American poets. We've talked about the Beat Poets from the 1950s, with their dazzling images. Today our focus will shift to contemporary writers who seek a kind of realism, a kind of coherence, in the same vein as Robert Frost. In these poems, a narrator describes a common incident using a conversational tone. The mundane scene nevertheless surprises the reader by delivering some extraordinary meaning. For example, Philip Levine may seem to be describing the weather in his poem "Our Valley," but when he catches a whiff of salt air from the ocean that he can't see, the poem becomes a meditation on human perceptions and on life itself.

So I would like to focus for a bit on a protégé of Philip Levine, Gary Soto. Some of his poems were in the assigned reading for today. Gary Soto writes poetry in the narrative style I just mentioned. He was a student of Philip Levine's at Fresno State University, and has gone on to publish more than 40 works, including novels, plays, and collections of poems.

Gary Soto's grandparents were immigrants from Mexico. They worked agricultural jobs in California's San Joaquin Valley, harvesting grapes and other crops, and their children did the same when they got old enough. Gary was born in 1952 in Fresno, where his parents worked at the Sun Maid Raisin factory. When Gary was 5, his father died in an accident at the factory. Soto's mother was left alone with three young children; the family had to move to a poorer neighborhood.

Fresno is a flat, unpretentious city that gets very hot and dry in summer. Soto's poetry and other works give voice to his experiences of trying to cope with loss, poverty and prejudice from a young age; but also, the unique and poignant moments of his life, the beauty and humanity in a place that may seem uneventful to the outside world. He provides just enough detail in each scene to make it feel familiar to the reader. For example, he may describe dusty bare feet making shadows in the stands of a local baseball game while the sun sets. The reader can fill in the warmth of the summer evening, the sounds of baseballs hitting leather gloves and shouting kids.

Male Student (FS): I think I read one of his books, maybe in middle school. Isn't he considered a Latino writer?

FP: That's a very important question. I think that Gary Soto might answer that he is Mexican American, and he is a writer, and obviously the two cannot be separated. But all writers seek to find something universal within personal experiences. So, while Soto clearly embraces being a Latino voice, he is so much more than that. I have here a quote I wanted to share with you, from Gary Soto himself, on this particular issue: "…as a writer, my duty is not to make people perfect, particularly Mexican Americans. I'm not a cheerleader. I'm one who provides portraits of people in the rush of life."

Soto's most famous and most anthologized poems don't have explicit Mexican-American images. In "Oranges," arguably Soto's best known poem, the narrator and the other characters are not identified by ethnicity. Instead, it's their common experience of poverty and intimacy that fuels the images of the poem. The adolescent narrator is on his first date with a girl. They walk to a small store, where the girl chooses candy that costs more money than the boy has. The lady working at the store deduces his dilemma, and, as though a silent message passes between them, she accepts a coin and an orange as payment.

In one of my favorite Soto poems, however, he addresses stereotypes of Latinos head-on. In "Mexicans Begin Jogging," the title suggests a news feature about Mexican Americans taking up the middle-class hobby of running for health. But the poem turns this notion upside down: the jogging Mexicans are undocumented workers running from U.S. border patrol officers.

The poem describes a time when Soto is working in a factory, and the border patrol raid the workplace. The boss assumes that Soto is lying when Soto says he is an American, and hurries him out the back door with the "other" Mexicans. Soto says: "Since I was on his time, I ran…" Soto runs away into a white neighborhood, and reflects on the absurdity of the situation; he imagines "…those sociologists/Who would clock me/As I jog into the next century/On the power of a great, silly grin." The poem thus uses ironic humor. The boss and the border patrol do not realize that Soto is as American as they are. He is suggesting that Latinos are an established and growing part of American life, and that an increasing number of them are achieving middle-class status. Probably even jogging for health…

Narrator: Now get ready to answer the questions.

PRACTICE 2 - TRACK 87

Narrator: Why does the professor provide this information?

FP: Gary was born in 1952 in Fresno, where his parents worked at the Sun Maid Raisin factory. When Gary was 5, his father died in an accident at the factory. Soto's mother was left alone with three young children; the family had to move to a poorer neighborhood.

PRACTICE 3 - TRACK 88

Narrator: Now listen to a lecture in a botany class.

Female Professor (FP): As you can see, I've brought some "friends" with me to class today. If you look at the table here, you will see specimens of what have become one of the most prized families of flowers in all of the world. Members of this family, called "orchids," are widely cultivated as house, garden, and greenhouse flowers. Perhaps you even have one in your dormitory or apartment.

So let's talk about some of the features of orchids, some of the things that make them so interesting to both scientists and amateur gardeners alike. First off, orchids are often regarded as the largest family of flowering plants, as there are well over 20,000 different species of orchid. As a result, orchids come in a huge variety of colors, scents, and shapes. Orchids are found on every continent except Antarctica, and they're particularly abundant in the tropics. Because there are so many varieties of orchids, and because they can survive in almost any climate, people have long been attracted to them. Another feature that attracts people to orchids is their wide range in size—the smallest orchid plant is only one-half centimeter high while the largest grows to over thirty meters long. The size range means there is always an orchid that can fit in any planting, indoors or out.

The popularity of orchids has almost been their undoing in some places. As I suggested before, orchids grow naturally where the weather is warm and humid, so they're particularly abundant in the tropics. Large numbers of orchids are imported annually from South America, the East Indies, the Philippines, and Australia. Because of this importation, to prevent the extinction of many orchid species, some of these region's governments have been forced to stop people collecting orchids from nature. And, get this, people have paid up to hundreds of thousands of dollars for a single rare orchid plant. So I guess you could say orchids are the diamonds or the ivory of the plant world.

Now let's get into some of the botany of orchids. First of all, if you look at any of the potted orchids I have here, you'll notice something interesting about them. Even though I have these orchids in pots, you'll notice that they are not growing in dirt or soil. In fact, they are growing in, well, basically, air. Actually, this way of growth is a defining feature of most orchids. The majority of orchids are what botanists call "epiphytes" or "lithophytes." Do those terms ring a bell with anyone, perhaps from a few weeks ago? If not, let me review: epiphytes are air plants that grow on tree trunks and branches, and lithophytes are air plants that grow on rocks. So, just what does that mean, that orchids are "air plants?" Well, it means that both of these types of orchids obtain their nourishment from long, spongy aerial roots that absorb moisture and nutrients from the air. That's why there are so many roots sticking out of these pots on my desk.

Now, then, let's look at the physical structure of orchids—that is, what the flowers themselves look like. Well, as you can see, all of the orchid specimens on my desk—and all orchids in general—have three petals as well as three petal-like structures called "sepals." However, unlike some other flowers with this pattern, orchids also have an extra central petal that's larger than the other petals. This petal, located in the center of the orchid is called the "lip." It may resemble a cup, a scoop, a trumpet, or a bag. The lip provides a landing spot for any passing pollinators, so insects or birds have access to it. And at the base of the lip sits the column, which contains "stamen"—the male reproductive part—and the "pistil"—the female part. The stamen bears pollen grains, which produce sperm cells, while the pistil contains egg cells.

Now onto one final point about orchids. Most orchids have elaborate mechanisms for ensuring pollination over time, another reason that they're so diverse. For example, in some orchid species, the plant's lip may look so much like a female insect that the male pollinator—an insect, in this case—will try to mate with it. In the process, the insect will get some of the orchid's pollen on itself, bearing the pollen on its body when it leaves. Or, the attraction in some other orchid species may be a tempting nectar within the flower or succulent tissue on the lip. Some orchids even expel nectar onto their visitors, like a shower, and make them crawl with wet wings past the waiting pollen. And that's why the column is located so close to the lip.

So, I'd like to stop now to see if you have any questions on what I've spoken about so far. Then, I'd like to show you some slides of various orchids from around the world so you can see their great diversity and beauty.

Narrator: Now get ready to answer the questions.

PRACTICE 3 - TRACK 89

Narrator: Listen to part of the lecture. Then answer the question.
FP: Members of this family, called "orchids," are widely cultivated as house, garden, and greenhouse flowers. Perhaps you even have one in your dormitory or apartment.
Narrator: Why does the professor say this?
FP: Perhaps you even have on in your dormitory or apartment.

ACTUAL PRACTICE 17

PRACTICE 1 - TRACK 90

Narrator: Listen to part of a conversation between a student and a professor.
Male Student (MS): Hello, Professor Park. I'm here for

my appointment.

Female Professor (FP): Oh, right, Liam. Come in, come in and have a seat.

MS: Thanks. Man, it's really pouring out there. I almost didn't show up.

FP: Well, I'm glad you did. Now, remind me, which one of my rhetoric classes are you in?

MS: Right now I'm in Rhetoric 150, Public Speaking for Persuasion.

FP: Okay. And are you a rhetoric major?

MS: No, I'm studying biochemistry. But I wanted to take this class because I've always been afraid to make speeches to big audiences. But I really want to be able to make speeches and make strong points.

FP: Great idea.

MS: Thanks, well, the only problem is that I'm kind of stuck on the final project.

FP: The final project—you mean the persuasive video essay?

MS: Yeah, the video essay. I want to talk about burning plastic in my video essay.

FP: Okay, that sounds promising. What about burning plastic?

MS: Well, burning plastic is… I want to talk about the negative effects of incinerating plastic. But maybe I shouldn't just stand there talking about toxic chemicals. It might be, you know, too much scientific information, a lot of names of chemicals.

FP: You're right, that doesn't sound like it'll persuade people. It sounds more like it'll put them to sleep.

MS: (*Laughing*) Yeah, that's what I'm afraid of.

FP: And remember, this assignment is to persuade the audience about a specific change that should be made, such as in a law or a public policy. You not only have to talk about the problem, you must suggest a way for people to change it.

MS: Oh, right! I didn't really think about that.

FP: So… maybe you need to address the question of what society should do about plastic waste?

MS: I get it… something like changing the laws? Like… maybe cities shouldn't be allowed to burn trash?

FP: That sounds like it'd be more in line with the assignment. Tell me, how did you get interested in this topic?

MS: Well, when I was a kid, my city built a trash incinerator in my neighborhood. A lot of smoke came out of it all the time. Everyone was mad about it and talked about it a lot. The city kept saying it'd be safe, but most of my neighbors didn't believe it.

FP: There you go, that can be your focal point. You can go back to your neighborhood and get video footage of the incinerator, and interview people who have lived near it and find out what their experiences have been. That could be very persuasive, and it would sort of personalize the topic. Personalizing is a good rhetorical strategy.

MS: Wow, I didn't even think of that! I didn't think of my own neighborhood as being a source. I guess I felt like that'd be cheating, because it's not something I found in the library or online.

FP: (*Laughing*) Well, when it comes to rhetoric, the rules are a bit different. Personal experience is very persuasive. The audience can identify with the speaker and understand his or her viewpoint better.

MS: That makes sense. But… don't I still have to talk about the other side?

FP: Hmm, yes, you can't just ignore the opposing viewpoint. How about this idea: try to find an international student who comes from a country where incinerators are really necessary, because there's no more land where they can bury trash.
Say, a student from Denmark, Switzerland, Japan? Somewhere like that? And see if you can get one of them to just talk about how they don't have room to bury trash?

MS: That's a great idea! In fact, I know some international students from my biochemistry classes. I'll ask around and see if I can find someone. Thanks, Professor!

Narrator: Now get ready to answer the questions.

PRACTICE 1 - TRACK 91

Narrator: Listen to part of the conversation. Then answer the question.

MS: Well, burning plastic is… I want to talk about the bad effects caused by incinerating plastic. But maybe I shouldn't just stand there talking about toxic chemicals. It might be, you know, too much scientific information, a lot of names of chemicals.

FP: You're right, that doesn't sound like it'll persuade people. It sounds more like it'll put them to sleep.

Narrator: What does the professor imply when she says

this?

FP: It sounds more like it'll put them to sleep.

PRACTICE 2 - TRACK 92

Narrator: Listen to a lecture in a biology class.

Female Professor (FP): Good morning, and welcome to Intro to Entomology. I hope everyone had a wonderful winter break. So for this first lecture, I'd like to introduce everyone's favorite insect: the honeybee. Although many people are allergic to the venom in a honeybee's stinger, these insects are important ecologically and commercially. These furry little bugs produce honey and beeswax and are also responsible for pollinating a variety of wild plant species and many agricultural crops.

Before we discuss the importance of honeybees as pollinators, however, I'd like to spend some time going over the life cycle of a honey bee. Bees form colonies that have remarkable ways of regenerating. Individual bees die, but the colony can survive indefinitely. It is quite fascinating to look at the life cycles of individual bees within their singular functions, and how they contribute to the whole.

So most species of honeybee lay eggs within the honeycomb of their hives. Eggs are laid by the queen bee, and there is only one queen in each colony.

Male Student (MS): Professor, how does the queen prevent another female from hatching out of one of her eggs and taking over the colony?

FP: That's a good question. Actually, she doesn't; in fact, all worker bees are females, but these workers are sterile. The current queen chooses a female larva to become a new queen shortly after it hatches. This larva is fed a special diet and she eventually becomes a queen herself and establishes a new colony or takes over for a dying queen in the existing colony.

MS: Okay, but what about male honeybees? What happens to them after they hatch from their eggs?

FP: Well, male bees are called drones, and they only hatch from unfertilized eggs. You see, the queen collects and stores sperm during mating. Later, when laying her eggs, she can choose which eggs to fertilize. The majority of bees are workers, so most eggs are fertilized. However, during the spring and summer, honeybee queens leave many eggs unfertilized to produce males drones, which are genetic clones of the queen.

These drones only live for a short amount of time and do not participate in any of the hive maintenance tasks which occupy the females. Instead, their primary role is to seek out and mate with a queen from a nearby hive. Drones do not mate with a queen from their own colony. Male honeybees die shortly after successfully mating with a queen; otherwise, they are removed from the hive come winter.

Okay, let's get back to female bees for a minute and we'll discuss the mating process more in depth later. So, after the larval stage, young worker bees take care of the hive and feed the larvae. They expand the honeycomb structure of the hive and receive and store nectar from older workers. Later, they guard the hive, then they eventually leave the hive to begin foraging. After that, workers spend most of their lives coming and going from the hive, searching for and storing nectar, and looking for water and other resources.

Female Student (FS): How do honeybees start new colonies?

FP: So, when a queen is ready to start a new colony, she sends worker bees to scout a new site. Then, a large group of workers escorts the queen to the new location and they begin building the hive. The queen immediately starts laying eggs for the next generation of worker bees and they gather food and take care of the hive for the new colony.

FS: And what happens to honeybees during the winter? You never see them out once the temperature starts to drop.

FP: Excellent observation. Well, as I mentioned earlier, honeybees spend a great deal of time searching for and storing food. So during fall and winter, all the workers retreat into the hive to keep each other warm. The workers cluster around the queen and shiver to increase the temperature in the hive. The whole colony participates, and workers rotate positions to prevent any one bee from getting too cold. During this time, they are able to survive on the honey they stored over the warmer months.

As temperatures begin to rise, the queen will start to lay eggs again. Once it gets even warmer, workers leave the hive to search for food once more. They will build up the hive's supply of honey in preparation for the coming winter. In addition, the queen will produce many drones during late spring and early summer to mate with queens from neighboring colonies.

Now, unless there are any more questions, I'd like to discuss the mating process of one particular species of honeybee…

Narrator: Now get ready to answer the questions.

PRACTICE 2 - TRACK 93

Narrator: Listen to part of the lecture, then answer the question.

FP: These drones only live for a short amount of time and do not participate in any of the hive maintenance tasks which occupy the females. Instead, their primary role is to seek out and mate with a queen from a nearby hive. Drones do not mate with a queen from their own colony. Male honeybees die shortly after successfully mating with a queen; otherwise, they are removed from the hive come winter.

Narrator: Why does the professor say this?

FP: Male honeybees die shortly after successfully mating with a queen; otherwise, they are removed from the hive come winter.

PRACTICE 3 - TRACK 94

Narrator: Listen to a lecture in a U.S. history class.

Male Professor (MP): One of the most sensational murder trials in United States history took place in Massachusetts in 1921. Today, however, the trial is all but forgotten by most Americans. Known as the Sacco and Vanzetti Trial, this case involved two Italian immigrant defendants, Nicola Sacco and Bartolomeo Vanzetti. They were convicted of and later executed for a crime that many people believed they didn't commit.

Female Student (FS): I remember reading about that in my high school history textbook. Sacco and Vanzetti were accused of killing two people in a robbery, right?

MP: Yes, that's correct, Grace. But before we get to the trial, let me just give you some background about these two men, and about the social and political atmosphere of the U.S. at the time. That's a really important part of the case.

Nicola Sacco and Bartolomeo Vanzetti emigrated from Italy to the United States in 1908. At that time, there was a great deal of discrimination and racism toward Italian immigrants by Anglo Americans. Immigrants from southern Europe in general were poor and poorly educated. They usually had darker skin, and many of them were Roman Catholic. These qualities were very different from the average American at the turn of the century.

Also, Sacco and Vanzetti were active in anarchist politics. They belonged to a group that advocated doing away with government and rebelling against authority. Most Americans feared this type of radicalism. They were afraid that immigrants brought political conspiracies and sought to overthrow the government. Remember that the early 1900s saw the rise of communist and socialist movements in Europe. A communist revolution had already started in Russia.

FS: So, is it safe to say this was right around the time of the "Red Scare?"

MP: Yes, that's correct, the first Red Scare. Many Americans at the time were afraid of communist politics and potential conspiracies. Also, the United States entered World War I in 1917. Sacco and Vanzetti didn't believe in fighting wars for any government, so they left the United States for Mexico to avoid military service.

After World War I ended, the two men returned to the U.S. and started working at a shoe factory in Boston, Massachusetts. While they were employed at the factory, there was a robbery. $15,000 dollars was stolen and a security guard and payroll clerk were killed. Sacco and Vanzetti were arrested and charged with the crime.

FS: Was there any evidence linking them to the crime? Did someone identify them?

MP: No one identified the men, but there was some circumstantial evidence. Both Sacco and Vanzetti owned guns. And Sacco's gun was of the same caliber as the one used to kill one of the murder victims.

But really, there was no hard evidence, and there were no witnesses to confirm their presence at the scene of the crime. Remember, this was before fingerprint databases and advanced forensic technologies, so many criminal investigations relied on circumstantial evidence.

But, this case lacked even indirect evidence. Really, these men were accused of this murder primarily because of their reputation. As I alluded to earlier, Sacco and Vanzetti were not well-liked by Anglo Americans and were regarded as "draft dodgers" and political rebels. In fact, that's how the prosecution described them during the trial. And the judge who tried the case, Webster Thayer, was openly prejudiced against Italians and refused to listen to the testimony of any Italian-born witnesses.

Male Student (MS): Sorry to interrupt, professor, but I don't understand. I thought these types of practices were illegal under the American system of justice.

MP: Well, there are supposed to be checks and balances to prevent any government officials from abusing their power. However, some exceptions still occur from time to time. As for Sacco and Vanzetti… the jury found them guilty of first-degree murder, and Judge Thayer sentenced them to death.

Naturally, Sacco and Vanzetti appealed the verdict while awaiting their death sentences. But Judge Thayer denied their motions, even after a notorious Italian mobster confessed to the murder. This caused a storm of protest. Famous American and European intellectuals campaigned for a retrial but were unsuccessful. Demonstrations were held in major cities. Still, the death sentence was carried out despite public objection. After it was over, this trial was regularly discussed in America for almost 50 years.

MS: So, did Congress or the President do anything to prevent this kind of thing from happening in the future?

MP: No, but the publicity from the trial helped to strengthen support for organizations that fight for people's rights, such as the American Civil Liberties Union.

Narrator: Now get ready to answer the questions.

ACTUAL PRACTICE 18

PRACTICE 1 - TRACK 95

Narrator: Listen to a conversation between a student and a librarian.

Female Student (FS): Hi, I was looking for information about the origins of several English words. I was wondering if you could help me.

Male Librarian (ML): Oh, certainly. We have a number of different resources for that.

FS: Awesome. Well, it's for a linguistics class on the history of the English language. We're doing group presentations. My group is doing a presentation about the influence of the Arabic language on English.

ML: That sounds interesting. Do you have to write about the Arabic influence on English in general? Or about specific words that came from Arabic?

FS: Specific words. My group found some words and broke up the list between us. I have to present information to the class about the words "lemon," "average," and "sofa."

ML: I didn't know those words came from Arabic! That's fascinating. Now, to trace their history, let's see… You already did a basic computer search on the words, correct?

FS: Yes, I did. But we're supposed to use academic sources, and they're not coming up.

ML: I see. Did you try looking in the *Oxford English Dictionary*? That's the source people traditionally turn to for information about words in English.

FS: No, I didn't… This is a pretty recent assignment, actually.

ML: That's okay. I'm glad you came to me early in the project. So, the print version of the *Oxford English Dictionary*, the OED for short, is located in our reference section. You'll see the signs above the shelves. It takes up several bookshelves—it has 20 volumes.

FS: Wow, that's great. Is it available online?

ML: Yes, I was just about to mention that. The library subscribes to the OED, so you can access it. You just log in to the library's website using your student I.D. number. Here, let's take a look on this computer, I'm already logged on.

FS: Sure.

ML: Okay, so you said that one of your words was "lemon"? Now, it looks like there's some history of the word, see where it says "etymology"?

FS: Yes, that traces the history back a little, but not all the way to its roots.

ML: You're right. The OED will be focused more on how the word has been used in English for the last thousand years or so. What you want is how it came into the language in the first place.

FS: Yeah… So, are there other resources?

ML: Of course, we have books on our shelves that are aimed at the general reading public that tell the histories of many words. Those would be easy to understand. And they might list their own academic sources, which you could look up.

FS: Yes, so to find those kinds of books on the shelves, I would access the library catalog and search for "word histories"? And it'll tell me where they are on the shelves?

ML: Yes, or look up "etymology." Now, besides books, another good option for you would be to access the digital academic journals that we subscribe to. If you click on this button on our website—see?—it takes you to the digital library. It contains all the past and present issues of more than 2,000 academic journals. So, if any academic researcher has published work on those English words, you're likely to find it there.

FS: Great! I'll get to work. Thanks so much!

ML: I have one more idea for you. It may not work, but you could keep it in mind if you don't find what you want any other way.

FS: What's that?

ML: The University does teach Arabic courses, so we have professors on campus who know Arabic fluently and probably have resources that I wouldn't know about. If you wanted to make your presentation really stand out, you might want to talk to them.

FS: That's a great idea! But, won't their resources be in Arabic?

ML: I thought about that, but they're teaching Arabic to students here, so I'll bet that they have a lot of material available in translation. At any rate, it's just a thought.

FS: Thanks! I see how that could really make our presentation special!

Narrator: Now get ready to answer the questions.

PRACTICE 2 - TRACK 96

Narrator: Listen to a lecture in a philosophy class.

Male Professor (MP): Good morning. Today, we begin our unit on ethics. As you may already know, ethics is the branch of philosophy that attempts to help us understand how to live the "good life" and how to determine which actions are right and wrong. Before the year 1500, many ethical theorists were followers of the ancient Greek philosophers Plato and Aristotle. These two thinkers revolutionized ethical discourse by defining the sort of life that is worth living and the sort of person who can live such a life.

So I'd like to start by discussing Plato's view of ethics and then moving on to Aristotle's. Plato based his ethical theory on the idea that all people desire happiness. Of course, people sometimes act in ways that do not produce happiness. But, according to Plato, they do this only because they do not know what actions will produce happiness.

Female Student (FS): Professor, that philosophy sounds like another philosopher we talked about in my Greek philosophy course last semester… Epicurus, I think his name was?

MP: Well, kind of, but not exactly. Epicurus was born after Plato, so his ideas were strongly influenced by Plato. Epicurus believed the "good life" consisted of seeking pleasure and avoiding pain, which sounds similar to Plato. But, really, Plato's philosophies are very different from those of Epicurus. Plato believed that all people desire happiness, but Plato related this "happiness" to a soul. Plato claimed that happiness is a natural consequence of a healthy soul. Epicurus was more concerned with physical life on Earth, so his idea of "happiness" had more to do with pursuing physical and social pleasures, like good food and good friends.

FS: Plato's view of the soul sounds a bit like the Christian view of the soul. You know, cultivate spiritual growth and you will be rewarded with eternal happiness.

MP: Well, that's not exactly right either. Plato was more liberal than Christian philosophers. For example, Plato would say a person who was behaving "badly" was doing so because he didn't know any better. Many Christian philosophers, on the other hand, would explain this "bad" behavior as a problem of the will. To a Christian, a person who behaves badly knows what is morally right, but he has willfully chosen to behave in a morally wrong manner.

FS: Okay. But there's something I don't understand. Plato believed that "good" people naturally seek happiness, right? But what if one person's "happiness" involves killing other people, or stealing people's money? Was that kind of thing acceptable to Plato?

MP: Oh, no, no. Plato thought that there were four virtues—wisdom, courage, self-control, and justice—and that all "good" or virtuous people seek to uphold these virtues. To Plato, the most important of these virtues was wisdom. A person who was wise naturally had all the other virtues.

Male Student (MS): So, does taking a philosophy class help me achieve wisdom? (*laughter*)

MP: Very funny. But you do bring up a good point here,

and it shows some of the limitations of ancient ethics. Plato merely describes virtuous behavior. He doesn't have any system of how a "bad" person can become "good," or any prescription for complex ethical choices.

FS: Professor, what about Aristotle? I know he was Plato's student. Did he try to extend Plato's ideas further, you know, filling in some of the blanks that Plato left out?

MP: Well, yes and no. As you pointed out, Aristotle was Plato's student. So, his views on ethics were similar to Plato's, but more complicated. For example, although Aristotle agreed with Plato's four virtues, he considered many other traits to be important, too. These included friendliness, generosity, gentleness, truthfulness, and wit.

Like Plato, Aristotle also believed that one trait is the source of all virtues—"good judgment." Good judgment is the ability to know what we should do by figuring out which course of action would lead to a "good life." Again, this is a major limitation of ancient ethics. Like Plato, Aristotle describes what a good person is like, but he provides no plan for how to get there. Aristotle just thought that people who were "properly brought up" usually see the right course and take it.

MS: I don't understand, Professor. I mean, how can Plato and Aristotle acknowledge that some people have virtues and others don't, but never tell us how to acquire them?

MP: Yeah, I understand where you're coming from. For whatever reason, ancient ethics didn't try to provide rules to guide us in making difficult choices. Modern ethics, on the contrary, does try to provide such rules. Ancient ethics is a theory of normal life, while modern ethics is a theory of life in crisis. We'll be discussing modern ethics more over the next few weeks.

Narrator: Now get ready to answer the questions.

PRACTICE 2 - TRACK 97

Narrator: Listen to part of the lecture. Then answer the question.

MP: Like Plato, Aristotle describes what a good person is like, but he provides no plan for how to get there. Aristotle just thought that people who were "properly brought up" usually see the right course and take it.

MS: I don't understand, Professor. I mean, how can Plato and Aristotle acknowledge that some people have virtues and others don't, but never tell us how to acquire them?

Narrator: Why does the student say this?

MS: I don't understand, Professor. I mean, how can Plato and Aristotle acknowledge that some people have virtues and others don't, but never tell us how to acquire them?

PRACTICE 3 - TRACK 98

Narrator: Listen to a lecture in a neuroscience class.

Female Professor (FP): Now we've been talking about how the brain is made up of specialized areas, which coordinate brain functions. These separate areas are part of a complex network. They collaborate on thinking projects, you might say. However, for a long time, researchers could only guess about the pathways between brain areas. When I say "pathways," of course, I am talking about the direction that information flows, as signals pass from one neuron to another, and to another, and so on.

For nearly 100 years we have had the ability to see electric signals in the brain through the use of EEG. Can anyone remember what EEG stands for? Yes, Dwayne?

Male Student (MS): Doesn't it stand for electro…encephalo…graphy?

FP: Excellent. And, while we're at it, can you explain how it works?

MS: Umm, okay, so they put sensors over a person's scalp, and then they can measure electrical activity in the brain. They can tell which area of the brain is most active, because it will have the strongest electrical signals.

FP: Yes, good explanation. So, as Dwayne indicated, we have been able to get kind of general information about activity in brain areas. But as I said, we have only been able to hypothesize about flow between areas. However, in 2014, a group of researchers at the University of Wisconsin tested out an algorithm created by Barry Van Veen, an engineer. So what does this algorithm do? Basically, the researchers found that using the algorithm allowed them to isolate the direction of particular electric signals in the brain.

So what they did was, they fitted volunteers with electrodes that recorded brain activity. Then, the volunteers watched video clips while EEG recorded their brain waves. The researchers found that during this process, not surprisingly, the subjects' brains were taking in visual information from the eyes, and the information flowed from the cerebral cortex's occipital lobe to the parietal lobe. That makes sense, of course, because the occipital lobe gathers and integrates visual information, and the parietal lobe processes it. So the images from the video flowed from the occipital lobe, where the sensory information is integrated, to the higher-order parietal lobe, where it becomes meaningful, perhaps recognized, you might say.

Now what was really interesting is that the researchers next asked subjects to imagine a moving scene. Specifically, the subjects were asked to imagine riding a bicycle through a terrain, paying close attention to imagined shapes and colors as they went. And during this period, the flow of information went the opposite way. Imagined information came down from "headquarters," you might say, from the higher-order parietal lobe to the lower-order occipital lobe that integrates the senses.

Female Student (FS): Wow, so, Professor Guzman, does that mean, is that saying that imagining something can affect our senses?

FP: Hmm, well, that is an interesting question, and worth considering. But all we can suggest based on this research is that during the imaginative process, the direction of electrical signaling is from higher-order to lower-order thinking.

But what I'd really like you all to grasp from this has to do more with the technological achievement. The significance of the research goes beyond an interesting fact about imagination. It is likely to turn out that the new algorithm will allow researchers to begin to understand more about connectivity in the human brain. There are a quite a few medical disorders like epilepsy, and schizophrenia, and more, that appear to be caused by abnormal connectivity. New abilities to analyze signals may offer new ways of treating such disorders. But it might also lead to insights about normal brain activities, such as sleeping.

Narrator: Now get ready to answer the questions.

ACTUAL PRACTICE 19

PRACTICE 1 - TRACK 99

Narrator: Listen to a conversation between a student and a professor.

Male Student (MS): Professor Frolander, may I speak with you for a moment?

Female Professor (FP): Of course. That's what office hours are for. How can I help you?

MS: My name is Walter, Walter Sears, and they told me at the Biology Department Office I needed to see you to apply for the summer field study on the Columbia River.

FP: Yes, you do. How much do you know about the marine biology field study program?

MS: I know that I need to complete all three marine biology classes and have at least a "B" average to apply.

FP: Good, good. Now, have you already finished all three classes?

MS: No, but I'll finish the third one this spring semester.

FP: Good! Most students apply while they're still completing the third course. What else do you know about the program?

MS: Well, my friends who did it said it was the best time they had in college. They say that they worked really hard, but they learned a lot and had lots of fun.

FP: That's what we like to hear! Yes, it's a lot of work, and a lot of it is very physical. Are you used to a lot of physical activity? Do you play a sport, or work out at the gym?

MS: I was a wrestler in high school, but not now. I don't really have time. I ride my mountain bike to school and around campus, and on the weekends my friends and I usually go for rides on the trails.

FP: Oh, I'm sure that's enough. We just need to make sure that our students are physically fit enough do the work. Now, I can give you an outline of the program, but it's also good if I give you an inkling of what to expect. Sound good?

MS: Yes, that'd be great.

FP: Well, the first thing is that you get up, Monday through Friday, at 5 am. That's so there's enough time for breakfast before you're on the bus. You'll be living in tents, but it's more like staying in a cabin than a tent. There's water and bathrooms, and a dining hall. Then, you get to the river about 7 am, and you'll be divided up into groups, and then you'll be supervised by whichever biologist or contractor is in charge of that group.

MS: Contractors? Like, construction work?

FP: Well, yes and no. Let me explain. You spend most of your time collecting and analyzing data for one of the experiments that the biologists are doing. But, everyone spends some time doing some of the physical work that scientists do. For example, there's a fish ladder that helps salmon get up and over a dam on the Columbia River. In the summer, before the salmon migration starts, we need to repair the ladder and calibrate the survey equipment. It's a wet, dirty job, and every student has to do some of it!

MS: Actually, that sounds like fun! I don't mind messy jobs. When I was in high school, I always tried to find a job where I could work outside.

FP: Well, then this program will be perfect for you. If you really like getting wet and dirty, every summer a couple of students have to volunteer for the wettest, dirtiest job in the program.

MS: What's that?

FP: Well, it's very important that the ladder have appropriate level heights. You want to have the flow of water over each level strong enough to stimulate the fish to head upriver, but not so strong that they get exhausted before they jump to the top level. So, a couple of students have to wade all the way up and down the fish ladder, and swim some parts of it, to make sure that it works and that the salmon can jump up each level to get over the dam.

MS: That sounds so cool! Can I volunteer now?

FP: (*Laughing*) No, Walter, that's something you'll have to wait on a little bit. So, still interested?

MS: You bet!

FP: Good! Fill out the application before the end of the semester, and I'll look forward to seeing it.

MS: Thank you, Professor Frolander.

Directions: Now get ready to answer the questions.

PRACTICE 2 - TRACK 100

Narrator: Listen to a lecture in a cultural anthropology class.

Male Professor (MP): Today, we're going to talk about eating dirt, a practice referred to as "geophagy." Geophagy is the scientific name for the regular or ritual eating of dirt.

Female Student (FS): Isn't that a kind of mental illness?

MP: Good question! There is a mental health disorder that involves eating non-food things, and sometimes that includes eating dirt. That's called PICA, and it's an obsessive desire to eat non-food items, such as buttons or coins or dirt. Geophagy is different. Geophagy is a behavior practiced around the world, usually in pre-industrial or agricultural societies, and involves regularly, and sometimes religiously, eating clay or soil. It's a practice as old as the human race. In fact, it may be older: evidence of eating clay soil has been found with the remains of *Homo habilis*, the human-like species that came just before *Homo sapiens*. That's us.

When European scientists first noticed this behavior, they thought it only happened in primitive societies. Alexander Humboldt observed geophagy among tribes in South America more than 200 years ago. But today, we know that geophagy happens on every continent except Antarctica. It's even practiced in Finland and Sweden! Sometimes, it's part of a religious ritual. Usually, it's considered a source of food or medicine. Humboldt reported that the Indians of the Amazon explained that they had been eating soil since ancient times.

For today's lecture, I'll divide our discussion of geophagy into two categories: first, the eating of earth as a food or as a medicine; second, a brief discussion of eating earth as a religious ritual.

Almost everywhere that earth is eaten, it's a special type of soil that provides something that's missing in the local diet. Like so many cultural practices, it probably developed for very practical reasons. For example, people in Sweden and Finland once ate the same kind of soil as the Amazon tribes described by Humboldt, for similar reasons: it is a thick, almost pure clay soil that contains important minerals that are not always available in the local diet.

The preferred soil is defined as an unctuous clay, meaning clay that's smooth and appears greasy or oily. It's a kind of clay that's often used to make ceramics, especially ceramics than can absorb great heat without being damaged or without absorbing any liquid. Pipes for smoking tobacco, for example, may be made from unctuous clay.

Geophagy is most common among children and pregnant women. Both these groups need minerals such as calcium and iron that may be available in the clay. But clay has also been used for medicinal purposes throughout the world. Some types may control stomach pain or diarrhea. Some types may have antibacterial or antifungal properties. Clay is still used in modern medicine. Even NASA uses clay for its astronauts' calcium needs in space.

Clay also plays a vital role in food preparation, by making certain important foods digestible. Native American tribes in North America use clay soil to neutralize tannic acid when preparing acorns. In other words, the clay helps make acorns edible, which allowed native tribes to flourish in areas such as California. South American tribes use clay to cook wild potatoes, because chemicals in that soil neutralize toxins. Also, in some cases clay replaces other foods in the diet. The Amazon tribes Humboldt studied in the 19th century couldn't hunt or fish for several months each year because of flooding rivers. During that time, they ate baked clay instead of fish or other food.

FS: Do people in the United States practice geophagy?

MP: Why, are you hungry? (*Laughs*) But really, that's an excellent question. And the answer is "yes." The modern American tradition primarily comes from Africa. The tradition grew in the southern U.S., where Africans and their descendants found clay soils similar to those in western Africa. The tradition was passed down through many generations. A survey in Mississippi in 1942 showed that more than 25 percent of all black children in the state ate earth sometimes. The practice moved north during the 20th century as black and white people migrated for work and opportunity. In fact, clay soils from the southern U.S. are still dug up, packaged, and shipped north. The clay food economy in the U.S. is nothing compared to Africa, however. Some villages in Nigeria export as much as 500 tons of edible clay each year!

Before we leave this subject, it's important to remember that geophagy can also have religious significance. Around the world, tribes in pre-industrial societies eat earth as part of religious rituals. Over time, these practices have been adapted by modern religions. In Central America, for example, Roman Catholic pilgrims who come to worship at particular sites can buy baked clay tablets that have images of the Virgin Mary and of saints. The tablets can be eaten or rubbed on the skin. In Pakistan, some Muslims eat cakes made from special clay dust, which is gathered from the tombs of important Muslim religious leaders.

Narrator: Now get ready to answer the questions.

PRACTICE 2 - TRACK 101

Narrator: Listen to part of the lecture. Then answer the question.

FS: Do people in the United States practice geophagy?

MP: Why, are you hungry?

Narrator: Why does the professor say this?

MP: Why, are you hungry?

PRACTICE 3 - TRACK 102

Narrator: Listen to a lecture in an economics class.

Female Professor (FP): Good morning. Today, we begin our unit on "industries," which can be thought of as a lot of individual businesses, which I'll often refer to as "firms" or "companies," that are grouped together. So, I'd like to review some of the terms we will be using to describe industries during this unit. You've no doubt heard these terms before, but I want to make sure everyone knows what each term means.

So, for starters, an important characteristic of industrial structure is its "concentration"—that is, the number of firms that supply its products. For example, a few large companies produce nearly all laundry detergents sold in the United States. A highly concentrated industry like this one, which is dominated by a few large businesses, is known as an "oligopoly." For instance, Proctor and Gamble, which controls a large share of the laundry detergent market, is said to have an oligopoly on that market.

The amount of concentration in an industry depends on how much increased production will lower the cost of making the product. If the cost of making the product decreases as the production increases, the business benefits from the principle of "economies of scale." Basically, this term implies, "the bigger, the better." For example, a large tennis shoe company like Nike benefits from economies of scale—that is, it makes so many shoes that it has a low cost-per-pair of shoes. A small tennis shoe company may not be able to negotiate the same low prices for supplies, manufacturing, and shipping. As a result, small companies may be forced out of business due to a failure to achieve "economies of scale."

And this concept—that is, economies of scale—explains why small, new businesses have so much trouble breaking into well-established markets: they don't have the resources to produce large quantities of a product at a low price.

So established firms often have advantages over a new company trying to enter the industry. For example, many types of manufacturing require such large factories and such expensive equipment that it's difficult for new businesses to invest in either. Established firms may also control the supply of raw materials. Obstacles that discourage newcomers are called "entry barriers."

Is everyone still with me? I see some confused looks in back of the class. Well, if you're confused, just focus on the key terms I've presented so far: concentration, economies of scale, entry barriers. A highly concentrated industry is one in which most of an industry's product comes from a few companies. In these concentrated industries, large companies benefit from economies of scale, meaning they can produce lots of something at a low price. And these economies of scale often prevent small or new businesses from entering a concentrated industry; thus, economies of scale can be considered entry barriers.

Okay, now that we've briefly reviewed those first three concepts, I'd like to introduce one more. A firm that produces a number of largely unrelated goods and services is said to be "diversified." A diversified company makes a variety of products. An example of a diversified company that everyone will be familiar with is Time Warner Corporation, which has Internet, publishing, film, communications, and television divisions. Diversification gives a company more financial security than it would have if it produced only one kind of product. Because a diversified company operates in various industries, it can sometimes offset losses in one industry with profits in another.

Narrator: Now get ready to answer the questions.

PRACTICE 3 - TRACK 103

Narrator: Listen to part of the lecture. Then answer the question

FP: If the cost of making the product decreases as the production increases, the business benefits from the principle of "economies of scale." Basically, this term implies, "the bigger, the better."

Narrator: Why does the professor say this?

FP: Basically, this term implies, "the bigger, the better."

ACTUAL PRACTICE 20

PRACTICE 1 - TRACK 104

Narrator: Listen to a conversation between a student and a financial advisor.

Male Student (MS): Hello. I was wondering if you could help me with a problem I've been having with my student loan.

Female Financial Advisor (FA): Well, I can certainly give it my best shot. What seems to be the problem?

MS: Well, I'm still waiting to receive my loan check for this semester. In the past, I've received all of my loan checks on time. I mean, it's already the second week of class, and I have to pay my tuition by the end of next week.

FA: Oh, I see. Let's figure out what's going on. Do you have your student I.D. card handy?

MS: Sure. My name is Noah Schmidt. Here's my student card.

FA: Great, Noah. Thanks. Now, let me just swipe your card and see what we come up with. (*Reading*) Huh, that's interesting. It says here that we sent out your loan check last week. So it should've arrived by now.

MS: Oh, how weird! As far as I know, it never arrived at my apartment. Of course, my roommate could've lost it without telling me. That guy is so out of it, it's like he's on another planet sometimes!

FA: (*Laughs*) Well, let's not blame your roommate yet. Do you still live at 4312 Crest Lane, Apartment 12?

MS: Oh, shoot! I must've forgotten to change my address with your office. Actually, I don't live there anymore. That's my old address. I moved to a new place this semester.

FA: Well, there you have it. Problem solved!

MS: Yeah, I guess. Or, "problem partially solved," at least. So, I'll need to fill out a change-of-address form for the student loan office, right?

FA: That's correct. The form should be available on our website.

MS: Okay. But what should I do about my situation now? I mean, I need to get my current semester check before next week.

FA: Well, you have two options. First, did you change your address with the post office?

MS: Yes, I submitted a change-of-address notice there.

FA: So, apparently that didn't take effect in time for this piece of mail. Hopefully the people who now live in your old apartment wrote on the envelope "please forward" or "not at this address" and put it back in the mailbox. That'll remind the postal workers to check your forwarding information and forward the mail to your new address. That may take some time, you never know.

MS: Yeah, or the new people may have just thrown it away.

FA: That's true. So your other option would be to fill out a form here requesting the student loan office to cancel the mailed check. Then the office would have to re-issue a new check, which you could pick up here, in the loan office. We could probably have it ready by tomorrow.

MS: Well, sounds like the second option is almost a guarantee that I'll get the check before tuition is due.

FA: Yep. All it means is that you will have to come all the way back here.

MS: That's okay.

FA: If you don't mind my asking, did you leave your old apartment because of the landlord?

MS: No. It was just too far from campus. Why?

FA: Well, I keep an eye on the landlords around the campus. A lot of our financial aid goes to pay for apartments around here, and we need to know if a landlord is taking advantage of students.

MS: No, no problems there. The refrigerator broke once, and the landlord had someone come out and fix it the same day. Otherwise, I never really saw the landlord.

FA: Okay. Thanks for the information!

Narrator: Now get ready to answer the questions.

PRACTICE 2 - TRACK 105

Narrator: Listen to a lecture in an American Literature class.

Male Professor (MP): So hopefully you all managed to read the novel we will discuss today, even if you already read it once in high school. *The Great Gatsby*, by F. Scott Fitzgerald, is worth re-reading. It is seen by most people as one of the best American novels if not the best. Yes, Ariana?

Female Student (FS): I didn't read the book in high school, and until I read it for today's class, I always just thought it was about the 1920s, parties, jazz, and glamorous people.

MP: Well, of course, it is about the parties of the wealthy. But, to be great, a novel has to show us our culture in a way that is beautiful, and at the same time, honest about ugliness. *The Great Gatsby* often reads like poetry, it is so beautifully written. So let's kind of go through the plot together, highlighting the tension between beautiful and ugly. Okay, so the story is told by Nick Carraway. Now Nick is a young war veteran who moves to a New York suburb. He comes from a rich family in the Midwest; he visits his cousin, Daisy, and her husband, Tom Buchanan. As a coincidence, Nick and Tom know each other from college. Now, what does this already suggest about American culture?

Male Student (MS): Maybe that rich people kind of all know each other?

MP: Exactly. On the other hand, Nick also meets his next-door neighbor Jay Gatsby, who is generous, courteous, and ultra-rich. Gatsby throws enormous open-invitation parties in his garden, offering jazz music and plenty of alcohol, which was illegal at the time. Yet no one knows Gatsby.

Nick discovers that Gatsby throws parties only because he hopes that Daisy--Nick's cousin--will show up. It turns out that Gatsby dated Daisy. It was years ago, when she was a teenager and he was a soldier preparing to ship out to fight in World War I. Gatsby has never loved anyone else, and he has dedicated his life to winning her back. So even though Daisy is married to Tom, Gatsby expects her to come back to him. Can anyone explain Gatsby's viewpoint?

FS: Well, it's as though Gatsby is living in the past. He thinks that because a rich girl loved him once, she must still love him, and that she has never loved her husband as much as she loved him. Also, Gatsby really thinks that because he is rich now, he is upper-class just like she is.

MP: Yes, he believes that he is a prince coming to rescue her from a tower, like some kind of fairy tale. Most characters in the novel do not look at themselves honestly, do not take any responsibility for their own choices. They lie to others and to themselves about their pasts, making them seem much better or worse than they were. The gangster Arnold Rothstein even speaks fondly of the past as he is recounting a brutal mob shooting.

FS: It seems like the book is really about the illusions that people create about themselves. Even Daisy acts all independent of Tom, making fun of him and stuff, but it turns out they are a unit, they think alike and they are never going to break up.

MP: Yes, Gatsby seems quite ridiculous for his dream, doesn't he?

MS: So, is it basically cynical? The novel is really saying that nobody can really move up in the world, or break into the top tier of society, even if they work hard and get rich?

MP: Maybe, or maybe the author was making another point entirely. You can explore this question in your essay this week. Before concluding today's discussion, I just want you to think about Gatsby for a minute. Nothing he says about himself turns out to be true. Even the name "Gatsby" is a lie; Gatsby is a name and personality he invented when he was a very poor teenager.

Gatsby wants to be a romantic hero, but actually, he's a gangster. We are left to imagine, in the end, just what his ethics are. We don't know what he has done, what he did in the war, what kinds of jobs he has done for his gangster boss. We don't know why he has no friends. He seems like the worst character in the story, and yet, Nick flips everything upside down and says that Gatsby was the best. What do you make of this paradox?

Narrator: Now get ready to answer the questions.

PRACTICE 3 - TRACK 106

Narrator: Listen to a lecture in an engineering class.

Female Professor (FP): Today, I'd like to talk about one of the greatest engineering inventions of the past 200 years. It's something that we use everyday, yet most of us probably take it for granted. Can anyone guess what I'm talking about? No? It's the light bulb.

The light bulb, when you think about it, greatly enhances modern living. It provided an alternative to earlier kerosene lamps which can easily cause fires. And even the first light bulbs could provide more light than kerosene lamps. Finally, well-lit streets became a reality because of light bulbs.

But the light bulbs you see in this classroom are not the type of light bulbs that were used when this invention first came into style. In fact, light bulbs are constantly being improved to be brighter, more energy-efficient, and longer-lasting.

The first electric light bulb to really come into mass circulation was the "carbon-arc lamp." This type of light bulb was produced by a man named C.F. Brush in 1878, and it came to be widely used for lighting streets in both America and Europe at that time.

Carbon arc lamps differ from their predecessor, the kerosene lamp, in every possible way. First of all, kerosene lamps are powered by an exhaustible fuel which constantly had to be replenished. Carbon-arc lamps, on the other hand, are powered by electricity. Second, carbon arc lamps are much more structurally complex than kerosene lamps—after all, a kerosene lamp is little more than a canister of flammable oil with a cotton wick. The carbon-arc lamp, on the other hand, consists of a pair of carbon rods, or electrodes, in contact at pointed ends. Electricity is sent through the carbon electrodes which causes them to pull apart slightly. As electricity flows, the electrodes heat up, causing some of the carbon to vaporize. These vapors produce the brilliant light for which the lamps are known. The lamp glows as long as the electric current is maintained.

So carbon-arc lamps seemed wonderful to people at first. I mean, they seemed to last forever and were very bright when compared with kerosene lamps. But some of their disadvantages eventually became apparent to people. For example, carbon-arc lamps are very bright, as I just said. In fact, they are so bright—so blindingly bright—that they can't be used to light the interiors of buildings. In addition, carbon-arc lamps are very hot. This was actually seen as benefit in some cities where the temperatures were very cold. But over time, the lamps can become so hot that they can actually burn people or, in rare occasions, start fires.

Because of these problems, arc lamps are no longer used on public streets or indoors. However, they're still used for searchlights and in some projectors for motion pictures. As you can imagine, carbon-arc lamps are perfect for those uses.

Male Student (MS): So how did engineers design light bulbs that don't overheat, like the ones in this classroom?

FP: Good question. So the first light bulbs were invented by Thomas Edison around 1880 and they were actually very similar to carbon arc lamps. However, there were a few major differences between carbon-arc lamps and Edison's light bulbs. First, carbon arc-lamps were, like kerosene lamps, housed in open glass containers. You know what those look like if you've ever seen the gas lamps on our downtown streets. In contrast, the first light bulbs were housed in vacuum-evacuated glass bulbs.

Another big difference is that carbon-arc lamps operate by using an arc, meaning that electricity is created between two carbon electrodes. But when Edison invented the first light bulb, he added something to this space: a filament of carbonized paper between the two electrodes. This filament, as well as the evacuated glass bulb, helped make Edison's invention more convenient than its predecessor. Remember the problems I suggested with the carbon-arc lamp? Well, these problems are eliminated when you add the piece of carbon paper and remove the air from the bulb.

Light bulbs are not nearly as bright as carbon arc lamps, and they are much cooler. So naturally, they became very popular following Edison's initial invention. In fact, some modern bulbs are still modeled after Edison's first bulb. However, there were problems with this early light bulb as well, and improvements have done much to make this convenience what it is today.

Narrator: Now get ready to answer the questions.

PRACTICE 3 - TRACK 107

Narrator: Listen to part of the lecture. Then answer the question.

FP: Because of these problems, arc lamps are no longer used on public streets or indoors. However, they're still used for searchlights and in some projectors for motion pictures. As you can imagine, carbon-arc lamps are perfect for those uses.

MS: So how did engineers design light bulbs that don't overheat, like the ones in this classroom?

Narrator: Why does the student say this?

MS: So how did engineers design light bulbs that don't overheat, like the ones in this classroom?

ACTUAL PRACTICE 21

PRACTICE 1 - TRACK 108

Narrator: Listen to a conversation between a student and a professor

Male Student (MS): Hi, Professor Zaman. Do you have a minute?

Female Professor (FP): Oh, yes. Come in,. What can I do for you, Mr. …?

MS: My name is Conner. I'm in your Tuesday-Thursday anatomy class.

FP: Ah, yes, you look familiar. I apologize for not knowing your name. That's a problem with the large lecture courses.

MS: Oh, it's okay, I totally get that.

FP: So, Conner, what brings you here today?

MS: Well, I just was looking for some advice or suggestions, kind of. I've gotten "Cs" on all the quizzes except one, where I got a "D." I'm a freshman and I declared my major as biology, but I'm kind of scared now. Like, maybe I'm not smart enough?

FP: Well, I doubt that you're not smart enough. To get some perspective, I think you should talk to some of the other students in the class about their grades.

MS: What do you mean?

FP: Well, right now, out of the 200 people in the class, only about 18 have "As." Another 20 are getting "Bs." About 100 students are getting "Cs," like yourself. And the other 50 or 60 students are getting "Ds" and "Fs."

MS: Really? So not that many people are doing better than I am?

FP: That's right. Even though the class is called "Introduction to Anatomy," it's difficult, no doubt about it. Many first- and second-year students are encountering this material for the first time. That makes it harder to learn.

MS: Huh. But I'm planning on going to medical school after I graduate. I don't want to mess up my grades.

FP: I understand your concern. But do you think doctors are born knowing what connects to the *posterior tibiofibular ligament*? Or how to pronounce *dorsal tarsometa-*

tarsal?

MS: (*Laughing*) No, I guess not.

FP: Every doctor that you see once had to struggle with all of this once, too. Gradually, though, it became like second nature to them. And, you know, there are some things you could do to improve your memorization process.

MS: Oh?

FP: Yes. For example, the university tutoring center can help you with memorization strategies. Tutoring sessions are available for no cost. Why don't you make an appointment there? You know where it is, yes? In the Student Commons Building?

MS: Oh, yeah, that's a good suggestion. I wasn't even thinking that a tutor could help with this.

FP: Well, I recommend trying that. Also, from what many of my past students have told me, forming study groups seems to improve grades in my anatomy classes.

MS: You mean getting together with other students to study for the class?

FP: Exactly. You'd be surprised how much better students perform, grade-wise, when they study in groups. In fact, one of my colleagues in the psychology department has done some interesting research in this area. He's found a strong correlation between grade improvement and study groups.

MS: Wow, that's good to know. I guess I'd better start talking more to other people in the class.

FP: An excellent idea, Conner. I'll bet that lots of the other students in the class would like to have someone to study with. Even if other students look confident, they might be just as worried as you are.

MS: Yeah, I guess you're right. Well, you've convinced me that things aren't as bad as I thought. I'm glad I came to your office hours.

FP: I'm glad you came, too. And, if you ever have specific questions or concerns in the future, please don't hesitate to stop by my office. You know my hours; they're posted on the syllabus.

MS: Thanks, Professor Zaman. I appreciate all your help.

Narrator: Now get ready to answer the questions.

PRACTICE 1 - TRACK 109

Narrator: Why does the professor say this?

FP: But do you think doctors are born knowing what connects to the *posterior tibiofibular ligament*? Or how to pronounce *dorsal tarsometatarsal*?

PRACTICE 2 - TRACK 110

Narrator: Listen to a lecture in a literature class.

Male Professor (MP): Today, I'd like to discuss a popular genre of literature: science fiction. The origin of modern science fiction as a literary genre goes back at least 200 years, to one novel in particular. Although we might not regard this tale as "classic" science fiction today, it certainly satisfies the definition: the plot creates a fictionalization of scientific discoveries that may be possible in the future. Does anyone want to guess which book I'm talking about?

Female Student (FS): Is it *Twenty Thousand Leagues Under the Sea* by Jules Verne?

MP: That's a great guess, but no. The novel I'm referring to is *Frankenstein* the horror classic by Mary Shelley. Although some elements of science fiction no doubt existed in literature prior to its publication, *Frankenstein* is the first truly modern science fiction novel.

FS: What makes it such a good example of science fiction?

MP: I'm glad you asked, Cecelia. Before I answer your question, I'd like to ask a question of my own: what makes a novel science fiction? What qualities are necessary for a good science fiction story?

Male Student (MS): Well, usually science fiction stories speculate about the future, and about technology. And, unlike fantasy, science fiction authors try to explain "mystical" or undiscovered technology, using references to modern science. You know, they try to make it understandable, so that the story seems more plausible.

MP: Great. So, as Mike was saying, two important elements of traditional science fiction are: speculating and explaining. To be precise, speculating about the future and new technology, and explaining imagined situations using real scientific discoveries and hypotheses. When you apply these standards to *Frankenstein*, you can easily see how it fits the mold. The idea of creating life from nonliving matter was revolutionary when the story was published in 1818. And, though the idea might seem mystifying at first, Shelley approaches this miracle as if it were any other scientific discovery.

For the next fifty years or so, the genre saw few noteworthy publications. It wasn't until the late 1800s that writers first expanded the genre into what it is today. Between 1864 and 1873, Jules Verne wrote classics such as *Journey to the Center of the Earth, Twenty Thousand Leagues Under the Sea,* and *Around the World in Eighty Days*. Verne created adventures to impossible locations that captivate movie-goers to this day.

Finally, at the turn of the century, British author H.G. Wells began writing what would become the archetypal science fiction stories for the next century. Three of his most popular novels, including *The Time Machine, The Invisible Man,* and *The War of the Worlds*, were published between 1895 and 1898. The popularity of stories that draw on these original science fiction classics has not diminished greatly over the years. Audiences never seem to tire of stories that incorporate time travel, alien invasion, or superhuman mutations.

Female Student 2 (FS2): What led to the explosion of science fiction as a literary genre? I mean, were there any social movements at the time that helped it build momentum?

MP: Well, science fiction, like any literary genre, can explore a wide range of social issues through storytelling. However, the primary reason for the rapid proliferation of science fiction works at the end of the 19th century was technological, not social. As you all know, the United States and much of western Europe was undergoing an Industrial Revolution and many new technologies were being introduced. Because of the growth of scientific understanding at that time, many authors began speculating about future discoveries.

As technology continued to advance through the 20th century, new science fiction stories emerged to explore the implications of continued scientific advancement. With the advent of computers, airplanes, automobiles, and factory automation, authors have found new subjects to scrutinize. For example, many modern books and movies deal with the idea of artificial intelligence or robot takeovers. Other stories, such as the popular film *The Matrix*, depict artificial, or virtual realities, leaving the viewer to ponder the question: "What is real?"

Undoubtedly, science fiction will continue to be an exciting genre in the future. With the continued advancement of human understanding, authors will have an abundance of inspiration. Where will their imaginations take the genre? What will be the next blockbuster sci-fi hit? The possibilities are limitless...

Narrator: Now get ready to answer the questions.

PRACTICE 2 - TRACK 111

Narrator: Listen to part of the lecture. Then answer the question.

MP: Today, I'd like to discuss a popular genre of literature: science fiction. The origin of modern science fiction as a literary genre goes back at least 200 years, to one novel in particular. Although we might not regard this tale as "classic" science fiction today, it certainly satisfies the definition: the plot creates a fictionalization of scientific discoveries that may be possible in the future. Does anyone want to guess which book I'm talking about?

Narrator: What does the professor mean when he says this?

MP: Although we might not regard this tale as "classic" science fiction today, it certainly satisfies the definition: the plot creates a fictionalization of scientific discoveries that may be possible in the future.

PRACTICE 2 - TRACK 112

Narrator: Why does the professor say this?

MP: Because of the growth of scientific understanding at that time, many authors began speculating about future discoveries.

PRACTICE 3 - TRACK 113

Narrator: Listen to a lecture in a physics class.

Female Professor (FP): So this week is all about radio waves. And today, I want to cover some of the basics. So can anybody tell me what, exactly, is a radio wave? Yes, Steve?

Male Student (MS): Well, radio waves are a form of energy, like visible light or x-rays.

FP: Excellent. Like all radiation, radio waves travel in a sine wave pattern. As you know, sine waves rise and fall as they travel through space. The height of a radio wave is called its "amplitude." The length of the wave is, appropriately, called its "wavelength." In addition, waves have a property called "frequency." Frequency is a measure of how often a radio wave passes through a single point in a given length of time. Frequency is typically measured in hertz, which tells us how many waves pass through a point in a second. And we'll come back to amplitude, wavelength, and frequency when we look at an example of radio waves in use. But first, I have another question for the class: why do we use radio waves to transmit information? (*To female student*) Yes, Carla.

Female Student (FS): I heard that radio waves can travel through clouds and walls. And it's better than other kinds of energy, like X-rays, because these can be harmful to humans.

FP: Great. In addition, radio waves travel farther than other forms of energy. X-rays, for example, only travel a few feet before they get absorbed into their environment. So, radio waves have become the go-to method of sending information. We use radio waves to transmit and receive information on our cell phones, our televisions, our computers, and, of course, our radios. But in order to send information using radio waves, you need a transmitter—that is, something to encode and send the radio waves—and you need a receiver, so something that picks up the radio waves and decodes the message stored within them.

The two most common ways to send information using radio signals are AM and FM. Now I'm sure most of you have heard of AM and FM before, but can anyone tell me what these terms mean? (To male student) Yes, go ahead, John.

Male Student 2 (MS2): I think that AM stands for "amplitude modulation." And FM means "frequency modulation."

FP: Wow, you guys are on fire today! So, basically, information gets stored on AM radio waves by changing the amplitudes of the waves. That way, the different heights of waves are encoded to store different pieces of information. And FM, as John mentioned, means "frequency modulation," so instead of sending information by changing the amplitude, you change the frequency of the waves.

Now, because I imagine that some of this information might be unclear to some of you, I want to look at how radio waves transmit and receive information. First, let's explore how radios receive AM signals.

So let's look at a local station—let's call it AM 750. The radio station uses a transmitter to send music to radios within range. In order to send a song to your radio, the transmitter first encodes the song into a sine wave with varying amplitudes. Basically, the transmitter translates the song into another language—the language of waves. It's like a computer, which constantly converts human language to binary code, then converts binary back into meaningful symbols. In this analogy, the song is like the meaningful set of signs and symbols that humans recognize and the radio wave is the code. After converting the song into a pattern of radio waves, the transmitter can broadcast this wave using an antenna. An antenna is just a piece of metal that sends out radio signals so nearby receivers can collect the information and decode it.

Now, say you want to listen to AM 750 on your car radio. The first thing you do is tune in to the station. When you tune in to a radio station, you're telling your radio to ignore all the signals that aren't broadcasting at the specified frequency, in this case 750,000 hertz. When you think about it, AM 750 really means, "this station sends out amplitude-modulated radio waves at 750,000 waves per second."

Once you've tuned into the AM radio station, your car antenna picks up the radio signal. A detector, located in your car radio, decodes the waves received from the radio station. That is, it translates the waves back into audio. Once decoded, the song plays out on your car's speakers.

Narrator: Now get ready to answer the questions.

PRACTICE 3 - TRACK 114

Narrator: Why does the professor say this?

FP: So radio waves have become the go-to method of sending information. We use radio waves to transmit and receive information on our cell phones, our televisions, our computers, and, of course, our radios.

ACTUAL PRACTICE 22

PRACTICE 1 - TRACK 115

Narrator: Listen to part of a conversation between a student and an advisor.

Male Advisor (MA): Hi there, what can I do for you? Do you have an appointment with one of the career counselors?

Female Student (FS): No. Actually, I just came in

because I need to get a part-time job, and I was wondering if you have, you know, part-time jobs listed here? I mean, it's not all just career-type jobs?

MA: Yes, we do. We have many listings for part-time jobs here. So is this your first time stopping in?

FS: Yeah, it is. I'm a freshman, so I'm still clueless about everything here.

MA: Ah, well, that's perfectly all right. Let me just take a minute and run through what we have for you. On the wall to your left there are notices for part-time jobs in the community. So that means that a business or agency from town has contacted us by phone or through our website, and has described an available job. We took down the information and posted it there.

FS: So, are those jobs that anyone can get? Or only students?

MA: Sometimes the company only lists the job with our office, because they really want to hire only college students. For example, a tutoring company may do that. But sometimes, the jobs are advertised in other places, too. It's up to the employer.

FS: Oh. And do you guys at this office kind of check the company out, make sure the job is legitimate and everything?

MA: That's a great question, and the answer is that we try to, but no system is perfect, and scams are not unheard of. We really urge students not to give anyone too much personal information up front, such as your social security number or passport number. The FBI publishes tips about how to be careful when sending information in response to job offers. You can find that link on our website, and I really recommend that you read it before you get started.

FS: Whoa, that's scary. Okay, I'll read that.

MA: We also cover that information in our employment workshops, which we give twice a month. We also can help you with interviewing strategies during those workshops.

FS: Okay, I'll sign up for one of those workshops, they sound great. But, to start, how does it work? You just read these notices? What if you want to apply for something?

MA: At the bottom of each notice, you'll see the employer's contact person and his or her email and phone number. If you're interested in any of those jobs, you can just copy down the information and respond to them on your own. They might ask you to email them a resume, or to fill out an online job application.

FS: Okay, that sounds good.

MA: Now, on the wall to your right, we have all of our on-campus jobs. That's pretty much the same process. So, out of the two walls, we really recommend checking the on-campus jobs wall first. Personally, I think it's great to have a job on campus. I mean, you're already here for classes. And of course, an on-campus job is a great way to meet other students. Also, all campus jobs can work around your class schedule.

FS: So, are there on-campus jobs like, at the food courts and stuff?

MA: Some are, and some are in campus offices, or at the student gym, at the sports stadium, and so on. But the biggest ones by far are the libraries and the bookstore. Those are also good because both places need student workers most at the beginning of the semester. Around finals, they won't need you as much.

FS: Wow, okay, I guess I'll look around for a bit if that's okay?

MA: Absolutely. Can I see your student I.D. card, please? Thank you.

Narrator: Now get ready to answer the questions.

PRACTICE 2 - TRACK 116

Narrator: Listen to a lecture in an evolutionary biology class.

Female Professor (FP): So in the past decade, there's been a staggering increase in the number of young people diagnosed with attention deficit hyperactivity disorder, which is commonly referred to as ADHD. People with ADHD generally have trouble focusing on one thing for long periods of time, making them inattentive and sometimes disobedient in school, at work, and at home.

Because ADHD has become so prevalent in recent years, researchers have spent a lot of time and resources trying to figure out what causes ADHD. And they've found that the dopamine receptors in many people with ADHD function differently than the receptors of people who do not have symptoms of ADHD. Some of you might know that dopamine is one of the chemical messengers in the brain. The absorption of dopamine by receptors leads to feelings of happiness and reward. Dopamine triggers happiness, and it signals your brain to focus on the experience so you can remember what you did to trigger that reward in the first place. But people with ADHD often have underactive dopamine receptors, meaning their brain doesn't absorb as much dopamine. And this helps explain why people with ADHD are often inattentive: they don't feel rewarded as early, certainly not from repetitive or "boring" tasks. Thus, those with ADHD often look for novel, unique experiences for stimulation. After all, only new and exciting experiences can really get the dopamine flowing in their brains.

Okay. So we know what ADHD is and, in very general terms, what causes it. Now let's look at how this relates to evolutionary biology. Today, most schools and jobs require focus. But a growing group of researchers suggest that in the distant past, the characteristics of ADHD might have had advantages in terms of survival.

As you know, humans evolved as hunter-gatherers. We tracked animals for meat and foraged for fruits, vegetables, and grains for hundreds of thousands of years. So, can anyone suggest why ADHD might have been an advantage?

Male Student (MS): Well, humans had to be constantly on the lookout both for food and for predators. I mean, both hunting and gathering are kind of unpredictable, so the desire to be on the move and searching for new experiences probably would have benefited a hunter-gatherer.

FP: Exactly so. But then, about 10,000 years ago, people began to settle more and more into a farming lifestyle. The rise of agriculture provided people with a steady supply of food, but it also required major lifestyle changes. Rather than adapting to an ever-changing environment to find food and fend off predators, farmers settled into a life of monotonous fieldwork. Suddenly, it wasn't so beneficial to be constantly looking for new experiences. Suddenly, those who could do repetitive, tedious farm work were benefiting from this new agricultural society. (*To female student*) Oh, I see there's a question in the front row. Go ahead.

Female Student (FS): Well, I have ADHD, and so I think that's a cool idea. But has it been proven in any way? I mean that ADHD was beneficial for hunter-gatherers.

FP: We can't prove it for certain, but a tribe in Kenya called the Ariaal has provided scientists with an opportunity to test this theory. So the Ariaal are a nomadic group of herders. As a result, their lifestyle is somewhat similar to the hunter-gatherer lifestyle: they're constantly on the move, attending to their herds while adapting to new environments. But recently, some of the Ariaal have broken away from this nomadic lifestyle, settling in one area and raising crops.

So here, researchers tested some of the men in both the nomadic and settled groups of Ariaal for a variation of a gene that has been linked to ADHD. To be more specific, the researchers looked for members of the Ariaal tribe with a variation of a gene that creates dopamine receptors. And, like I said, this variation has been linked to symptoms characteristic of ADHD.

And what these researchers found was quite astonishing. The nomadic members of the Ariaal tribe with the variation of the dopamine-receptor gene were found to be better nourished than the average nomadic Ariaal tribesman. And the settled, agricultural members of the Ariaal tribe with the variation of the dopamine-receptor gene were *less* nourished than other members of the tribe. So this research does suggest that symptoms of ADHD may have benefited our nomadic, hunter-gatherer ancestors. But these findings *must* be taken with a grain of salt: we need more data before we can draw any conclusions.

Narrator: Now get ready to answer the questions.

PRACTICE 3 - TRACK 117

Narrator: Listen to a lecture in an U.S. history class

Male Professor (MP): Now, you know we've been talking about America's most popular presidents, including Washington, Lincoln, and FDR. Today, let's consider a president with a more complex legacy: Lyndon Baines Johnson, also known as "LBJ."

In 1963, when President John F. Kennedy was assassinated, his vice-president, Lyndon Johnson became president. JFK had been an incredibly charismatic president. He was young and handsome, had a beautiful wife and family, and was very popular around the world.

Johnson was very different. Johnson was much older than Kennedy, he spoke with a Texas drawl, and he did not look like a movie star. He had been elected to Congress in 1937 as a strong supporter of Roosevelt's New Deal, a controversial government program with a strong liberal bias. But Johnson became increasingly conservative over the years. This change was necessary to succeed politically in his home state of Texas, a very conservative state. He gradually rose in the senate until he was the Senate Majority Leader, a very powerful position. He joined Kennedy's 1960 presidential campaign as the vice presidential nominee to help Kennedy win in the conservative South.

Two major issues dominated LBJ's time in office, and the public's lasting impression of him. First is his achievements on civil rights and social issues. Second is his role in escalating the war in Vietnam.

Female Student (FS): Wasn't the civil rights legislation started by Kennedy?

MP: Yes, Kennedy had proposed sweeping civil rights legislation, but the Senate wouldn't take action. It was going nowhere.

Johnson had a mixed voting record in the Senate when it came to civil rights, although he had helped push through an earlier 1957 version of the Civil Rights Act, which ended up being largely symbolic. But Kennedy's proposal was radical. Kennedy proposed to make any racial segregation in schools, public places, and employment illegal. Before his assassination, it seemed unlikely to pass through Congress.

However, President Johnson made it the primary goal of his presidency. The Civil Rights Act of 1964 was passed and signed into law less than eight months after Kennedy's death. It included almost 80 new laws. But Johnson wasn't done! After winning the presidential election of 1964, Johnson pushed through several more important laws. For instance, in 1965, Johnson signed into law Medicare, which guaranteed medical care to every American over 65 years old. He also signed the Voting Rights Act, which specifically outlawed many of the practices that had been used to keep African Americans from voting, such as poll taxes and literacy tests.

Some historians believe that the anti-poverty and civil rights laws passed during Johnson's presidency had more impact than any legislation since Lincoln signed the Emancipation Proclamation.

Male Student (MS): But wasn't Johnson also blamed for the Vietnam War?

MP: Yes. Many Americans, and people around the world, blame Johnson for the Vietnam War. He is responsible for greatly increasing the number of U.S. troops in Vietnam, but the actual history of the war is more complex.

The United States began sending military advisors to Vietnam in the 1950s. The U.S., along with England, France, and West Germany, was very concerned with the spread of communism from the Soviet Union and China. Americans worried about the countries of South East Asia and beyond falling like dominoes if communists won in Vietnam. In hindsight, this seems like nonsense, but it was a very real fear at the time.

President Johnson knew everything about domestic politics and the domestic economy, but he wasn't an expert on foreign policy and the Cold War. He kept Kennedy's foreign policy advisors and took their advice. In August, 1964, Johnson used a small fight between the U.S. Navy and the North Vietnamese Navy to push the Gulf of Tonkin Resolution through Congress. This gave Johnson the power to greatly increase the U.S. presence in Vietnam, although it stopped short of being a declaration of war. By 1966, the United States had 325,000 soldiers in Vietnam.

The war became increasingly unpopular in the United States and Europe. The anti-war movement became as important in the media as the Civil Rights Movement. Johnson was stunned by the reaction of the public, and by the damage to his reputation and power. He decided not to run for reelection in 1968. This was a radical decision for an incumbent president. No other modern president has chosen not to run for a second term in the White House.

Robert Kennedy, John F. Kennedy's younger brother and a U.S. Senator, was sweeping toward the Democratic nomination when he was assassinated in June, 1968. All through that summer there were protests, riots, and demonstrations. Republican Richard Nixon won the Presidency in November, 1968.

Narrator: Now get ready to answer the questions.

PRACTICE 3 - TRACK 118

Narrator: What does the professor suggest when he says

this?

MP: The war became increasingly unpopular in the United States and Europe. The anti-war movement became as important in the media as the Civil Rights Movement. Johnson was stunned by the reaction of the public, and by the damage to his reputation and power.

ACTUAL PRACTICE 23

PRACTICE 1 - TRACK 119

Narrator: Listen to a conversation between a student and a professor.

Male Student (MS): Thanks for meeting with me today, Professor Silva. I just wanted to go over some things about my research paper for your American Studies class.

Female Professor (FS): Oh, certainly, Aiden, I'm happy to meet with you. So, where are you in the research process right now?

MS: Well, uh, at the beginning. Because we're supposed to come up with a topic about shifts and changes in American culture, I've been thinking about the effect of films, I mean, like, movies… and I'm having problems… well, I think my topic may be too broad.

FP: So, okay, are you thinking about researching how films and movies changed American culture when they first appeared? Hmm, yes, Aiden, that's probably a topic that needs to be narrowed down. If you try to write about such a broad topic, you may have a hard time organizing it all.

MS: Right, that topic is huge, so, I'm trying to narrow it down to a particular film. I was thinking about the silent film *Birth of a Nation*, from 1915. I remember hearing that it was the first big blockbuster silent film.

FP: Ah, yes, that film was quite significant.

MS: Yeah, it re-wrote history to portray the Ku Klux Klan as heroes instead of criminals. So maybe my thesis could be that the film caused a change in America. For the first time, that idea about the KKK as heroes was on the big screen, and it probably seemed to have some real authority. You know, like, "this is how things really are."

FP: Yes, that would be a relevant topic. *Birth of a Nation*, as you suggest, was followed by huge growth in KKK membership during the 1920s. The KKK really terrorized African Americans.

MS: Yeah, I could write about how the movie made African Americans seem so dangerous, when actually, it was the KKK that was dangerous.

FP: Oh yes, that's putting it mildly.

MS: Yeah, but what's weird is that even though the filmmaker, umm, D.W. Griffith? Yes, even though Griffith falsified historical events, he tried to show very realistic battle scenes, right? I mean, he depicted what combat was really like during the Civil War. I read that the film was the first ever to show huge, epic shots of a battlefield, and then cut to close-ups. And, Griffith used huge crowds of extras, so it was different from plays.

FP: Yes, the film is still considered brilliant for its realistic portrayal of battle during the U.S. Civil War. But remember to stick to the assignment: research a shift or a change in American culture.

MS: So the way the film depicts battle realistically wouldn't be a good topic?

FP: Well, if you were writing an essay for a film-studies class, you could describe the film's battle scenes in terms of technique. And as for the cultural impact of the battle scenes, well, if you had a lot of time to research, you might be able to trace connections between the film and public opinion about war. But I don't want you to get overwhelmed with too much information. For the purposes of your paper now, I think the best approach is to look at measurable effects of the film.

MS: Okay, but, what do you mean exactly?

FP: Well, you want to avoid just writing a description of the film. And you want to avoid speculating about the film's impact on American culture. So, you might want to find factual evidence for what I mentioned earlier; the rise of the KKK after the movie's debut.

MS: That sounds like a pretty focused topic.

FP: Yes, it would be. You could trace the Klan's membership and political clout following the movie's appearance. Another possible way to focus on your topic would be to examine the backlash to the movie. You could describe the growth of organizations such as the NAACP, groups demanding civil rights for African Americans.

MS: Oh, yeah! I could write about the growth of both the KKK and the NAACP.

FP: That would be fabulous. Or, another measurable effect on society would be how *Birth of a Nation* inspired some African-American filmmakers to make films that countered its stereotypes. Let's see, now… a man named Oscar Micheaux made a silent film in 1920 called *In Our Gates*. You could write about that film and others made by black filmmakers at the time.

MS: Wow, professor, thanks for all these ideas. I wrote them down here. I kind of get it now about narrowing down the topic.

FP: Good, I look forward to reading your paper.

Narrator: Now get ready to answer the questions.

PRACTICE 1 - TRACK 120

Narrator: Listen to part of the conversation. Then answer the question.

FP: Yes, that would be a relevant topic. *Birth of a Nation*, as you suggest, was followed by huge growth in KKK membership during the 1920s. The KKK really terrorized African Americans.

MS: Yeah, I could write about how the movie made African Americans seem so dangerous, when actually, it was the KKK that was dangerous.

FP: Oh yes, that's putting it mildly.

Narrator: Why does the professor say this?

FP: Oh yes, that's putting it mildly.

PRACTICE 2 - TRACK 121

Narrator: Listen to a lecture in a U.S. history class.

Female Professor (FP): Historians' views of presidents vary over time, so sometimes, it is difficult to predict how a president will be remembered and what he will be remembered for. Case in point: Richard Nixon. Nixon resigned in disgrace in 1973, the only American president ever to resign. If he had not resigned, he was facing even more disgrace as the first president to be removed from office by the U.S. Senate. His image has become synonymous with abuse of power due to the Watergate Scandal. So it's sometimes difficult for historians see an obvious fact: Richard M. Nixon was an environmental president.

Female Student (FS): I always thought that Teddy Roosevelt was the most concerned about the evironment.

FP: President Roosevelt—Teddy Roosevelt, that is—established the National Park System, which was a great achievement. He also created the National Forest Service to protect, supervise, and grow the more than 100 forests that the government owned and maintained. Also, Teddy Roosevelt signed the Pure Food and Drug Act, the first legislation that protected Americans from dangerous foods and drugs. Teddy Roosevelt was a very important environmental president. But Roosevelt never came close to what Nixon accomplished for the environment.

And Nixon's achievements are all the more remarkable because Nixon was a Republican, and because the nation's economy was obviously on the edge of a steep and long recession. Nixon came to power as the post-WWII economic boom had ended. America's industries, especially mining and manufacturing, were beginning to die a slow, painful death. Those huge companies, like Ford Motors, General Motors, and U.S. Steel, wanted nothing to stand in their way, even though competition from international markets, automation, and other factors were leading to their decline. They were dying, but they wanted the best life-support money could buy, and they didn't want any new laws getting in the way. Any legislation that threatened industry would be strongly opposed.

But that's exactly what Nixon did. He began by signing the National Environmental Policy Act of 1969. This declared national environmental policies and goals, and established the Presidential Council on the Environment. Most importantly, this act required that Environmental Impact Reports (EIR) be done for most federally funded projects. Today, this requirement has filtered down to every city and school system in the country. If you want to build a bridge, drain a swamp, or extend an airport runway, you need to show how your project will affect the environment with one of these Environmental Impact Reports.

In 1970, Nixon made history when he established the Environmental Protection Agency (EPA). Before that, the United States had no central authority overseeing environmental protection. The EPA writes and enforces regulations protecting human health and the environment.

Nixon followed up by extending the Clean Air Act. The newly extended Act required the EPA to write and enforce laws making air safer to breathe, and targeted levels of sulfur dioxide, carbon monoxide, and lead in the environment. It was the most important air pollution law in American history. President Nixon continued his commitment to the environment in 1972, when he signed the Marine Mammal Protection Act. This was the first federal law to protect dolphins, whales, manatees, sea otters, polar bears and other animals. It also made provisions for subsistence hunting of whales and other mammals in Alaska. Shortly after this, Nixon signed the Ocean Dumping Act, which regulates the dumping of anything into the ocean that is harmful to humans or the marine environment.

Nixon's final achievement in environmental law came in 1973, when he signed the Endangered Species Act. It has been called the Magna Carta of the environmental movement. The Act gave the government broad powers to act to protect animal species. The Act, and its enforcement, still makes headline news in America today.

Nixon also worked on legislation that became the Safe Drinking Water Act of 1974. Although this became law after his resignation, it was conceived and written during his presidency. No other law has done as much to protect America's water.

Although everyone in the environmental movement was opposed to Richard Nixon, his contributions to environmental law were surprising to them. Although Nixon was the only president ever to resign from office, that doesn't change the legacy he left as an environmental president. As Doug Scott, a 45 year veteran of The Wilderness Society points out, "He is correctly remembered as one of the greatest environmental presidents, and that is not a very long list."

Narrator: Now get ready to answer the questions.

PRACTICE 2 - TRACK 122

Narrator: Listen to part of the lecture. Then answer the question.

FP: His image has become synonymous with abuse of power due to the Watergate Scandal. So it's sometimes difficult for historians to see an obvious fact: Richard M. Nixon was an environmental president.

Narrator: What does the professor suggest when she says this?

FP: So it's sometimes difficult for historians to see an obvious fact…

PRACTICE 3 - TRACK 123

Narrator: Listen to a lecture in a Cultural Anthropology class.

Male Professor (MP): The only indigenous people in Europe are the Sami. About 10,000 years ago they settled in what is now Finland, as well as parts of Norway, Sweden, and even part of Russia. As other groups moved into these territories, the Sami were pushed north above the Arctic Circle. They are small in number today, but even so, there is diversity; there are at least nine different Sami languages spoken in different areas. Yes, Devin? You had a question or comment?

Male Student (MS): Yeah, I had a friend who went to Norway, and she went on a tour where they met a Sami family that herded reindeer. Until I heard about that, I didn't know that reindeer were real. (*laughter*)

MP: Yes, reindeer are real. And the Sami did eventually domesticate herds of reindeer. They also sometimes did use them to pull sleds before they had snowmobiles. So, as I think you are saying, some aspects of ancient Sami culture have been made "cute" for the Santa Claus story.

MS: Yeah, Santa's flying reindeer.

MP: Yes, but few Sami people depend completely on reindeer anymore. In general, the Sami are struggling to retain their language and culture. This is a culture that, for thousands of years, helped people adapt to living in a harsh environment, dominated by coastline, snowy mountains, and windswept plains. In summer there is nearly nonstop daylight; but for a couple of months in winter, the sun does not rise above the horizon at all.

The Sami did not have much edible plant material available to them. They therefore adapted to eating mainly fish and meat, whether it was stewed, dried, fried, or so on. Their crafts and clothing mainly came from animal bones and hides, or reindeer antlers. They were able to trade with other people for cloth and other goods. But how do you think they managed to hunt, fish, and trap animals in winter, when there was deep snow on the ground?

FS: Did they use skis?

MP: Good, you got it. Thousands of years ago, Sami people began skiing. It's not clear whether they were the first people to ski, but at any rate, they developed skis made of light wooden frames covered by animal skins. Their boots were held to the skis with bindings;

the boots also curved up in the front, to help keep the boots secure in the bindings when going downhill. So when you see Santa's elves wearing shoes that curl up at the toe, you will now know where that image came from!

Another adaptation was to rely on Man's Best Friend, the dog. Dogs helped keep watch, discourage wolves and bears, and track game. The Sami bred medium-sized dogs that are intelligent, friendly, and covered by double coats of fur that keep them warm and dry.

Sami languages enable speakers to convey highly specific information about conditions in their surroundings. There are literally hundreds of words for "snow" in Sami languages. These words can indicate different qualities of snow, such as its depth, density, texture, and also when it fell, whether it is marked by tracks, whether it is on plants and trees, and so on.

The Sami traditionally lived in tents or homes made of sod, in small communities called *siidas*. One way that they coped emotionally with the long, dark winters and the freezing temperatures was to create a beautiful storytelling and singing tradition. The traditions fostered strong social ties within the siida.

A major part of this tradition consists of chants called *yoiks*. These are syllabic phrases that people sing; they refer to particular people or things, almost like, you might say, melodic names. Yoiks could be combined as a way of recalling events, or referring to people. Yoiks could be accompanied by a traditional drum, especially by shamans, or healers, who were believed to communicate with the spirit world.

Traditionally, each person receives a personal yoik upon reaching adolescence. To sing a person's yoik is to invoke that person. It is as if the song is that person. If someone has died or is away, for example, you can "yoik" the person by singing his or her personal yoik, and you feel that the person is with you. Singers can blend yoiks into narratives, although their meaning will be understood only by one's own inner circle. Over the centuries, Christian missionaries and governments tried to ban the Sami from drumming and yoikking. Their music was thought to be a kind of sorcery or magic.

Narrator: Now get ready to answer the questions.

PRACTICE 3 - TRACK 124

Narrator: Listen to part of the lecture. Then answer the question.

MP: Yes, reindeer are real. And the Sami did eventually domesticate herds of reindeer. They also sometimes did use them to pull sleds before they had snowmobiles. So, as I think you are saying, some aspects of ancient Sami culture have been made "cute" for the Santa Claus story.

MS: Yeah, Santa's flying reindeer.

Narrator: What does the professor imply with this statement?

MP: So, as I think you are saying, some aspects of ancient Sami culture have been made "cute" for the Santa Claus story.

ACTUAL PRACTICE 24

PRACTICE 1 - TRACK 125

Narrator: Listen to a conversation between a student and a writing tutor.

Male Writing Tutor (MT): So your assignment was to read this opinion piece, and respond by analyzing and evaluating the writer's strategies?

Female Student (FS): Yes, the author of the essay is a math teacher. She wrote this opinion piece and it was in the newspaper. Her opinion is that we should continue making high school students study algebra. Because, you know, recently some experts have been saying that algebra is not necessary.

MT: Okay, so this math teacher supports high school algebra. Let's take a look at your response. Now, looking at your essay here, I can already see that there is a problem. It looks like you have summarized the article, and then given your own opinion of algebra.

FS: Well, the prompt said to explain her points and then evaluate them. So, I thought that meant to tell what she said, and then give my opinion on algebra.

MT: Not exactly. Actually the prompt says to "explain and analyze the writer's strategies, and evaluate their effectiveness." So, it's more like you have to analyze *how* she's making her point and what strategies she uses to make that point. And, you have to evaluate whether it works—you know, whether it's persuasive.

FS: Yeah.... But to tell you the truth, I don't really know what to write.

MT: Let's work on an example then. Now, in the math teacher's essay, she argues that each student should learn algebra because it builds basic knowledge and teaches kids how to think, right? So, how does she support that point?

FS: Well, one thing is that she compares learning algebra in middle school or high school to learning the alphabet in kindergarten. She says that all kids learn the alphabet so they can read. She says that everyone agrees that reading is important, even for people whose jobs won't need it. So, algebra is like that. We need it as a foundation.

MT: Okay, so let's see if we can name that strategy. You said that she compares learning algebra to learning the alphabet. When a writer compares one thing to another related thing, remember, that can be called an *analogy*.

FS: So I say that one of the writer's strategies is making an analogy?

MT: Very good. So, one of your paragraphs can focus on that. You could start the paragraph with the sentence, "The writer uses analogy to support her position." So you're labeling her strategy.

FS: Is that okay to say that, though? Just make my own label?

MT: Yes, that's analyzing. You're pointing out the strategy. So, your next sentence would explain the analogy, so the reader knows what you're talking about. So, something like, "The writer claims that learning algebra is like learning the alphabet."

FS: Isn't that kind of a summary though?

MT: Kind of, but it's still different from the writer's words. You can also write that she 'makes an analogy between' learning algebra and learning the alphabet.

FS: Okay, so I say something like, "The writer uses analogy to support her argument. She says that algebra provides basic knowledge—she compares learning algebra to learning the alphabet." Is that all?

MT: No, no, then you continue to label and evaluate. For example, did that analogy persuade you?

FS: No, not really, not until she added more information about how algebra helps people understand patterns and variables, and stuff like that. That seems like basic knowledge.

MT: So you could write some sentences like, "Not many readers will see, at first, that algebra is as fundamental as reading." That describes how you felt at first.

FS: So, I'm just saying that whatever I think is what most other readers will think?

MT: Yep, you are evaluating the argument for everyone. Kind of like somebody doing an on-line review of a new movie. Now, you said that the math teacher *did* convince you with other information, right? So you could say something like, "The writer, however, provides convincing information about how algebra assists people in understanding many concepts." What's another word for "information?"

FS: Facts? Details? And that shows that I was convinced?

MT: Yes. I think you're starting to get it! Think like that movie critic. You label the writer's different strategies, judge their effect, and then tie it all back in to the main point.

FS: So name and label the strategies and talk about whether they persuaded me—whether they are persuasive, in my judgment—that everyone needs algebra? Okay, so… can I come back on Thursday with a new draft?

MT: I think so, I do have some openings. Let's take a look at the schedule.

Narrator: Now get ready to answer the questions.

PRACTICE 2 - TRACK 126

Narrator: Listen to a lecture in a neuroscience class.

Male Professor (MP): I want to start today's class by throwing out a question: Where does the term "neuroscience" come from? (*To female student*) What do you think, Caroline?

Female Student (FS): Well, it comes from a Greek word for "nerve," right? The "neuro" in neuroscience has the same meaning as "nerve" I think.

MP: Yes, exactly. And of course, neuroscience is the study of the nervous system, and especially of the brain. So the name seems appropriate. After all, nerve cells send the electrochemical signals that tell our body what to do and when to do it. But today, I'll argue that this name is misleading because it leaves out a group of cells that are absolutely crucial to the central and peripheral nervous systems. I'm talking about glial cells, which are commonly referred to simply as glia.

When glia were first discovered in the 20th

century, they were dismissed as "support cells." Most scientists believed that glia simply held neurons in place. After all, glia don't communicate with one another in the same way that neurons do, so they must not play a crucial role in the nervous system. Or so the thinking went. But as our knowledge of the brain increases in scope and depth, so too does our appreciation of glia.

But before we start discussing the types and functions of glial cells, we need to return to the "stars" of the nervous system: neurons. Now we've already discussed much of this in class, but let's do a bit of reviewing. So the three most basic components of every neuron are dendrites, the cell body, and the axon. These three components work together to send electrochemical signals throughout the body, and these electrochemical signals tell the body what to do. So now let's briefly look at *how* these signals are sent. And keep in mind, nerves and glia exist throughout the body, but today we're just focusing on how these cells interact in the brain.

So in the brain, neurons are surrounded by a "soup" of chemical elements, mainly potassium and sodium. Both of these elements are positively charged, and relative to these elements, the cell bodies of neurons are negatively charged when not sending a signal. A cell membrane separates the positively charged outside from the negatively charged inside. When the brain receives a signal from the environment—maybe the organism senses danger, or smells good food, or sees a prospective mating partner—the brain signals neurons to "fire," which means they send signals to the rest of the body.

To send a signal, a neuron's cell membrane will let in some of the positively charged sodium and potassium into the cell body, giving it a more positive charge. Then, the cell body works to restore its original, negatively charged state by pushing the charge down the axon. And a neuron's axon always connects to another neuron's dendrites. So these dendrites pick up the electrochemical charge, and send it to the cell body where it's pushed through to the axon, and so on. Thus, all these impulses we all have—the need to scratch itches and drink water—are controlled by little electrical signals traveling from the brain to the rest of the body.

And because neurons give us the signal to do, well, pretty much everything, they get all the attention among neurologists. But without glia, none of this signaling would be possible. In the brain itself, there are two main types of glial cells. There are some different kinds of glia in the peripheral nervous system, but we'll worry about them later.

So let's start out with arguably the most important type of glia, which are called "astroglia." So the "astro" part of the name comes from the Greek for "star" because astroglia are often star-shaped. And while neurons are busy sending electrical signals to the body, the astroglia are busy doing everything else. Astroglia connect neurons to a blood supply, which provides neurons with the nutrients they need to survive and send signals. Astroglia also remove excess potassium from a neuron's immediate environment; this ensures that neurons have the right chemical balance to send signals. And astroglia even send signals to one another to meet the needs of neurons. So the astroglia are starting to make neurons look downright lazy by comparison, right?

Another type of glia found in the brain are called oligodendroglia. These types of glial cells surround a neuron's axon, forming something called a myelin sheath. And for now, don't worry too much about what exactly a myelin sheath *is*, just know that it helps electrochemical signals travel more efficiently from one neuron to the next.

So to review, neurons send electrical signals from the brain to the rest of the body to tell it what to do, and glia provide structural and nutritional support for the neurons, making these glia much more important than researchers once believed.

Narrator: Now get ready to answer the questions.

PRACTICE 2 - TRACK 127

Narrator: What does the professor suggest when he says this?

MP: But before we start discussing the types and functions of glial cells, we need to return to the "stars" of the nervous system: neurons.

PRACTICE 2 - TRACK 128

Narrator: Listen to part of the lecture. Then answer the question.

MP: Astroglia connect neurons to a blood supply, which provides neurons with the nutrients they need to survive and send signals. Astroglia also remove excess potassium from a neuron's immediate environment; this ensures that neurons have the right chemical balance to send signals. And astroglia even send signals to one another to meet the needs of neurons. So the astroglia are starting to make neurons look downright lazy by comparison, right?

Narrator: Why does the professor say this?

MP: So the astroglia are starting to make neurons look downright lazy by comparison, right?

PRACTICE 3 - TRACK 129

Narrator: Listen to a lecture in a physics class.

Male Professor (MP): Today I thought we'd explore a very simple question that has a surprisingly complex answer. That question is, "Why is the sky blue?"

To answer this question, let's talk about light for a minute. The visible light we see is just a type of electromagnetic radiation. X-rays, microwaves and radio waves are all examples of electromagnetic radiation that humans can't detect with our senses.

Imagine that any type of radiation is a river containing a certain amount of water. As the space between the riverbanks shrinks, the river flows faster; as that same space widens, the river flows much slower. Like these rivers, some forms of electromagnetic radiation are very thin, but incredibly fast, while others are wide and slow. All radiation, including light, is classified according to its speed, or frequency, and its width, or wavelength.

Now, humans can only see visible light, the steady, but gentle "rivers" in the middle of the spectrum. Radiation in this range of frequencies is responsible for "coloring your world," so to speak. And different wavelengths within the visible spectrum produce different colors. Deep, dark blue and vibrant violet are the narrowest bands we can see: the shores of their rivers are so close together, we can nearly leap across the raging rapids. (*laughter*) At the other end, reds and oranges flow gently by, across great leagues.

So what happens when all this radiation enters Earth's atmosphere? Well, as you know, most of the visible light enters Earth and interacts with objects we encounter everyday. These interactions are responsible for the diversity of colors in the natural world. However, just as solids and liquids clearly absorb and reflect specific colors, or wavelengths of light, gases, too, interact with visible light from the sun and other sources.

When light enters Earth's atmosphere, some of it gets absorbed by the gases that comprise the atmosphere. All frequencies and wavelengths are absorbed, but blue is retained more often than any other color of light. We'll discuss the reasons for this later.

Now, the gases in our atmosphere don't actually absorb this light, per say. What's really happening is a process known as "Rayleigh scattering." Unlike an opaque solid or liquid, the transparent gases in our atmosphere don't react chemically with incoming light, so once it's absorbed, it has nowhere to go. The gas molecules simply radiate this light back out, and it scatters across the sky.

Female Student (FS): Professor, what do you mean when you say it "scatters across the sky"? Does this light just float around in the atmosphere forever?

MP: Not exactly. If it stayed there forever, we'd never be able to see it down on Earth. Think of it like this: after a pebble falls into a pond, ripples spread outward, even after the pebble has settled on the bottom of the pond. If the pond is very small, the ripples may reach the shore and start a new series of ripples. However, some of this energy escapes; with each ripple, the wave transfers a small amount of energy to the surrounding atmosphere. Over time, the ripples fade and, eventually disappear altogether.

In this analogy, light waves are like the pebble, bombarding Earth's atmosphere. The atmosphere is like the water in the pond, absorbing the impact of the lightwaves, creating a sort of rippling effect on the surrounding gas particles. The ripples affect other gas particles, creating new ripples. It ends up being a confusion of ripples, so we say it is "scattered." However, as in the pond, some of this energy escapes. Light waves are constantly being ejected from the "ripple" of absorbed energy.

When we look up at the sky, we can see those waves which are sent in our direction. As I mentioned earlier, the majority of light scattered is in the blue spectrum, so humans tend to perceive the sky as being blue during daytime hours. Once the last wave of light passes through the atmosphere, however, the "ripple" in the sky calms and dies down altogether. So the sky, like the pond, becomes calm once more; without the scattering of incoming blue light, the sky goes dark pretty quickly.

Now, let's discuss the reasons blue light is more likely to interact with atmospheric gas particles...

Narrator: Now get ready to answer the questions.

PRACTICE 3 - TRACK 130

Narrator: Listen to part of the lecture. Then answer the question.

MP: So what happens when all this radiation enters Earth's atmosphere? Well, as you know, most of the visible light enters Earth and interacts with objects we encounter everyday. These interactions are responsible for the diversity of colors in the natural world. However, just as solids and liquids clearly absorb and reflect specific colors, or wavelengths of light, gases, too, interact with visible light from the sun and other sources.

Narrator: What can be inferred from this?

MP: Well, as you know, most of the visible light enters Earth and interacts with objects we encounter everyday. These interactions are responsible for the diversity of colors in the natural world.

ACTUAL PRACTICE 25

PRACTICE 1 - TRACK 131

Narrator: Listen to a conversation between a student and a professor.

Male Professor (MP): So, Zoe. You wanted to talk about the results of your first quiz?

Female Student (FS): Yes, well, just a quick question. I was wondering if maybe there was a mistake, because I got a "B" on the quiz even though my score was only 65 percent. Normally, isn't 65 percent a "D"?

MP: Yes, but do you remember the first day of class, when we went over the syllabus and I explained my grading policies?

FS: Well, actually, I missed the first day of class because I dropped another course and added this one to my schedule later.

MP: That's okay, we can go over it now. My system is a modified version of "grading on a curve," if you have heard of that? No? Well, let me go over it now, then. To begin with, this calculus class is tough. I mean, to be honest, most students tend to struggle in this class.

FS: Yeah, I've noticed!

MP: So I've learned over the years that, well, the traditional grading system, where 90 percent and above is an "A," and so on, was discouraging to students.

FS: Oh, so... were all the students failing?

MP: No, no, but students who said they were used to getting top grades were earning lower scores on my quizzes and tests. For example, students who were used to getting "As" on all of their quizzes and tests in other classes were getting "Cs" and even "Ds" in this class.

FS: Oh, wow. They must've been complaining.

MP: That's right, they were. Yet it was a dilemma. I wanted the students to pass the class, but I couldn't just water-down the tests. There are a number of concepts that must be mastered in this course.

FS: Yeah, making the tests easier doesn't seem like a solution.

MP: So what I began to do was to apply a "curve" to the grades. That means I base all the grades for quizzes and tests on the highest score in the class. So let's say that the highest score on a test is 86 percent. So, 86 percent becomes the new "A-plus." Then from 86 percent down to 76 percent is an "A."

FS: Oh, I see, so the test doesn't change, just the way you give letter grades, "As" and "Bs" and stuff.

MP: Pretty much, yes. The idea is to be more fair. So, even if the quiz or test is insanely difficult, the students who demonstrated the most knowledge will still get "As" and "Bs."

FS: Ah, I see. Grades are still 10 percentage points apart?

MP: Yes, that's right. For example, on this last quiz, the highest score was 79, and a few more people scored in the high 70s. So, I felt comfortable designating scores above 70 as an "A," above 60 as a "B," above 50 as a "C," and above 40 as a "D."

FS: Huh. Well, that's how I ended up with a "B" for a score of 65 percent. All teachers should use your system!

MP: Well, of course many instructors feel that it would make their classes too easy. The decision needs to be made case-by-case. And on the other hand, you get some tough instructors who curve the grades even more than I do by pegging the lowest score in class as an "F." At least one person in the class always fails.

FS: Yeah, that seems harsh. What if everyone in the class does about the same on the test, and the unlucky person who gets a *slightly* lower score gets an "F."

MP: Exactly. While with my system, everyone could theoretically get an "A."

FS: That'd be nice, wouldn't it!

MP: Yes, indeed! I'll see you in class, Zoe.

Directions: Now get ready to answer the questions.

PRACTICE 1 - TRACK 132

Narrator: Listen to part of the conversation. Then answer the question.

MP: That's okay, we can go over it now. My system is a modified version of "grading on a curve," if you have heard of that? No? Well, let me go over it now, then. To begin with, this calculus class is tough. I mean, to be honest, most students tend to struggle in this class.

Narrator: Why does the professor say this?

MP: To begin with, this calculus class is tough. I mean, to be honest, most students tend to struggle in this class.

PRACTICE 1 - TRACK 133

Narrator: Listen to part of the conversation. Then answer the question.

MP: And on the other hand, you get some tough instructors who curve the grades even more than I do by pegging the lowest score in class as an "F." At least one person in the class always fails.

FS: Yeah, that seems harsh. What if everyone in the class does about the same on the test, and the unlucky person who gets a *slightly* lower score gets an "F."

Narrator: Why does the student say this?

FS: Yeah, that seems harsh. What if everyone in the class does about the same on the test, and the unlucky person who gets a *slightly* lower score gets an "F."

PRACTICE 2 - TRACK 134

Narrator: Listen to a lecture in an economics class.

Male Professor (MP): You know, it's incredible that the income tax system in the United States is only about 100 years old. In fact, before an income tax amendment to the U.S. Constitution was adopted in 1913, income tax was declared unconstitutional many times by the U.S. Supreme Court.

Female Student (FS): Wait a second, Professor. How did our government pay for everything if there wasn't any kind of income tax?

MP: That's a good question. Well, many services we now expect from our government did not exist when the U.S. was established. For example, there were no public schools or highways. In addition, the U.S. didn't have a large military until World War II. Without these expenses—you know, military, education, and public works programs—the U.S. could exist without an income tax. Does that make sense?

FS: I guess I hadn't considered those things. But what about all the land the United States was buying prior to the 20th century? How did the government pay for that?

MP: So, the U.S. government has relied on many different forms of income since its inception, including tariffs on both imports and exports, property taxes, and excise taxes. With the development of a larger government and the introduction of social services, additional taxes became necessary. In addition to income taxes, estate taxes and sales taxes all evolved very recently to help meet growing budget requirements.

Let's take a minute and discuss the history of taxes in the U.S. before we examine the political climate that made additional taxation necessary. So, following the Revolutionary War, the U.S. relied heavily on tariffs. Early on, most of the federal government's income was from tariffs. Of course, the government was much smaller. Imported goods were taxed at a much higher rate back then, too, so the government was able to support its budget needs primarily from the revenue brought in by tariffs.

However, the United States relied on other sources of income as well. Property taxes have always been a popular method for states to meet their budgetary needs. And excise taxes have come and gone when other sources of income couldn't meet the government's need. If you don't remember, an excise tax is a tax added to specific products, like alcohol, tobacco, hotel rooms, and gasoline. Though unpopular, excise taxes tend to receive little organized opposition, so governments pass them fairly frequently.

The U.S. held a considerable amount of debt following the Revolutionary War and had raised the rates on tariffs. To increase revenue without further burdening importers and exporters, Alexander Hamilton proposed an excise tax on alcoholic beverages produced within the country. This tax was so unpopular it eventually led to a minor insurrection known as the "Whiskey Rebellion." Later the tax was abolished. Following the Civil War, however, it was reinstated, again to help reduce national debt. Today, many products are subject to excise taxes by local and federal governments.

FS: So, where does income tax come in? Why did the government find the need to add additional taxes?

MP: There are a few factors that led to the development of income tax and, later, sales and estate taxes. Remember, at the beginning of the lecture, I mentioned the increase in social services and public works in the early 20th century? Well, as a result of the Industrial Revolution and changing perceptions during this time, people started becoming more aware of social injustices and wealth inequality. Men like John Rockefeller and Andrew Carnegie accumulated massive amounts of money while the average American remained very poor.

It was during this time that philosophies like socialism and communism developed. Workers began forming labor unions in order to advance bargaining rights with employers. In addition, public schools were becoming more common, and children were spending more time in school before joining the workforce. The government was was getting more involved in the daily affairs of its citizens in an attempt to ensure equality and social justice.

The downside to all this social reform is its cost; in order to pay for the increased services offered to the public, the U.S. government had to increase taxes. So, Congress finally amended the Constitution in 1913, imposing an income tax on all citizens. Since then, rates have fluctuated, and additional taxes have been levied in order to balance the budget.

Narrator: Now get ready to answer the questions.

PRACTICE 3 - TRACK 135

Narrator: Listen to a lecture in a biology class.

Male Professor (MP): Now, one of the eternal questions for biologists is, of course, how life began. So humans have been seeking answers in very far-away places. The European Space Agency, in 2014 I think it was, managed to land a robotic lander spacecraft called *"Philae"* on a comet. Now can anyone tell the class why researchers would go to the effort to land a robotic craft on some chunk of ice that's careening through space?

Female Student (FS): Wasn't *Philae* sent to do some chemical analysis testing? Like, it was supposed to gather rock and ice samples, right?

MP: Yes, very good. Scientists want to know if any of the compounds they extract from the comet match substances found on Earth. And, to be more specific, *Philae* was looking for organic compounds. And, just as a reminder, organic compounds are combinations of chemical elements that contain hydrogen and carbon, and they form the "backbone" for life here on Earth. Thus, if organic compounds found by *Philae* match those found on Earth, it could tell us a lot about the origins of life here on Earth. And this search for non-living, organic compounds brings us to our main topic for the day: abiogenesis.

Abiogenesis is the idea that life can naturally arise from non-living matter, given the right conditions. And for centuries, most people believed that most living things came into existence through abiogenesis. When people observed maggots hatching from rotting meat, they assumed that the raw meat created the maggots. Or when people saw frogs emerge from muddy lakes and swamps, they assumed that the mud produced the frogs. The concept of these creatures hatching from eggs had not quite caught on yet.

But then, beginning in the 1600s, some scientists started to question this type of abiogenesis. And over the following 200 years, a number of experiments refuted the notions that life could arise from rotting meat or mud. These experiments proved that all existing life forms came about through biogenesis—that is, the idea that living organisms come from other living organisms.

So from this little story, it would be rational to think that abiogenesis has been thoroughly disproved. After all, the idea that all life comes about through reproduction is common sense, and the notion that frogs come from mud is nonsense, right? This brings us back to the beginning of our lecture: How does *Philae*'s search for non-living, organic compounds on a distant comet relate to abiogenesis?

Well, clearly biogenesis does a great job explaining how organisms reproduce, but it doesn't explain how life got started here on Earth. So some researchers suggested that perhaps, billions of years ago, simple organic compounds underwent a series of chemical reactions that produced more complex organic compounds. And these complex organic compounds underwent changes that produced life. (*To male student*) Go ahead.

MS: But how could we ever prove that's how life started? I mean, without a time machine, we can't know what happened on Earth billions of years ago.

MP: This is true. But scientists have designed experiments that replicate the chemical and environmental conditions on Earth about 4 billion years ago—that's the earliest point that most scientists believe life could have developed.

In the 1950s, researchers Stanley Miller and Harold Urey combined water, methane, ammonia, and hydrogen. All these substances were almost certainly present in abundance on Earth 4 billion years ago. They then added heat and humidity to the mixture, and they fired electrical sparks into the solution to imitate lightning strikes. After a week, they extracted samples of the chemical solution, and found that it contained several complex organic compounds, including amino acids necessary for life on Earth.

Since this first attempt to recreate the conditions of an early Earth, many others have tried different chemical combinations in their experiments, and virtually all of them have produced complex organic compounds. Not life, mind you, but a good start.

So because of efforts such as the Miller-Urey experiment, abiogenesis stands out as the most accepted scientific theory for the origin of life on Earth. And the comet that *Philae* landed on may give us clues about how simple organic compounds got to Earth in the first place.

In the days before life, Earth was bombarded with icy comets, which provided Earth with water and a host of other chemical substances. So what scientists want to know from *Philae* is whether any organic compounds that might be found there match the ones that led to life here on Earth.

So now let's take a closer look at the amino acids that I mentioned earlier...

Narrator: Now get ready to answer the questions.

PRACTICE 3 - TRACK 136

Narrator: What can be inferred from this?

MP: And for centuries, most people believed that most living things came into existence through abiogenesis. When people observed maggots hatching from rotting meat, they assumed that the meat created the maggots. Or when people saw frogs emerge from muddy lakes and swamps, they assumed that the mud produced the frogs.

PRACTICE 3 - TRACK 137

Narrator: What does the professor suggest when he says this?

MP: Since this first attempt to recreate the conditions of an early Earth, many others have tried different chemical combinations in their experiments, and virtually all of them have produced complex organic compounds. Not life, mind you, but a good start.

APPENDIX

Answer Key

CHAPTER 2

ACTUAL PRACTICE 1 - PRACTICE 1

Notes

TA meeting with stu. to review research paper
stu. has not written much of the paper
→ stu. has done research (minimum wage in U.S.)
→ trouble narrowing topic down
→ wrote draft, too unfocused
TA says to meet tomorrow to look over stu. draft
stu. begins to discuss history of minimum wage

1) A

   Main Idea Question

   The teaching assistant explains the main topic when she says to the student, "the primary purpose of this meeting is… to review what you've written so far," or check *the student's progress.*

2) C

   Detail Question

   The student explains his problem when he says, "I can't really seem to narrow anything down" when writing the research paper.

3) D

   Inference Question

   The teaching assistant spending much of the conversation trying to fix the student's problem, as well as her exclamation of "Uh-oh," indicate that she is *concerned* about the student's progress on the research paper.

4) A

   Purpose Question

   Because the teaching assistant thinks that "maybe there's something in that paper [the student's rough draft] you can actually use," we can infer that she wants to see the rough draft *to suggest parts that the student can use.*

5) B

   Inference Question

   At the end of the conversation, the teaching assistant says to the student, "let's discuss it [minimum wage in the U.S.] chronologically then." Thus, we can assume that the student will *describe the history of minimum wage* to the teaching assistant.

ACTUAL PRACTICE 1 - PRACTICE 2

Notes

finger painting = simple form of art expression
started for children, now used by all ages (no training necessary)
→ created by Ruth Faison Shaw
→ she was inspired by child writing on walls in Rome (1920s)
finger painting technique:
→ spread paint by sweeping fingers, hands, arms
→ stand when painting
→ vary movements (no repetition)
uses special paint (no stains, mix w/ water, mix colors on paper)

1) B

   Main Idea Question

   The professor spends the majority of the lecture discussing "some background information" on finger painting, including *the history and techniques of finger painting.*

2) C, D

   Detail Question

   Toward the beginning of the lecture, the professor says that finger painting is popular "because there is no technique to master," and it allows people to express their "creative instincts."

3) A

   Detail Question

   According to the professor, Ms. Shaw developed finger painting after watching a student who was "absorbed in decorating the bathroom door with a finger dipped in iodine."

4) D

   Inference Question

   When the professor says, "whatever works, goes," she means that any painting strategies that work (prove effective) are acceptable when finger painting. Form this, we can infer that finger painting *is a free and spontaneous activity.*

5) A, C, D

   Detail Question

   The finger-painting techniques mentioned by the professor include, "spread paint with sweeping movements of the hands," "stand up when working," and "make a variety of movements rather than just one single movement."

6) C

Inference Question

The professor tells the students to "sprinkle some water in it [the finger paints] using the glasses of water I've left." Thus, we can infer that the paint *dries out fairly quickly when uncovered*.

ACTUAL PRACTICE 1 - PRACTICE 3

Notes

coyote = indigenous to N. America
relative of wolf (Canis)
differences
→ *smaller than wolves*
→ *coats thinner than wolves*
similarities
→ *social unit = breeding pair*
→ *sometimes hunt in packs*
→ *older pups proctect younger ones, then leave to breed*
diverse diet/social groups → *live in many environments*
recent ↑ in SW American pop.
→ *humans displace large predators, coyotes populations grow*

1) D

Main Idea Question

At the beginning of the lecture, the professor says, "Today, I want to discuss… the coyote." She then goes on to describe the coyote's *physique, environment, and behavior*, especially how these traits compare to those of the wolf.

2) B, C

Detail Question

According to the professor, coyotes and wolves "belong to the same genus, *Canis*." Additionally, "like the wolf, the coyote's basic social unit is the breeding pair," so coyotes and wolves *live in similar social groups*.

3) A

Detail Question

After mentioning that coyotes are social animals, she says that "one of the biggest misconceptions people have of coyotes" is that of "the 'lone coyote'." Thus, coyotes' depiction in popular culture is *a common misconception*.

4) D

Inference Question

The professor implies that her class had an "ecology unit." Moreover, because she asks students to explain the relationship between animal populations and human developments, we can infer that the class previously covered *the ecological effects of human developments*.

5) C

Detail Question

According to the professor, "Because coyotes have such an adaptive social organization (*flexible social groups*) and varied diet (*diverse diets*), they can thrive in a wide variety of habitats."

6) B

Detail Question

The professor says, "When humans push out wolf populations, coyotes multiply," or in other words, coyotes *lack natural predators*.

ACTUAL PRACTICE 2 - PRACTICE 1

Notes

stu. apologizing for leaving early, he feels anxious in class
→ *stu. can't borrow notes, b/c classmates older*
→ *taking Advance Spanish as freshman, nervous when other stu. talk*
→ *prof. will put stu. in group w/ sophomores for presentation, help stu. socialize*
→ *prof. tells stu. to sit by door, easy to leave*
prof. recommends stu. go to health center

1) D

Main Idea Question

The student explains why he is visiting the professor when he says, "I just wanted to apologize for leaving class early over the last few weeks."

2) B

Detail Question

The student claims that he does not talk to other students in class because "they're all older," and the professor responds, "I can see how that would feel a little intimidating."

3) A

Purpose Question

Because the professor tells the student, "you'll be fine

as long as you keep trying," we can infer that she is *encouraging the student to keep putting effort into her class.*

4) B, C

Detail Question

The professor says, "I think you'll feel more comfortable [in class] when you get to know some of the other students (*interact with classmates*)," and she tells the student to "sit near the door" during class.

5) C

Inference Question

Because the professor gives the student helpful advice to deal with his anxiety, we can conclude that the professor's tone is *sympathetic and understanding.*

ACTUAL PRACTICE 2 - PRACTICE 2

Notes

endemic animals of New Zealand (mostly bird species)
→ *NZ isolated island for 65-mil. years, no land mammals arrived*
→ *birds fill many eco. niches, flew to island*
→ *lack of predators makes many birds flightless*
arrival of humans (Maori first, then Europeans) led to many species extinction
→ *introduced rats, outcompeted many birds*
→ *destruction of forests, overhunting led to extinctions*
over half of bird species now extinct, preservation efforts to save remaining species

1) D

Main Idea Question

At the beginning of the lecture, the professor says, "I want to talk about the endemic animals of New Zealand." Because he talks about the *history* of these endemic animals, we can conclude that the main topic is *the ecological history of New Zealand.*

2) B

Purpose Question

The professor emphasizes the fact that "the Galapagos tortoise is *endemic* to the Galapagos Islands," so we can infer that the professor mentions it *to give an example of an endemic, island-dwelling species.*

3) B

Detail Question

After the professor asks about "why there are so many unique species" in New Zealand, a student responds that is has "to do with how long New Zealand has been isolated from other major landmasses."

4) A

Purpose Question

The professor says that the moa "was hunted to extinction by 1400," so the moa is an example of *an endemic bird species that was driven to extinction by human activities.*

5) B, C, E

Detail Question

The professor says, "Maori people hunted some of the endemic bird species to extinction;" "Many other endemic bird species went extinct due to habitat loss;" and "the biggest cause of extinction… was the introduction of invasive mammal species."

6) D

Inference Question

The professor emphasizes that humans have driven "nearly half of New Zealand's endemic bird species" to extinction, and that "humans have decimated a fragile… ecosystem." From this, we can assume that the professor believes that humans *have irreversibly damaged New Zealand's ecosystem.*

ACTUAL PRACTICE 2 - PRACTICE 3

Notes

jazz music = American art, from New Orleans (1800s)
→ *Influenced by African/Euro. music*
prof: what makes jazz unique?
→ *stu: instruments? (no)*
→ *stu: rhythmic structures? prof: syncopation" (accents on weak beats)*
→ *prof. gives ex. of syncopation using Getty. Address*
→ *stu. guesses improv. (prof. agrees, says much of jazz is improv.)*
next class will listen to jazz improv. solo

1) C

Main Idea Question

The professor spends the majority of the lecture asking the students, "What is it that makes jazz 'jazz'?"

In other words, the professor wants the students to *describe some unique characteristics of jazz music.*

2) B

Inference Question

Here, the professor's tone is playful, so we can infer that he is joking when he calls "eating hamburgers with French fries" an "art." Thus, the professor is simply implying that—like jazz music—these food items *are often associated with the United States.*

3) D

Purpose Question

Here, the professor mostly talks about the different instrumentation of different types of jazz bands, so we can infer that he mentions this *to explain that jazz music uses a wide variety of instruments.*

4) B

Purpose Question

Shortly before quoting the Gettysburg Address, the professor says, "Let's illustrate syncopation with language." Thus, he is using the Gettysburg Address *to help students understand* syncopation, which is *a feature of jazz music.*

5) B

Detail Question

Because the professor says, "Improvising is more important than the 'basic musical framework' in jazz," we can conclude that improvisation *is more central to jazz compositions* than it is to other genres of music.

6) A

Inference Question

At the end of the lecture, the professor discusses the importance of improvisation in jazz music, then he says, "Let me play you a song to show you what I mean." From this, we can infer that he *plays a piece of jazz music for the class* to give an example of improvisation.

ACTUAL PRACTICE 3 - PRACTICE 1

Notes

stu. feels overwhelmed by prof.'s Chem. 201 class
→ stu. did well in lower-div. classes
→ stu. wants to go to vet. school (needs good grades)
prof. says class is difficult for many
prof. recommends "homework schedule"
→ plan out assignments on a calendar
→ break works into "chunks"
stu. decides to stay in prof.'s class

1) C

Main Idea Question

The student explains her reason for visiting when she says, "I just wanted to get in here before the deadline for dropping Chemistry 201." Thus, she visits the professor *to talk about dropping the professor's difficult class.*

2) B

Inference Question

If something is "a walk in the park," then it is an easy, relaxing activity. So if lower-division classes are "no walk in the park," then we can infer that *the lower-division classes are difficult.*

3) D

Detail Question

The student says to the professor, "I was hoping to get good enough grades to get into veterinary school."

4) C

Detail Question

The professor tells the student "to make a homework schedule," so she can break "the huge tasks into smaller 'chunks'." In other words, he tells her to *break down the assignments into a study plan.*

5) B

Inference Question

The professor emphasizes how difficult his class is by saying, "a lot of students have struggled to keep up in this class." From this, we can infer that *most students find it very difficult.*

ACTUAL PRACTICE 3 - PRACTICE 2

Notes

debate in edu. field = Progressive Ed., 1880s-1920s, typical schoolroom 19th cent. stu. practice writing, arithmetic
→ used slates to practice, memorize
students tested orally on memorized info. (similar to European monasteries)
→ 1880s more factory jobs, people living in cities, kids going to work
→ reformers: children should be in school

→ *increase in supplies (edu. more practical)*
→ *Progressives: stress thinking critically*
→ *still active debate (memorize info. vs. explore and express.)*

1) D

   Main Idea Question

   The professor begins the talk by referring to "a debate within the field of education that began more than a century ago," or *two opposing approacheds to education in the U.S. since 1880.*

2) A

   Detail Question

   The professor says that learning activities included "students using their slates to practice penmanship, English grammar, spelling, or arithmetic."

3) B

   Purpose Question

   The professor says that in monasteries, education was passive and emphasized handwriting and memorizing. Thus, he mentions them as possible *historical sources of the 19th century emphasis on rote learning.*

4) C

   Inference Question

   According to the professor, supporters of progressive education "associated education with democracy. What they meant by that was that education should produce people who could think critically." The implication is that when voting, they would make more informed choices *(vote wisely).*

5) B, D

   Detail Question

   The professor describes how people moving to cities meant children were not involved in farm work; and how access to reading and writing materials meant that students could read and write more freely.

6) D

   Inference Question

   The professor describes the historical roots of traditional American educational practices leading up to the progressive movement. After describing the background of the debate between traditional and progressive approaches, he says he will "open it up for discussion" and *asks students to share current examples from classroom observations.*

ACTUAL PRACTICE 3 - PRACTICE 3

Notes

plant hormones = chemical messengers to coordinate plant growth (3 hormones)
   1) *auxins = most impt. hormone, cause stems/roots to grow, ↑ fruit growth, ↓ branch growth (auxins ensure plant growth occurs in impt. parts of plant)*
   2) *cytokinin = controls cell division, decides which cells become root, leaf, branch cells (prof. compares to guidance counselor)*
   3) *gibberellins = cause plant to grow larger (mostly seed and flower growth)*
prof. to use diagrams in PP

1) B

   Main Idea Question

   At the beginning of the lecture, the professor says that the focus of his lecture will be on the roles of hormones in plants.

2) A

   Detail Question

   According to the professor, "one characteristic of hormones is that they're produced in one part of an organism, but they actually affect a different part of the organism."

3) C

   Inference Question

   Because the professor says that cytokinin's determine the functions of developing cells much like "guidance counselors," we can infer that *they are most active in young, developing plants.*

4) A

   Purpose Question

   The professor says, "You can think of cytokinins like career or guidance counselors," so he mentions counselor *to compare a plant hormone (cytokinins) to something more familiar to students (visiting a guidance counselor).*

5)

	Auxins	Cytokinins	Gibberellins
			✓
	✓		
		✓	

Detail Question

According to the professor, "Auxins cause plants' stems and roots to lengthen"; the hormone cytokinin "controls cell division in plants"; and "gibberellins mostly cause the seeds and flowers of plants to grow."

ACTUAL PRACTICE 4 - PRACTICE 1

Notes

stu. switched, psychology → poli. sci.
needs letter of rec. for politics internship
→ stu. will study abroad in Geneva, Switz.
→ optional internship to work with intl. org.
→ stu. wants to study global environment issues
→ student speaks Korean, learning French, taking int'l poli. Classes to prep. for trip
stu. will email prof. with info. for letter of rec.
stu. will sign up for prof.'s upcoming poli. class

1) B

Main Idea Question

The student explains to the professor, "the reason I came to see you today was to ask you to write a letter of recommendation for me for a politics internship."

2) A

Detail Question

The student says, "I started out as a psychology major, but this semester I switched my major to political science."

3) C

Inference Question

After the student says that he will study political science in Geneva, the professor responds, "Well, Geneva is certainly the place to be for that." Thus, we can infer that Geneva *is a good place to study political science.*

4) B, D

Detail Question

When the professor asks the student how he is preparing for the program, he responds, "I'm taking French," and "I'm getting in all my applications for scholarships and financial aid."

5) D

Purpose Question

The phrase, "I'll bet!" means that you agree with someone enthusiastically. Because the student says this phrase after the professor describes her upcoming class, we can infer that the student is *expressing enthusiasm regarding the professor's upcoming class.*

ACTUAL PRACTICE 4 - PRACTICE 2

Notes

eucalyptus tree = native to Australia, found in many warm climates
most eucalyptus in CA = blue gum species (main topic of lecture)
→ can grow over 50 meters tall, grows quickly
→ flower color varies by species
→ leaves face sideways to conserve water (face away from sun)
why so many eucalyptus in CA?
→ south CA lacks lumber, eucalyptus planted to provide lumber (eucalyptus bad for building, cracks and warps when dry)
→ today, eucalyptus used as wind block, + cough syrup, decoration
next prof. explains why eucalyptus hazardous

1) C

Main Idea Question

The professor explains, "during today's lecture, we're going to look at the botanical characteristics and practical industrial uses of the blue gum" eucalyptus tree.

2) A

Purpose Question

According to the professor, "unlike other tall trees, such as the redwood and Douglas fir, blue gums grow incredibly quickly." From this, we can conclude that the professor is *contrasting the growth of these trees to that of eucalyptus trees.*

3) C

Detail Question

The professor says that "some of [the trees'] water-saving adaptations have made them hazardous" (*dangerous*).

4) D

Detail Question

After the professor asks the student to guess why eucalyptus leaves are turned edgewise, the student guesses, "does it have something to do with conserving water?" Thus, *edgewise direction* of eucalyptus leaves helps prevent evaporation.

5) B

Detail Question

Many people stopped planting eucalyptus trees when they "realized that lumber from eucalyptus trees bends, warps, and cracks as it dries out," making it *inadequate number*.

6) C, D

Detail Question

According to the professor, "eucalyptus trees make great wind block," so they *protect crops and buildings from strong winds*, and "the oil within the tree is still used in some cough syrups," so parts of the tree *can be used in certain medicines*.

ACTUAL PRACTICE 4 - PRACTICE 3

Notes

Laetoli fossil site, in Tanzania; in 1970s, Leakey found Australopithecus fossils & footprints
fossil footprint discovery:
→ *volcano deposits ash (3.6 mil. years ago)*
→ *rain falls, dampens ash*
→ *hominid leave footprints in ash*
→ *ash dries, preserving footprints*
at the time, footprints oldest on record, since then newer ones
Leakey covered footprints; re-excavated/reexamined in 1990s

1) C

Main Idea Question

The professor explains the main topic when he says, "today I want to talk about a couple of very important fossil sites that are essential to understanding our human origin" (*help explain hominid evolution*).

2) A, B

Detail Question

The professor says, "the fossil footprints were preserved at the Laetoli site by a rare… sequence of events," and that "there are tracks made by two, perhaps three, hominids."

3) C

Detail Question

According to the professor, "a volcano erupted near the site"; "Rain fell after the eruption"; "Many animals, including hominids, walked across the wet ash"; and "The sun then dried the ash into cement-like hardness."

4) D

Purpose Question

The professor says that the fossilized footprints "show a pattern of upright walking (*bipedal locomotion*) similar to that of modern humans," which reveals that the fossils were left by hominids. Thus, bipedal locomotion *highlights an important characteristic of the fossilized footprints*.

5) C

Detail Question

The professor says, "Leakey and her team covered the [footprint fossil] site with sand to protect the footprints," so she was *maintaining the site for future investigation*, which happened in the 1990s.

6) B

Inference Question

Because the "erosion and vandalism" of the footprint fossils were such big concerns to scientists only a couple of decades after their discovery, we can infer that *once uncovered, fossil sites are difficult to preserve*.

ACTUAL PRACTICE 5 - PRACTICE 1

Notes

man asks about shared rental
→ *woman says she wants to live off campus, thinks both will live well together*
→ *man thinks they should find 1-2 more people*
→ *woman wants affordable, but thinks they need to consider transp. costs*
→ *suggests finding house w/ her friend Ashley, asks if man okay w/ cat*
→ *man says okay, woman going to call Ashley, man will check uni. housing website*

1) B

Main Idea Question

The man says he is "wondering about trying to set

up a shared rental situation for the fall semester," and asks the woman about her plans and whether she would like to share a rental. Thus, his purpose is *to suggest that they share a rented house.*

2) C

Inference Question

The woman implies that because the speakers have similar lifestyles and personalities, sharing housing "might really work out," because they *should be able to live together peacefully.*

3) A

Detail Question

The man says that if the two speakers could "find another person, or maybe even two," to share a three-bedroom house, "the overall rent and utilities would be a lot cheaper for each person." In other words, they could *split expenses.*

4) D

Inference Question

The woman says that "it would be so perfect to find something near campus," but that might be "too costly," implying that *rents may be higher closer to campus.*

5) A, D

Detail Question

The woman says that her friend Ashley "has to move because all of her roommates are graduating," and she wants to live in a place where she is allowed to have a cat. Thus, *Ashley's roommates are graduating and moving away,* and *she wants to live in a pet-friendly place.*

6) C

Detail Question

The man says, "I like cats because they kind of act like wild animals, but they still want you to pet them and play with them," or *they seem wild, but they like attention from their owners.*

ACTUAL PRACTICE 5 - PRACTICE 2

Notes

indentured servants = workers in British colonies (now U.S.) = temp. slave

→ *colonies struggling, needed perm. citizens, laborers*

→ *people start importing servants to work land*

→ *recruited from Europe, become ind. servant for free fare to U.S.*

→ *very popular, 75% workers = ind. servants in some colonies*

→ *pop. b/c new possibilities, opportunity for work, avoid prison, some kidnapped*

→ *workers unaware of conditions (many never survived to be free)*

1) C

Inference Question

The professor describes the reasons that colonists needed workers, and the reasons that people signed work contracts to come; she also describes how the system began and ended. Thus, the main topic is *why and how* indentured servitude *(a labor system) developed.*

2) A

Purpose Question

The professor says that for farmers, raising crops that "needed lots of workers" was a problem that was first solved by importing poor Europeans. Describing the crops as "labor-intensive" helps *explain the demand for indentured servants.*

3) D

Inference Question

The professor refers to the national anthem calling the U.S. "the land of the free," when in some areas, a majority of the earliest colonial settlers were not free. The difference between the popular perception and the reality is an *irony.*

4) B

Detail Question

The professor says that "Convicted criminals were sometimes allowed to choose indentured servitude in the colonies instead of going to prison," so some were motivated because *they could avoid prison.*

5) B

Inference Question

The professor is describing what workers were agreeing to when they signed on to become indentured servants. That they were willing to take such a huge risk because it was temporary implies that they expected to gain their freedom, or *they assumed they would outlive their contracts.*

6) B, C

Detail Question

The professor says that a "typical" punishment for

indentured servants was to add time to their indenture (*their freedom was delayed as a form of punishment*); and that the majority of indentured servants died during their period of indenture because of "overwork, poor food rations, and inadequate housing" (*their needs for food, shelter, and rest were not met*).

ACTUAL PRACTICE 5 - PRACTICE 3

Notes

class trip to Mammoth-Flint Ridge Cave (longest system in world)

main topic = solution cave formation (formed from limestone)

→ *underground water dissolves limestone*
→ *top of saturated water zone = water table*
→ *limestone dissolved by CO2 in water (acid)*
→ *water dissolves limestone, then drains*

how do cave entrances form?
→ *sinkhole = rock above cave collapses, forming entrance*
→ *otherwise, entrance formed by stream flowing out of cave*

1) B

   Main Idea Question

   The professor explains that the main idea is to describe "how cave systems such as the ones in Mammoth-Flint are formed." In other words, she is discussing *how a certain type of cave is formed*.

2) C

   Inference Question

   Because the professor says, "mapping out caves is a pretty new field of research, so there's a lot about caves that we have yet to uncover," we can infer that *many cave systems remain undiscovered*.

3) D

   Detail Question

   According to the professor, "caves that form in limestone are referred to as solution caves."

4) A

   Purpose Question

   Here, the professor is discussing the formation of solution caves, and he is explaining that, contrary to popular belief, limestone is not a soft stone. Thus, the professor is *addressing a common misconception about cave formation*.

5) A, B

   Detail Question

   The professor explains that cave openings form when "the rock above part of the cave collapses" *and forms a sinkhole*, or when "a spring or stream flows from the cave," usually *on a hillside*.

6) B

   Inference Question

   Because the professor says, "Most caves... form in limestone," we can infer that limestone must be *a fairly common type of rock*.

ACTUAL PRACTICE 6 - PRACTICE 1

Notes

stu. wants to add prof.'s art class to schedule
→ *deadline for adding classes already passed*
→ *stu. missed deadline b/c of emergency surgery (appendix removed)*
→ *class was full when she tried to enroll before (stu. on waiting list), class still full*

stu. wants to take the prof.'s year-long series; this is first class
→ *stu. graduating, last chance to take series*
→ *prof. will put student at top of wait list, stu. should go to his class*

stu. asks to take class as independent study; prof. will ask dean about that

1) C

   Main Idea Question

   The student states her reason for visiting when she says to the professor, "I'd like to add you painting class." Thus, she visits the professor *to ask him if she can enroll in his art class*.

2) D

   Purpose Question

   The student explains, "I didn't really have time to get my schedule set up" because of the emergency surgery.

3) A

   Inference Question

   The professor says that his art "class is completely full," and he also says that students are still asking him if they can join the class. From this, we can infer that Art 209-A *is a very popular class*.

4) B

Inference Question

Here, the professor is explaining to the student why she cannot sign up for his class. Because the student has a legitimate reason for missing her chances to enroll in the class, we can infer that the professor is *apologetic* toward the student.

5) A, D

Detail Question

The student says that she wants to take the art class because she "wanted to take the year-long series of painting classes," and because the professor's "students say that they learned so much" from him, or in other words that he *is an excellent teacher*.

ACTUAL PRACTICE 6 - PRACTICE SET 2

Notes

Postmodernism = shift in expression
→ away from categorizing
(ex) TV in '60s = mediated
→ omniscient narrator (not postmod.)
postmodern: truth = subjective
(ex) MTV = music video channel
→ videos seem random, chaotic (viewer interprets meaning)
→ diverse styles: Thriller (what is real?)
(ex) internet, shift from mediation
→ YouTube (choose programming, participate)

1) C

Main Idea Question

The professor states his main focus when he begins the lecture by saying that he will "attempt to explain what makes a work of fiction 'postmodern.'" He then defines post modernism using an extended metaphor.

2) A

Purpose Question

The professor says that all programming during the era "could be contained in a weekly magazine called TV Guide," therefore indicating *the limited choices available at the time*.

3) D

Detail Question

The professor says that in talk shows, "someone has decided who should be invited to be on the show, and there is a familiar host who kind of guides everyone along," which, he says, is like having a book's narrator *making selections and decisions for the audiences*.

4) A

Detail Question

The professor describes the music videos that appeared on MTV as mainly "an incoherent mix of images, sort of suggesting a story, but not explaining it," or in other words, *having unclear meaning*.

5) B

Purpose Question

The professor has said that he is "using the TV metaphor" to explain postmodernism, and later says that the Internet represents "a more complete shift against mediated programming," and is thus a "perfect metaphor for postmodernism." Thus he mentions the Internet *to expand a metaphor*.

6) D

Inference Question

Listeners can infer that the professor is *enthusiastic* about postmodernism in the arts because of his focus on benefits for audiences—such as more diversity to choose from, and more opportunities to make choices. His diction has mostly positive connotations, such as the words "delightful" and "playful."

ACTUAL PRACTICE 6 - PRACTICE SET 3

Notes

Epi- or hyper-parasite infests another parasite
   (ex) mistletoes → mistletoes → trees
   (classic ex) protozoan → flea → cat
Host species successful → opens an ecological niche
(Hyper-hyperparasites do the same)
(ex) Lepidaptera (butterfly) successful,
→ Braconid wasp (eat butterfly caterpillar) → Chalcid wasp infests

1) D

Main Idea Question

In the beginning of the lecture, the professor says, "…now I would like to introduce epiparasites." He spends the majority of the lecture describing characteristics of *epiparasites and their hosts*.

2) A

Purpose Question

The professor says, "a classic example of this type of parasitism is the infestation of a flea by a small protozoan." In other words, he gives an *example of a parasite with its own parasites*.

3) B

Detail Question

The professor states that the braconid wasp's success is due to its parasitism of a widespread group of insects (moths and butterflies).

4) B

Inference Question

The professor alludes to the abundance of mistletoe species in the world and explains that they have evolved to infest many different plants, including other species of mistletoe. Thus, we can infer that mistletoe *has a large number of host plants*.

5)

Lepidoptera	Braconid Wasp	Chalcid Wasp
✓	✓	
	✓	✓
		✓

Detail Question

The professor explains that braconid wasps invade Lepidoptera species and chalcid wasps invade braconids. Therefore, *Lepidoptera and braconid wasps host parasites, and braconid and chalcid wasps are parasites*. Finally, chalcid wasps infest braconid wasps, which are themselves a parasite, so the *chalcid wasp's host is a parasite*.

ACTUAL PRACTICE 7 - PRACTICE SET 1

Notes

stu. has to miss 2 weeks of class (mother hurt back, needs help)
→ TA seems sympathetic
TA tells stu. to look at syllabus and keep up w/ reading
→ class discussing Portugal's colonialism
→ prof.'s PowerPoints online
→ stu. should email research paper (10 pages on sugar cane)
stu. wants to go to law school (needs good grades)

1) B

Main Idea Question

At the beginning of the conversation, the student reveals her reason for visiting when she says to the teaching assistant, "I'm going to have to miss a couple of weeks of lectures and sections."

2) D

Purpose Question

The teaching assistant seems shocked when the student says that she will miss two weeks of class. Thus, he mentions the length of a quarter *to emphasize how much class time the student will miss*.

3) A

Detail Question

The teaching assistant says, "Be sure to look at the syllabus for all assignment information."

4) C

Inference Question

When talking about sugar cane, the teaching assistant says, "there will be more than enough information to analyze in 10 pages. Even in 500." Because one could write 500 pages on sugar cane, we can infer that *there is an abundance of information on the topic*.

5) B

Detail Question

The student says, "I have to keep my grades up because I'm going to be applying to law schools."

ACTUAL PRACTICE 7 - PRACTICE SET 2

Notes

irrigation necessary when not enough rainfall
1. simplest method = flooding field with diverted water (flood irrigation)
  → works w/ crops like rice and alfalfa, not good for heavy soils and clay
  → inefficient (water evaporates, runs off), expensive
2. Sprinklers if pressurized water available (more control than flood)
3. Subirrigation (underground pipes, control water table)
  → trenches or raised rows (ex. strawberries)

1) B

Main Idea Question

The professor begins the lecture saying that she will focus on "groundwater" and the "impacts of agriculture." For the rest of the lecture she describes different *methods for diverting* water (*a resource*) from rivers, lakes, or wells, and applying it to crops.

2) B, C

Detail Question

The professor agrees with the student that where

there are "*heavier soils* with less drainage," flood irrigation can fill in all the air pockets around plant roots, killing them. She also says that with flood irrigation, about half of the water is lost; thus "farmers who have to buy water would see (flood irrigation) as inefficient," and therefore *expensive*.

3) D

Purpose Question

The professor describes the invention of elevated sprinkler systems that can be moved where water is needed, or moved out of the way during planting or harvesting, because they are mounted on "huge wheels." In other words, she mentions the wheels to *describe how elevated sprinkler systems are moved.*

4) D

Inference Question

The professor says that sprinkler irrigation "is only an option in places with pressurized water, which requires a power source and a network of delivery pipes." The implication is that sprinklers are not feasible in some places that have *less modern infrastructure*.

5) B

Purpose Question

After the professor describes irrigating by putting water in trenches and letting it seep to the plants' roots horizontally, the student asks if watering elevated strawberry plants by irrigating between rows is "kind of the same idea." Thus, he is *suggesting an example of horizontal subirrigation.*

6) D

Inference Question

The professor describes factors in choosing each type of irrigation: flood irrigation works best where "water is already abundant," sprinkler irrigation works "in places with pressurized water" but only "depending on the dryness of the air," and subirrigation works best when there is "already a fairly high water table." We can conclude that *the "best" system for a given farm depends on many factors*.

ACTUAL PRACTICE 7 - PRACTICE SET 3

Notes

McDonalds history = founded in CA (1930s)
→ *started selling hot dogs/BBQ, food delivered to car*
→ *started making only hamburgers*
→ *1948, simplified menu, made assembly style (inspired by Ford); pioneered "fast food"*

McDonalds restaurant
→ *no waiters (order at window)*
→ *kitchen visible to all*

Ray Kroc, first to franchise McDs.
→ *1961, buys out McDonald bros.*
→ *rewrites McDonald history (claims he was founder)*

1) A

Main Idea Question

The professor mainly discusses "the origins of the American fast food industry" by focusing on McDonalds, *a specific fast food restaurant in the United States*.

2) C

Purpose Question

The professor says the McDonald brothers were "inspired by the assembly line of Henry Ford" to begin producing food "on a continuous basis (*fast food*)."

3) A, C

Detail Question

According to the professor, McDonalds "offered a simple menu" that was "produced on a continuous basis," and it served "everything in paper bags and cups."

4) B

Inference Question

The professor mentions that "Kroc bought out the McDonald brothers for 2.7 million dollars," which implies that he was *ambitious* because he bought a successful fast food chain. Later, the professor implies that Kroc is *aggressive* because he wrote the McDonald brothers out the company's history in order to improve his own image.

5) C, D

Detail Question

According to the professor, "Kroc rewrote McDonald's history to show himself as the founder," *leaving the brothers out of it*. Kroc also opened a new McDonald's nearby to force the original restaurant out of business."

6) D

Inference Question

When referring to someone's knowledge of

something, "to fill in any holes" means to include any important pieces of information. Thus, the professor *wants to include details that the students may not know.*

ACTUAL PRACTICE 8 - PRACTICE SET 1

Notes

stu. asks about changing majors: English lit. Chinese taken Into. Mandarin, Intermed. Mandarin, 2 history classes
→ *needs Adv. Mandarin, Conv. Mandarin, Modern Chin. Culture*
→ *needs upper-division courses, soc. sci., lab. sci.*
→ *adv. suggests adding minor, not changing major*
→ *minor only needs: Adv. Mandarin, Chin. Culture*
stu. not sure, no progress to Lit. major
→ *adv. gives both forms, tells stu. to think about it*

1) A

Main Idea Question

In the beginning of the conversation, the student says, "I would like to change my major."

2) D

Inference Question

The advisor suggests that the student declare Chinese as a minor because she has nearly completed the requirements already. Because the Chinese major requires a much greater commitment, we can infer that the advisor believes declaring a minor *might be easier than changing majors.*

3) A, D

Detail Question

The advisor lists the required courses for Chinese major, including *Advanced Mandarin* and *Modern Chinese Culture.*

4) B

Purpose Question

The student believes her course, Consumer Chemistry, fulfilled her laboratory science class requirement. Thus, she suggests that *the course description was incomplete.*

5) D

Detail Question

The student says "studying Chinese just makes more sense for my future career plans." In other words, *she thinks it will be helpful for her future career.*

ACTUAL PRACTICE 8 - PRACTICE SET 2

Notes

Dead Sea, between Israel and Jordan
→ *416 m. below sea level (lowest place on Earth's surface)*
→ *saltiest body of water in world*
→ *mineral-rich (minerals used in manufactured products/health spas)*
→ *very little life (only brine shrimp, few plants)*
→ *18 km. wide, 80 km. long*
water levels falling in last 100 years (global warming)
formed w/ Great Rift Valley (2- to 7-mil. years ago)
mentioned in Greek writing, Bible (Lot's wife = salt)

1) B

Main Idea Question

The professor says, "Today, I want to talk about... the Dead Sea." He then goes on to describe the sea's *physical makeup and its historical background.*

2) A

Purpose Question

The professor mentions the depth of Death Valley immediately after mentioning the greater depth of the Dead Sea. From this, we can infer that the professor mentions Death Valley to compare the depths of the two locations and *to give students an idea of how far below sea level the Dead Sea lies.*

3) A, C

Detail Question

According to the professor, "many people believe that the high mineral content of the Dead Sea can impart health benefits (*health-promoting qualities*)," and "few plants and no fish other than brine shrimp can survive in" the sea's *mineral-rich waters.*

4) B

Detail Question

The professor says that the water level of the Dead Sea "has been slowly falling" over the last century. She also says, "Scientists are beginning to think that global warming is the culprit here."

5) C

Detail Question

The professor claims that the Dead Sea formed at the same time as "the longest split in Earth's crust," and that both of them were caused by "volcanic eruptions" whose origins remain mysterious.

6) D

Inference Question

We can infer that the professor mentions Sodom and Gomorrah to tell the related story of Lot's wife, who "supposedly was turned into a pillar of salt." The professor says that *salt formations near the Dead Sea help explain the origin of ... the story.*

ACTUAL PRACTICE 8 - PRACTICE SET 3

Notes

Spanish Flu (1918) killed more than AIDS, Black Death
→ *viral, no vaccine*
→ *transferred from birds to men in French military base*
→ *spread very quickly, targeted healthy people (caused overreaction of immune system)*
→ *outbreaks in 3 waves, 25 weeks = 25 mil. deaths*
spread by modern transport (steam trains/ships transport people with virus quickly)

1) B

Main Idea Question

The main topic of the lecture is the 1918 Spanish Flu, *an epidemic during the early 20th century.*

2) D

Detail Question

The professor says, "what really made the virus unique was who it killed." He goes on to say, "The Spanish Flu... was most deadly to the healthiest, most robust patients."

3) B

Purpose Question

At the beginning of the lecture, the professor compares the death tolls of the Spanish Flu to other major health crises in order *to emphasize the deadliness of the Spanish Flu.*

4) B

Detail Question

According to the professor, "the virus mutated and successfully crossed from birds to men at a military base."

5) D

Detail Question

The professor explains that the Spanish Flu spread so quickly because it "was the first pandemic moved around by modern transportation," so the flu spread because of *new methods of transportation.*

6) C

Inference Question

At the end of the lecture, the professor says that the Spanish Flu "left us with so many questions." Moreover, because there is no vaccine for the virus, we can infer that *doctors and scientists still do not know a lot about it.*

ACTUAL PRACTICE 9 - PRACTICE SET 1

Notes

stu. wants to learn about spring break trips w/ rec. dept. (wants to take trip w/ roommate)
→ *stu. has heard good things about trips*
→ *stu. wants to go somewhere warm, inexpensive employee recommends trips to Florida, N. Carolina, California*
→ *stu. likes trip to CA best*
→ *stu. decides overseas trips too expensive*

1) C

Main Idea Question

The student reveals her reason for visiting when she says to the employee, "are you the person to talk to about Rec Department trips for spring break?" From this, we can conclude that she is visiting *to ask about trips sponsored by the recreation department.*

2) C

Detail Question

The student says, "my roommate and I heard someone talking about these [spring break] trips in the bookstore."

3) A

Detail Question

After the employee asks the student, "What kind of trip are you interested in?" the student responds, "A trip to some place that's warm!"

4) A

Detail Question

The employee says, "for most students, really, the most important variable is money." In other words, most students are concerned with *how much the trip costs.*

5) D

Purpose Question

Although the locations that the employee lists are *located near beaches* and in *warm locations*, we can infer that the employee actually lists them in response to the student's request for a "cheap" vacation. Thus, they are *the most affordable trips*.

ACTUAL PRACTICE 9 - PRACTICE SET 2

Notes

Post-impressionist = abstract, flat images (ex. Gauguin, Picasso)
→ *critics said looks "childish"*
→ *Ellen Bixby Smith paintings called "old school".*
her husband, Paul Jordan-Smith, made joke painting + phony school "Disumbrationists," phony photo receives praise → paints more
Q: purposely use racist, sexist images to mock critics?
→ *eyeballs painting: man going home to angry wife*

1) B

Main Idea Question

The professor implies that Smith started the hoax because he felt that some art critics were "fools," and that he did not like Modern art or "its enthusiastic supporters," so his *joke targeted the art criticism of the day.*

2) B, D

Detail Question

The professor said that Smith created the phony "Disumbrationist" school of art and "had a mock-serious photo taken of himself with comically raised eyebrows," or *made up a school of art* and *submitted a photo of himself making a strange expression.*

3) D

Purpose Question

The professor says Post-Impressionists were experimenting with "abstract, flat" images. She later says that Smith's painting looks "like it was painted by a Post-Impressionist child" to acknowledge that it included characteristics of the style. Thus, the professor says it *to explain why Smith's art might have fooled critics.*

4) C

Inference Question

The student says that "it's almost like he's making fun of the women," or that *the pictures display a superior attitude toward their subjects.*

5) A

Detail Question

The professor quotes the description of the painting as the conscience of a man "anticipating a storm from his indignant wife. He sees her eyes and the lightning of her wrath…" In other words, it supposedly depicts *a man imagining his wife's critical eyes.*

6) B

Inference Question

The professor describes how Paul Jordan-Smith set out to prove that art judges and art critics of his day were easily impressed by bad art, as long as it fit current trends. Thus, Smith could be described as mocking and ridiculing the critics; being, in other words, *irreverent.*

ACTUAL PRACTICE 9 - PRACTICE SET 3

Notes

Death Valley = hottest, driest, lowest place in W. hemisphere
→ *deep channel surrounded by mountains*
→ *formed by earthquakes, called "graben"*
→ *during ice age, housed a large lake*
→ *little rain; has desert plants, animals*
→ *1873, borax deposits discovered*

1) B

Main Idea Question

The professor discusses Death Valley, "which is located in the eastern part of California," and has *some interesting features*, such as being the "hottest, driest, and lowest place in the Western Hemisphere."

2) C, D

Detail Question

The professor claims that Death Valley "is known as the hottest… place in the Western Hemisphere," and that "parts of it lie 86 meters below sea level."

3) B

Detail Question

According to the professor, Death Valley formed from "a large block that dropped down when two earthquakes occurred along its sides."

4) A

Detail Question

The professor says, "during the last ice age (in ancient times)… a large lake occupied Death Valley."

5) D

Detail Question

The professor says that people originally searched Death Valley for gold, but "their real 'goldmine discovery'… was borax deposits."

6) C

Inference Question

According to the professor, there were once many towns in Death Valley, but "the towns died when the [borax] ores were exhausted." Because Death Valley is an extremely hot and dry location, we can infer that today, *Death Valley contains very few human inhabitants*.

ACTUAL PRACTICE 10 - PRACTICE SET 1

Notes

stu. wants to make sure he'll graduate on time
→ *stu. studying lit. and classical studies*
→ *4 of stu.'s lit. classes count toward classical studies major, too*
→ *stu. closer to graduating than he realized*
→ *stu. can graduate 2 quarters early*

1) B

Main Idea Question

The student explains his reason for visiting when he says to the advisor, "I wanted to make sure that I'm on-track with graduation," so the purpose of the conversation is *to determine when the student can graduate*.

2) C, D

Detail Question

The advisor says to the student, "so you're pursuing a double major, in literature and classical studies."

3) C

Purpose Question

In regards to a conversation, the phrase, "I follow you" means, "I understand you." Thus, the student says this *to show that he understands what the advisor is saying*.

4) A

Detail Question

The professor says to the student, "many of your literature classes count toward both majors."

5) D

Inference Question

After the advisor tells the student, "you will be able to graduate two quarters early," the student responds, "Wow, that's great news!" From this interaction, we can infer that the student *can graduate earlier than he expected*.

ACTUAL PRACTICE 10 - PRACTICE SET 2

Notes

living fossil = last species of its kind
lungfish = native to southern continents
→ *breathes air using special bladder*
→ *lives in marshes (low oxygen), gets extra oxygen from breathing air*
→ *around for 400 million years, maybe one of first land animals*
→ *eel-like appearance, up to 2 ½ meters*
→ *scavengers, prey on small swamp animals*
→ *live off air when swamps dry in summer, goes into estivation (summer sleep)*

1) C

Main Idea Question

The professor mainly discusses the lungfish, which is an ancient type of fish with interesting characteristics, such as the ability to survive off air.

2) B

Detail Question

The professor explains that the lungfish "can breathe out of water… by means of a lung-like organ called an air bladder."

3) A

Purpose Question

Here, the professor is explaining that the lungfish has an *odd appearance* because it evolved 400 million years ago, when many organisms had appearances that would be considered strange today.

4) B, D

Detail Question

According to the professor, "lungfish eat mainly small fish, frogs, and snails."

5) C

Detail Question

The professor says, "when the swamps and marshes

ANSWER KEY ♦ APPENDIX 267

where they [lungfish] live dry up (*its habitat becomes too dry*)… they tunnel into the wet mud and remain inactive for months at a time."

6) D

Inference Question

The professor defines hibernation as "a period of little to no activity during the winter," so we can infer that the term translates to *winter sleep*.

ACTUAL PRACTICE 10 - PRACTICE SET 3

Notes

We all like praise
→ *N. Brandon psych. paper: self-esteem = success*
→ *parents, teachers falsely inflate kids' self-esteem*
→ *studies monitor pos. effects of self-esteem (found no support)*
Carol Dweck: how parents praise matters
→ *saying child is intelligent = less learning (fixed mindset)*
→ *praise for learning process = more learning (growth mindset)*
→ *progress is ongoing (brain plasticity)*

1) C

Main Idea Question

The lecture mainly focuses on how praise affects children's motivation to learn. Thus, the lecture addresses *how people's attitude toward learning can be shaped by feedback*.

2) A

Purpose Question

The professor asserts that everyone loves to receive praise and compliments. Thus, he pretends to ask for praise as the "best lecturer ever," admitting in a humous way that he feels the same.

3) C

Detail Question

The professor explains the influence of a 1969 publication connecting high self-esteem to success. It led to adults trying to boost children's self-esteem. They did so by just telling children that they were special or good, or that they were all winners. In other words, *they gave unearned rewards and general praise*.

4) B

Detail Question

Dweck found that in classrooms where teachers praised learning process behaviors such as effort, students learned significantly more. Thus, she concluded that *praise should mainly emphasize specific actions, not overall qualities.*

5) D

Purpose Question

The professor says that "Dweck maintains that the ideal 'growth mindset' does not see failure, but rather achievements that have not been made yet." In other words, "growth mindset" is the view that one can achieve a learning goal with time and effort, and thus *summarizes an optimistic self-concept*.

6) D

Inference Question

A student asks whether the research indicates that people do not have a certain "IQ." The professor does not give a definite answer, but he says that the research he discussed is "pointing" toward brains being more plastic (changeable) than fixed. The implication is that *traits such as intelligence can change*.

ACTUAL PRACTICE 11 - PRACTICE SET 1

Notes

woman's project partners dropped class, she asks to join man's group, project on psych. case study
case study: Genie, "Wild Child" couldn't learn to talk (isolated)
→ *woman will search images of brain, kids talking, for PowerPoint*
Will email anything she finds on language development.

1) B

Main Idea Question

The man correctly guesses the woman's reason for talking to him when he asks, "You want to join my group?" From this, we can conclude that the woman wants to ask the many *if she can join his group for a project*.

2) A

Purpose Question

To be "flustered" means to be "nervous." From the man's tone, we can infer that he commenting on the woman's seeming nervousness *to express concern* for her and to make sure she is okay.

3) C

Detail Question

The woman says that, for the project, groups are supposed to "analyze a famous case study" in psychology.

4) A

Inference Question

The group is presenting information about a child who "couldn't learn to speak," so we can infer that the man asks the woman to find images that will *address normal language development* in the brain.

5) D

Inference Question

After the woman says that the man is more prepared than Sam and Cody, the man says that Sam and Cody "seemed like nice guys, but I wouldn't exactly call them the hardest workers." Here, the man is using understatement to imply that Sam and Cody *put little effort into completing the group project*.

ACTUAL PRACTICE 11 - PRACTICE SET 2

Notes

pop art (1950s/1960s) = art w/ pop culture & consumerism elements
→ *rejected "elite" artistic standards*
→ *influenced by abstract expressionism (shapes, lines, colors*
→ *pop art = anyone can be artist, led to many styles*
Andy Warhol: repeated, enlarged consumerist/pop culture images
Roy Lichtenstein: giant comic strips, make everyday life melodramatic
Claes Oldenburg: large, soft sculptures of everyday objects (beauty of everyday life)

1) C

Main Idea Question

The professor mainly discusses pop art, which is *a style of art that emerged during the mid-twentieth century* (it "flourished mostly during the 1950s and 1960s").

2) D

Detail Question

The professor says, "the term 'pop art' was coined by an art critic during the height of the trend, in 1956," so pop art was most popular in *the 1950s*.

3) B

Inference Question

Because "pop artists were rejecting long-held" beliefs about art by creating new and unusual works, we can infer that they *wanted to redefine what was considered "art."*

4) C, D

Detail Question

The professor explains that "pop artists were rejecting the long-held" beliefs that art has to be "inspired by certain 'proper' themes." In other words, pop art was *a reaction to the strict* artistic *standards of the past*. Moreover, the professor says that pop artists wanted to incorporate "elements of popular culture and consumerism" into their art.

5) A

Purpose Question

When describing abstract expressionism, the professor claims, "abstract expressionism... greatly influenced pop art."

6) A

Inference Question

The professor says, "each pop artist created his or her own style." Thus, the artists in the lecture *had very different styles*, but because they are all mentioned in a lecture about pop art, we can infer that they *are still considered pop artists*.

ACTUAL PRACTICE 11 - PRACTICE SET 3

Notes

continental drift = continents once connected, moving apart (supported by the shapes of continents)
Alfred Wegener = 20th c. scientist, compiled evidence for continental drift
→ *found paper saying that same plant found across ocean*
→ *found tropic plant fossils in Arctic (Arctic once tropical, then moved)*
→ *used geographic evidence (Brazil and Africa have similar features)*
→ *published that all continents once together, Pangea (1915)*
→ *no one believed him b/c he didn't explain how continents move*
1950s/1960s, sci. discover valleys/mountains on ocean floor, shows sea-floor movement, tectonic plates
→ *earth crust = lithosphere, sits atop asthenosphere (magma)*

1) D

Main Idea Question

The main topic of the lecture is the theory of continental drift, which was a *controversial theory* when it was first proposed, but it *slowly gained acceptance* because of the work of Alfred Wegener and because of the discovery of plate tectonics.

2) B, C

Detail Question

The professor says that Wegener developed his theory of continental drift after reading "a scientific paper stating that fossils of the same plant species were found on… either side of the Atlantic Ocean (*a document of a fossil discovery*)," and after noticing "that the continents appeared to fit together."

3) C

Purpose Question

After the professor mentions that early cartographers noted that the continents appeared to "fit together like puzzle pieces," he points out that "this observation led to early proposals of continental drift."

4) A

Purpose Question

Because the professor makes a point of saying that "Wegener was not the first person to" suggest continental drift, we can infer that the professor is *clarifying that Wegener was building on the assertions of previous scientists* rather than introducing an entirely new theory.

5) B

Detail Question

The professor says, "when the scientific community read about his idea of continental drift, they absolutely hated it," so the attitude of the scientific community was *skeptical*, at best.

6) C

Detail Question

According to the professor, the lithosphere "sits atop the asthenosphere, which is… constantly being moved around by heat current from below."

ACTUAL PRACTICE 12 - PRACTICE SET 1

Notes

stu. wants to learn about being an RA

how to become RA:
→ *fill out application, interview, answer questions*
RA duties:
→ *ensure student safety (check for drugs), enforce rules, ensure student comfort*
→ *prof. understanding if RA duties get in the way of schoolwork*
RA benefits:
→ *free food and housing*
→ *getting to know first-year stu.*
RA downsides
→ *time consuming (affects social life)*
stu. going to fill out RA application

1) D

Main Idea Question

The student explains the purpose of the conversation when he says to the RA, "I was wondering if you could tell me a little bit about being an RA."

2) A, C

Detail Question

The RA says, "Our number one goal is to ensure the students' safety." She also says that RAs "are also supposed to enforce dorm rules."

3) B

Inference Question

Because professors allow resident assistants to put their RA duties before schoolwork on occasion by giving extensions on assignments, we can infer that *most professors understand that RAs have busy schedules*.

4) C

Detail Question

The RA says, "the free dorm room and meal plan are the best part of being an RA."

5) B

Purpose Question

The RA says this when she is describing the benefits of being an RA. We can infer that she finds helping first-year students rewarding, so she says this *to explain why she enjoys interacting with first-year students.*

ACTUAL PRACTICE 12 - PRACTICE SET 2

Notes

Gettysburg Address = speech by Lincoln during Civil War

(1863)
→ *during dedication of Gettysburg as cemetery*
→ *powerful speech, meant to inspire Union*
→ *Lincoln wrote 5 version of the speech, changed it as he spoke*

myth that many disliked speech (Rep. liked, dem. disliked)

Edward Everett main speaker that day, praised Lincoln's speech

Next class will read speech from textbook

1) D

   Main Idea Question

   In the lecture, the professor mainly gives *some background information* about the Gettysburg Address, which is *a famous American speech.*

2) B

   Inference Question

   Because the professor says that Lincoln's speech "reshaped the nation," and remains "among the best remembered in American history," we can infer that *the speech resonated with Americans even after the Civil War had ended.*

3) B

   Detail Question

   The professor says that Lincoln "held this second version in his hand during the address," so we can conclude that he read from the *second version* of his speech during the Gettysburg Address.

4) A

   Inference Question

   The professor says that Lincoln's speech "reshaped the nation by defining it as one people dedicated to one principle—that of equality." Thus, we can infer that he changed the speech to emphasize the need for unification during the Civil War. In other words, Lincoln hoped *to convey sentiments that could unite the entire country* by appealing to the nation's shared belief in God.

5) D

   Detail Question

   The professor says that one of the "many false stories" about the Gettysburg Address is that "the people of Lincoln's time did not like the speech."

6) C

   Purpose Question

Everett's letter to Lincoln said that Lincoln's speech was concise and powerful, so we can infer that Everett wanted *to praise the speech Lincoln made at Gettysburg.*

ACTUAL PRACTICE 12 - PRACTICE SET 3

Notes

ozone = rare form of oxygen
→ *ozone in low atm. combines with carbon dioxide and makes smog*
→ *ozone in upper atm. (ozone layer) blocks radiation*
→ *ozone layer repairing*

ozone layer = stratosphere
→ *blocks all UV-c, most UV-a/-b*
→ *20th c. = CFC/human activity damaged ozone layer*

1978, U.S. bans CFCs; 1983, Canada bans CFCs; 1995, Europe bans CFCs
→ *1987, Montreal Protocol (22 nations agree to reduce CFCs)*

recent years have shown evidence of ozone repair

1) C

   Main Idea Question

   The professor spends most of the lecture talking about the efforts taken to repair the ozone layer through *international bans on some chemical compounds* called CFCs.

2) C

   Detail Question

   The professor says, "The ozone layer is vital for Earth's health because it blocks harmful radiation from the sun."

3) D

   Detail Question

   According to the professor, scientists thought that "CFCs were a perfect chemical product: inexpensive, inflammable, and non-toxic."

4) A, C

   Detail Question

   The professor says, "In 1978, the U.S. banned the use of all CFCs…. It was not until 1983 that Canada did the same."

5) D

   Purpose Question

   The professor says that the U.S. "began an important movement to change international attitudes toward CFCs," so we can infer that he mentions the U.S.'s actions *to show that individual countries can take initiatives on global issues.*

6) B

Inference Question

At the end of the lecture, the professor says that "the ozone layer was showing early signs of becoming thicker" as of 2014. Because the professor is focusing on the improvements to the ozone layer, we can infer that he is *optimistic*.

ACTUAL PRACTICE 13 - PRACTICE SET 1

Notes

stu. 1st day of work, training, dining hall
→ *stu. worked in her aunt's restaurant*
manager: jokes, "you train me"
→ *discusses hand-wash policy (sing "Happy B-day")*
stu. asks about dining hall scheduling
→ *manager scheduled stu. for Mon, Wed, Fri, Sat, Sun (20 hrs./week)*
→ *senior workers get priority for scheduling*
→ *weeknight shifts most difficult, weekend shifts usually easy*
stu. gets free dining hall meals when on duty

1) B

Main Idea Question

The manager reveals the main topic of the conversation when he says to the student, "I'm to train you as a server, is that it?" Thus, the purpose of the conversation is for the student *to receive training for a new job.*

2) C

Inference Question

The student reveals that she has a lot of experience working in food service, so we can infer that the manager says this to imply that *the student seems very qualified for her new job* as a server.

3) D

Purpose Question

The professor tells the student to wash her hands "for at least as long as it takes you to sing 'Happy Birthday'." From this, we can infer that he mentions the song to explain the university's *hand washing policies for employees.*

4) A, B

Detail Question

The manager explains to the student, "we have you put your class schedule and other commitments on your job application" so that the manager can *work around* employees' *school schedules and other commitments.* He also says that "students who have worked here longer have the opportunity to pick and choose their hours more."

5) A

Inference Question

The manager claims, "weeknight shifts… can be really hard," while "weekends, on the other hand, can be positively quiet." From this, we can infer that working on weekends is *often much easier than working on weeknights.*

ACTUAL PRACTICE 13 - PRACTICE SET 2

Notes

Vesuvius = Italian volcano, destroyed Roman cities of Pompeii and Herculaneum
→ *erupted in 79 CE, killed 16,000*
→ *eruptions preserved Roman cities, giving archaeologists useful info.*
Pompeii = trading city, SE of Vesuvius
Herculaneum = resort town, W of Vesuvius
Romans didn't realize Vesuvius was volcano
events of the eruption:
→ *ash and debris blown over Pompeii, no Herc.*
→ *pyroclastic surge (hot rock/gas) covers Herc, killing all left in city*
excavation of Pompeii begins in 1500s, Herc. excavated 150 years later
→ *1981 = skeletons found (Roman skeletons rare b/c of cremation)*

1) C

Main Idea Question

The professor talks about the *volcanic eruption* of Vesuvius, and she described *its effects on* the *nearby Roman cities* of Pompeii and Herculaneum.

2) B

Purpose Question

The professor says, "Vesuvius is located on Italy's western coast, very close to the present-day city of Naples." Here, the professor mentions Naples *to help explain the geographical location of Vesuvius* by naming a city that may be familiar to students.

3) D

Detail Question

According to the professor, "as far as we can tell, the inhabitants didn't even realize Vesuvius was a volcano."

4) B

Inference Question

Later in the lecture, the professor reveals that the Romans who waited in Herculaneum's port were killed by a pyroclastic surge. Thus, the professor is implying that they would have fled the city, but *they did not realize the how much danger they were in.*

5) A

Inference Question

Pompeii was primarily covered by ash from Vesuvius' initial eruption while Herculaneum was "covered with nearly 75 feet of volcanic ash" from a series of pyroclastic surges. From this, we can infer that *Herculaneum was buried under more debris than Pompeii was.*

6) A

Detail Question

According to the professor, "Romans traditionally cremated their dead, meaning Roman skeletons are very rare."

ACTUAL PRACTICE 13 - PRACTICE SET 3

Notes

tariffs raise $ for gov.; three types

1) *transit tariff*

   tax on goods that pass through a country on their way to another; no longer used (popular 16th-19th c.); transportation/changing attitudes led to decline

2) *export tariff*

   meant to encourage domestic industries; + meet local demand (ie. food); first used by England (13th c.); free trade principles lead to its demise (19th c.)

3) *import tariff*

   most common tax today; makes imports to more expensive, protects domestic industries, raise: $ for gov.; hard for gov. to predict

1) A

Main Idea Question

The professor talks about *the history and purposes of three different types of tariffs*: transit tariffs, export tariffs, and import tariffs.

2) C, D

Detail Question

The professor reveals two reasons for imposing tariffs when he says, "One primary purpose of tariffs is to raise money for the governments that impose them. But tariffs may also be used to protect domestic industries."

3) D

Purpose Question

At the end of the lecture, the student claims that governments estimating revenue from import tariffs is "like the government trying to predict the stock market." Thus, the student is *creating an analogy that helps him to understand import tariffs*.

4) D

Inference Question

When something "comes into the picture," it means that something has become relevant or important. Thus, we can infer that the student believes that *import tariffs started*, or became relevant, *when export tariffs ended*.

5)

A, F	B, E	C, D

Inference Question

The professor claims that **transit tariffs** were important "from the 16th century until the middle of the 19th century." He also describes these tariffs as "taxes placed on things that originate in one country, pass through a second country, and arrive in a third." The professor says that **export tariffs** "were very common during the early stages of the Industrial Revolution," and they were meant "to keep goods from leaving a country." Finally, the professor says that **import tariffs** "are the most commonly used trade tariffs today," and "they tax goods coming into a country."

ACTUAL PRACTICE 14 - PRACTICE SET 1

Notes

stu. needs help finding info. for research project (pine trees)

→ *lib. recommends encyclopedia (has general info.)*

→ *stu. says he needs a "field guide,"*

project = identify types of pine trees on campus

→ *lib. wonders if there's an app. for identifying trees (ie., one for identifying birds)*

→ lib. recommends photographing trees, then using reference guides

1) A

Main Idea Question

The student explains the purpose of the conversation when he says to the librarian, "I was wondering if you could help me locate some information for a research project I'm doing."

2) D

Detail Question

The librarian says, "I still recommend paper-and-print encyclopedias sometimes. After all, they are very reliable sources (*trustworthy*), and easy to use."

3) A

Inference Question

After the student describes his assignment, the librarian says, "Oh, how interesting! That sounds like a fascinating project." From this, we can infer that the librarian is *enthusiastic* about helping the student on his assignment.

4) B

Purpose Question

The librarian says that the bird identification application was very useful, so she implies *that there may be a similar app for identifying trees* that the student can use for his project.

5) D

Purpose Question

At this point in the conversation, the librarian has helped the student find many resources for his project. Thus, we can infer that the student says, "That kind of thing sounds perfect," to show that the librarian has provided good advice and *to express appreciation for the librarian's efforts*.

ACTUAL PRACTICE 14 - PRACTICE SET 2

Notes

1930s Jews forced out of Germany (Nazis), influenced culture in U.S.
→ *Kurt Weill teen years → played for opera during WWI*
→ *after WWI, Weill = composer in Berlin*
→ *wrote The Three-Penny Opera (incl. song "Mack the Knife")*
→ *criticized Nazis with The Pledge, The Silver Lake*
→ *In U.S. wrote music for Broadway (ex. Street Scene w/ Langston Hughes), included jazz and blues*

1) D

Main Idea Question

The professor mentions that many European Jews who immigrated to the U.S. in the 1930s had a "profound effect on American arts and sciences," and then focuses on Weill. We can conclude that *she mainly wants to describe a unique contribution to American culture*.

2) B

Inference Question

The professor says that during the 1920s, the city was a "fabulous" place for a "budding composer." She describes a thriving music scene with eager audiences. Thus, we can conclude that there were *many opportunities for musical composers to find work*.

3) D

Detail Question

The professor explains that in *The Three-Penny Opera*, "Weill's cheery, jazzy tunes" are ironic because the characters "betray and cheat each other." Thus, *the music's mood is upbeat even when its characters are acting despicably*.

4) C

Detail Question

We learn from the lecture that Weill worked on plays that could be seen as "allegories of the Nazis seizing power and exiling intellectuals and Jews." Thus, *Weill's work indirectly criticized Nazi goals and policies*.

5) B

Detail Question

The professor says that Weill wanted to "synthesize a new American sound" using classical music with jazz and the blues, and fuse "European opera with more natural spoken dialogue." Thus he wanted to be involved in *productions that would combine classical opera, jazz, and naturalistic spoken word*.

6) A

Purpose Question

Langston Hughes is admiring Weill's artistry in the quote, particularly because it is "truly universal." The quote suggests that, in Hughes' opinion, Weill sincerely and capably used what he absorbed from hearing African American performers. Thus, the quote asserts *Weill's open attitudes and musical skill.*

ACTUAL PRACTICE 14 - PRACTICE SET 3

Notes

"shooting stars" actually matter from outer space
meteoroid = before Earth
meteor = in atmos.
meteorite = landed
→ *meteoroids composed of stone, silicon and oxygen (come from asteroid belt btwn. Mars and Jupiter) or metal (from ast. belt, too),*
→ *nickel, iron (like planet core) shows that asteroid belt may be unformed planet*
tektites: debris from Earth, ejected when meteorite hits
→ *falls back near met. impact site*

1) B

Main Idea Question

Throughout the lecture, the professor discusses the origins and different types of meteoroids, so we can conclude that the main topic is *the characteristics and classification of meteoroids.*

2) A

Detail Question

The professor says that "before they encounter Earth's atmosphere," they are called "meteoroids"; once they are in the atmosphere, they are meteors; and when they reach Earth, they become meteorites. Thus, the different labels are based on *their location in relation to Earth's atmosphere.*

3) C

Purpose Question

The professor says, "Like almost all meteoroids, stony meteoroids are thought to come from the asteroid belt," so mentioning the "asteroid belt" *explains where most meteors originate.*

4) B, D

Detail Question

The female student says, "And aren't the cores of most planets also made of iron and nickel?" The professor confirms her answer, indicating that *iron and nickel comprise the cores of most planets.*

5) C

Detail Question

The professor says, "most astronomers believe that tektites are actually chunks of debris from Earth."

6) B

Purpose Question

The professor adds this disclaimer to emphasize that the information to follow is merely one among many theories about tektites. Therefore, she is acknowledging *other explanations for tektites.*

ACTUAL PRACTICE 15 - PRACTICE SET 1

Notes

stu. needs to find parking, looking for "Tremont Theater"→ going to see friend's concert
→ *stu. can't remember theater name, clerk tries to help by looking on school website*
→ *stu. texts friend, friend says concert at "Tree Frog Café," stu. asks for directions there*
→ *clerk gives directions, says to park in Student Lot 8*
stu. purchases temporary parking pass
clerk says campus parking = confusing

1) C

Main Idea Question

The student reveals her reason for visiting when she says to the clerk, "I'm looking for a place to park by the theater." From this, we can conclude that she is *asking about on-campus parking for an upcoming event.*

2) B

Purpose Question

After the clerk says, "let's figure out which theater we're talking about here," the student responds, "I'll try texting my friend." From this, we can infer that she is texting her friend *to find out the location of an event.*

3) A

Purpose Question

The student is talking to the clerk to get directions to an on-campus event, so when she says, "I have no idea how to get [to the café] from this side of campus," we can assume that she is *explaining why she needs directions to the café.*

4) D

Inference Question

The clerk notices that the student's car does not have parking sticker, and he tells her that she can buy a temporary one for $2. The student responds, "Good idea," implying that she will buy one from him.

5) C

Inference Question

Because the professor says, "a lot of students have trouble understanding the on-campus parking system. Heck, sometimes I don't even understand it," we can infer that the campus parking *frequently causes confusion*.

ACTUAL PRACTICE 15 - PRACTICE SET 2

Notes

déjà vu = "already seen," feeling "I've experienced this before"
→ 70% of people
→ still poorly studied
déjà vecu = "already experienced," more specific described by Dickens
déjà visité = "already visited," familiarity with a new place, ex. of familiar museum
déjà vu causes:
→ misfiring neurons (brain mistake)
→ still a mystery

1) B

Main Idea Question

The professor discusses déjà vu experiences, which are feelings "of already having experienced something." Thus, déjà vu is *a strange experience related to memory*.

2) A, B

Detail Question

The professor says, "about seventy percent of the population (*a majority of people*) have reported experiencing déjà vu at least once," and "in laboratory settings, it is extremely difficult to invoke… déjà vu."

3) D

Inference Question

If someone claims that a description "paints a pretty good picture," it means that the description was clear and accurate. Thus, we can infer that *Dickens' description of déjà vécu is very accurate*.

4) C

Purpose Question

After the professor describes déjà visité, he says, "For instance, say you're walking through a museum." Thus the phrase "For instance" indicates that the museum serves *to introduce an example of déjà visité*.

5) B

Detail Question

According to the professor, déjà vu occurs because "brain cells are firing to create the impression that one has been somewhere or done something before, when in fact one has never had these experiences," so it is caused by *misfiring brain cells*.

6) A

Inference Question

The professor indicates that *déjà vu experiences remain poorly understood* when he says, "little research has been done on the phenomenon," and "it remains a poorly studied topic."

ACTUAL PRACTICE 15 - PRACTICE SET 3

Notes

scams offer quick, easy money = "get-rich-quick schemes"
→ two kinds: employment scam, investment seminar
emp. scam: no exp., pay too much, work @ home, require investment
→ job is sales, person buys product from scammer, but prod. hard to sell
→ easy to spot: targets young, ignorant
invest. seminar: advertise "secret formula" for wealth
→ person buys ticket to learn
→ invest. strat. no good
→ use testimonial for advert.
real way to get rich quick: high risk stock
→ not guaranteed, could lose lots

1) D

Main Idea Question

The professor says, "Today, I would like to talk about scams that promise participants a quick, fast, and easy method for making large amounts of money." In other words, *scams about getting rich*.

2) B

Inference Question

The professor says, "The advice given by these so-called experts turns out to be mediocre and certainly never produces the level of profit promised." Thus, we can infer that *almost no one really makes money from the strategies outlined in investment seminars.*

3) A

Detail Question

The professor says that employment scams are easy to catch, so victims are often young and desperate.

4) A, D

Detail Question

When the professor introduces employment scams, he mentions that they "offer the 'employee' the opportunity to work from home." He also says they "require participants to provide an initial investment."

5) C

Purpose Question

The professor discusses the potential of high-risk stock to produce high returns and uses Microsoft and Apple as examples of this. Thus, he is *giving examples of high risk investments that succeeded.*

6) A

Detail Question

The professor explains that high-risk stock has the potential to produce high returns, or to lose its entire value. Therefore, *risky stocks have the potential to produce high returns.*

ACTUAL PRACTICE 16 - PRACTICE SET 1

Notes

prof.: upset with midterm grade?
stu.: no, extension on assignment, having trouble, has work tonight (at radio station)
prof.: Ok, turn in Fri. to class website
stu. understands material, ok on midterm, talked to TA, stu. thinks she wrote "bad code"
prof.: coding addicting, asks stu. about her job
stu.: radio station technician, fixes transmitter

1) D

Main Idea Question

The student explains her reason for visiting when she says to the professor, "I was wondering if I could get an extension on the programming assignment that's due tomorrow."

2) C

Detail Question

The professor says to the student, "You upset about your grade on the midterm? I've had a lot of students in here about that today." From this, we can conclude that many students *are upset with their low midterm grades.*

3) D

Purpose Question

After the student requests an extension, the professor says, "Just submit it via the class website." Thus, the professor mentions the website *to tell the student where to turn in her assignment.*

4) A

Purpose Question

We can infer that the professor is trying *to encourage the student* because he makes supportive comments such as "you are on the right track."

5) B

Inference Question

The student says that her friend "loves coding so much, he forgets to eat and sleep," which implies that her programmer friend is *extremely committed to his work*, and the professor agrees that this is true of most programmers.

ACTUAL PRACTICE 16 - PRACTICE SET 2

Notes

contemporary writers w/ conversational tone and extraordinary meaning
(ex) Gary Soto, grandson of Mexican immigrants
Soto's parents and grandparents worked ag. jobs in CA
→ father died in factory, family moved
Soto's poetry: coping w/poverty, prejudice
→ Soto = Mex. American but not all poems Mex. Am. images
→ (ex) "Oranges" wordless communication w/clerk
→ (ex) "Mexicans Begin Jogging" = ironic b/c Soto is American, running from Border Patrol

1) D

Main Idea Question

The professor starts the lecture by announcing that she will talk about "contemporary writers who seek a kind of realism, a kind of coherence…" She then focuses on one example, Gary Soto, and describes his *background and artistry.*

2) C

Inference Question

The professor describes Gary Soto as a protégé of

Philip Levine. She describes how Philip Levine typically wrote about a "mundane scene (that) nevertheless surprises the reader by delivering some extraordinary meaning." Thus, we can infer that Levine *inspired Soto to write meaningful poetry about ordinary events.*

3) B

Purpose Question

Since later in the lecture the professor points out that "all writers seek to find something universal within personal experiences," the professor probably offers information about Soto's childhood to *suggest connections between Soto's life and his writing.*

4) A

Detail Question

The professor summarizes the poem by saying that the narrator and a girl walk to a small store, where the girl picks out candy that he does not have enough money to buy. The professor says, "The lady working at the store deduces his dilemma, and, as though a silent message passes between them, she accepts a coin and an orange as payment;" *she helps him.*

5) C

Purpose Question

The context of the quote is a discussion about to what extent Soto is a "Latino writer." Using a quote allows Soto to explain his personal artistic goal: "As a writer, my duty is *not to make people perfect, particularly Mexican Americans.* I'm not a cheerleader. I'm one who provides portraits of people in the rush of life."

6) D

Inference Question

The professor says that the poem is one of her favorites. She describes how it uses ironic humor and how it turns the reader's expectations "upside down." Thus, she explains the cleverness of the poem, and we can infer that her attitude is *admiring.*

ACTUAL PRACTICE 16 - PRACTICE SET 3

Notes

orchids = over 20,000 species; various colors, sizes, shapes; on every continent but Antarctica
→ *many exported from tropical areas, some must be protected from extinction*
orchid characteristics
→ *some are epiphytes (air plants), some lithophytes (rock plants)*
→ *absorb nutrients from the surrounding air*
→ *3 petals, 3 sepals, 1 central 'lip'*
→ *lip structure: for pollinators to land on, has stamen (male) and pistil (female)*
→ *many ways of attracting pollinators:*
  make lip look like female insect, attract males
  attract using sugary nectar
  spray nectar, pollen sticks to pollinator

1) C

Main Idea Question

The professor talks "about some of the features of orchids," including their *physical and botanical characteristics.*

2) D

Purpose Question

The professor wants *to emphasize the popularity of orchids* when he says that orchids "are widely cultivated," and "Perhaps you even have one in your dormitory or apartment," implying that many people keep them as houseplants.

3) B, C

Detail Question

According to the professor, people like orchids because they "come in a variety of colors, scents, and shapes," and "because they can survive in almost any type of climate."

4) B

Purpose Question

The professor says, "orchids are the diamonds or the ivory of the plant world" because like these valuable products, rare orchids were being collected in a way that threatened the extinction of species, or some other harm.

5) A

Detail Question

The professor says, "orchids obtain their nourishment from long, spongy aerial roots that absorb moisture and nutrients from the air."

6) A, D

Detail Question

According to the professor, in some orchids "the plant's lip may look so much like a female insect" that it attracts male pollinator insects. Other orchids "expel nectar onto" pollinators to "make them crawl with wet wings past the waiting pollen."

ACTUAL PRACTICE 17 - PRACTICE SET 1

Notes

stu. visiting rhetoric prof.
→ *stu. studies biochem., wants to improve public speaking*
→ *main topic: stu. having trouble with final project (making persuasive video)*
→ *wants to discuss burning plastic, right now too boring*
→ *stu. talks about trash incinerator in his hometown; prof. says he should focus on that, interview townspeople*
prof. explains that personal experience good for rhetoric
→ *recommends that stu. find int'l stu. to interview for counterargument*

1) A

Main Idea Question

The student explains that he needs *advice on his final project* when he says to the professor, "the only problem is that I'm kind of stuck on the final project."

2) C

Detail Question

The student reveals why he wants to study public speaking when he says, "I have always been afraid to make speeches to big audiences. But I really want to be able to make speeches."

3) C

Inference Question

Because students would not be interested in a presentation where someone simply gave the "names of chemicals," we can infer that the professor's comment means that *the student's presentation may bore his classmates* if it contains "too much science information."

4) B, C

Detail Question

For the student's project, the professor recommends that the student go to his old neighborhood to "get video footage of the incinerator, and interview people." The professor also says to the student, "you can't just ignore the opposing viewpoint," and she recommends that he *include an opposing viewpoint in his presentation.*

5) D

Purpose Question

After the professor asks, "how did you get interested in this topic?" the student starts by saying, "when I was a kid." From this, we can infer that the student mentions his childhood *to explain how he got the idea for his project's topic.*

ACTUAL PRACTICE 17 - PRACTICE SET 2

Notes

Bees: important ecologically & commercially
life cycle: colonies regenerate
→ *eggs in honeycomb hive, laid by queen*
→ *all workers female, larva w/ spec. diet = queen*
→ *males: unfertilized egg, only mate, then die*
young workers: feed larvae, store nectar, expand hive
→ *later, guard hive, then search for food most of life*
workers scout place for new hive, then queen escorted and new hive built
→ *queen lays eggs, populates new colony*
during winter, bees stay in hive, shiver to keep warm
→ *spring, queen lays eggs, workers find food*

1) D

Main Idea Question

At the beginning of the lecture, the professor says, "I'd like to introduce everyone's favorite insect: the honeybee." Throughout the lecture, she describes the birth, death, and work of honeybees. In other words, she discusses *the lifecycle and habits of honeybees.*

2) B

Detail Question

When describing worker bees, the professor says, "workers spend most of their lives coming and going from the hive, searching for and storing nectar, and looking for water and other resources." In other words, they are *looking for food.*

3) B

Inference Question

The professor explains that queen bees lay eggs in the honeycomb of the hive. Because queen bees spend the majority of their lives laying eggs, we can infer that *queen bees rarely leave the hive.*

4) C

Purpose Question

The professor explains that males (drones), either die after mating, or get forced out of the hive. Therefore, in terms of daily life in the hive, she *emphasizes the insignificance of drones.*

5) B, D

Detail Question

The professor explains that "young worker bees take care of the hive and feed the larvae." She adds, "Later, they guard the hive."

ACTUAL PRACTICE 17 - PRACTICE SET 3

Notes

murder trial 1921: Sacco and Vanzetti Trial
S. & V. convicted, executed for crime they didn't do
S. & V. immigrated to U.S. when racism against Sicilians common, involved in anarchy, draft-dodgers
S. & V. worked at shoe factory, factory robbed, 1 employee killed
→ S. & V. accused b/c reputation
judge biased, racist, refused testimony from Italians
→ S. & V. convicted, executed despite public outcry, gangster confessing

1) B

Main Idea Question

The professor describes the main topic as "one of the most sensational murder trials in United States history...." In other words, the main topic is *an American legal case that caused a great deal of strife and agitation.*

2) A

Purpose Question

The student says, "I remember reading about [the Sacco and Vanzetti Trial] in my high school history textbook." From this, we can infer that she mentions her textbook *to indicate where she first learned of the case.*

3) D

Purpose Question

The professor explains that "there was a great deal of discrimination and racism toward Italian immigrants" at the time of the Sacco and Vanzetti Trial, and many people feared "political conspiracies," so they did not trust anarchists. Thus, these facts *explain why many Americans distrusted Sacco and Vanzetti.*

4) C

Inference Question

After the student says, "I thought these types of practices [judge and jury bias] were illegal under the American system of justice," the professor responds, "They are. But that didn't stop the judge and jury from doing it!" From this, we can infer that Judge Thayer *broke the law to ensure that Sacco and Vanzetti were found guilty.*

5) C

Purpose Question

The professor says, "Famous American and European intellectuals campaigned for a retrial," implying a high-profile effort and thus *showing that many people felt the trial was unjust.*

6) B, D

Detail Question

The professor claims that the trial "strengthened organizations that fight for people's civil liberties," and it "was regularly discussed in America for almost 50 years," so the trial *became a part of American history.*

ACTUAL PRACTICE 18 - PRACTICE SET 1

Notes

stu. needs help finding Arabic roots of English words
lib.: sounds interesting
→ recommends looking in OED, print and online versions; not detailed enough
→ recommends looking up "word origins" or "etymology" to find info. in library/digital library
→ recommends asking Arabic profs. about other resources

1) C

Main Idea Question

The student explains the main topic of the conversation when she says to the librarian, "I was looking for information about the origins of several English words. I was wondering if you could help me."

2) A

Inference Question

Because the student says, "This is a pretty recent assignment, actually," we can infer that *she has not had much time to work on* her project yet.

3) A, C

Detail Question

The librarian says that the OED is "the source people traditionally turn to for information about words in English," because *it contains much valuable information*. And when the student asks if the OED is "available online," the librarian says, "Yes…. The library subscribes to the OED."

4) C, D

Detail Question

The librarian says, "we have books on our shelves that… tell the histories of many words," and he recommends that the student "access the digital academic journals that we [the library] subscribe to."

5) B

Purpose Question

The librarian says that the Arabic professors on campus "probably have resources that I [the librarian] wouldn't know about," so we can infer that the student should visit professor of Arabic *to ask them for resources for her project*.

ACTUAL PRACTICE 18 - PRACTICE SET 2

Notes

ethics = study of "good life," right and wrong
Plato and Aristotle revol. philosophy
Plato: all people desire happiness
→ diff. from Epicurus (Plato includes idea of soul)
→ diff. from Christian view (Plato says bad behavior from not knowing)
→ 4 virtues = wisdom, courage, self-control, justice
Aristotle: Plato's student
→ extended many ideas, added new virtues
→ did not describe how to achieve "good life"

1) A

Main Idea Question

The professor spends most of the lecture describing *the ethical systems of two Greek philosophers*: Plato and Aristotle.

2) C

Purpose Question

The student says that Plato's "philosophy sounds like another Greek philosopher… Epicurus." From this, we can infer that she mentions Epicurus *to try to connect Epicurus' and Plato's* philosophical *views*.

3) B

Detail Question

The professor claims, "for Plato, the basic problem of ethics is a problem of knowledge," but for Christian philosophers, "'bad' behavior is a problem of the will." Thus, *Plato claimed that ethical behavior requires knowledge, not will.*

4) B, C

Detail Question

According to the professor, Plato believed that wisdom is the source of all other virtues, and similarly, Aristotle credited "good judgement." Both men also described what the good life or a good person is like, but not how to get there.

5) D

Detail Question

The professor says that "like Plato, Aristotle describes what the good life or a good person is like, but he provides no prescription for how to get there." Thus, *they do not explain how a person can become virtuous.*

6) B

Inference Question

The student criticizes Plato and Aristotle for discussing virtues without explaining how to become more virtuous. Therefore, *he believes Plato's system of ethics is missing an important component.*

ACTUAL PRACTICE 18 - PRACTICE SET 3

Notes

brain areas are part of a network
question: pathways between?
EEG: sensors on scalp, shows elec. signals in brain
→ Uni. Wisconsin research shows direction of elec. signals
→ part. watch video: signals flow from occipital to parietal lobes (from low to high processing)
→ part. imagine scenery: signals flow from parietal to occipital (high to low)
→ research may help discoveries/cures
   (ex. epilepsy, schizophrenia); (ex. sleep)

1) D

Main Idea Question

The professor primarily describes a study on an algorithm that researchers used "to isolate the direction (flow) of particular electric signals in the brain."

2) B

Purpose Question

The professor introduces the experiment by saying, "...in 2014, a group of researchers at the University of Wisconsin tested out an algorithm..." In other words, she mentioned the university *to explain where the experiment described in the lecture took place*.

3) A

Inference Question

The professor says that before the experiment, researchers were only able to hypothesize about the direction of signals in the brain. Thus, the goal of this experiment was to see if a new algorithm could isolate them.

4) A, C

Detail Question

The professor says that when subjects were asked to watch a video, the sensory information flowed from a (lower-order) integrating center to a (higher-order) processing center; when they were asked to imagine, the signals went the *opposite* way.

5) C

Purpose Question

The professor uses the specific disorders as examples of conditions that "appear to be caused by abnormal connectivity" in the brain.

6) D

Inference Question

The professor says that the new algorithm may "lead to insights about normal brain activities, such as sleeping," which indicates that sleeping is not well understood and is *somewhat mysterious to neurologists*.

ACTUAL PRACTICE 19 - PRACTICE SET 1

Notes

stu. wants to apply for summer field study on Columbia R.
→ *to apply stu. must complete 3 marine bio. classes w/ "B" average, be in good shape*
→ *stu. qualified (good grades, used to wrestle, rides bikes) about the field study:*
→ *stay in cabin/tent, wake up early*
→ *most time spent analyzing data, some time repairing fish ladder (stu. likes outdoor work)*

1) A

Main Idea Question

The student says that he wants to "apply for the summer field study," which is a *special marine biology course*.

2) B, C

Detail Question

The student describes a prerequisite when he says, "I know that I need to complete all three marine biology classes." In addition, the professor says that he needs "to make sure that students are physically fit enough to do the work," so they *must be in good physical condition*.

3) A

Detail Question

The student says, "I was a wrestler in high school," and "I ride my mountain bike to school and around campus."

4) D

Inference Question

The student says, "When I was in high school, I always tried to find a job where I could work outside," so we can conclude that *he enjoys working outside and does not mind messy work*.

5) B

Inference Question

The professor mentions that a fish ladder "helps salmon get up and over a dam" on the river; thus he implies that *the salmon run's natural course has been blocked by a dam*.

ACTUAL PRACTICE 19 - PRACTICE SET 2

Notes

geophagy = practice of eating dirt
→ *practiced for millions of years, mostly in pre-industrial societies*
→ *Documented in S. America 200 years ago, thought to be practiced by primitive cultures (also practiced in N. Europe)*
As dietary supplement:
→ *geophagy most common among children/pregnant woman, supplies minerals ie. calcium, iron,*
also for stomach ache, antibacterial etc.
useful in food prep. to neutralize toxins in food
In U.S., African immigrants in South ate clay
As religious ritual
→ *Central Amer. Catholic eat clay cakes w/ religious images*

→ Pakistani Muslims eat special clay dust

1) C

Main Idea Question

The professor discusses wide-ranging cases of geophagy, which is the *worldwide dietary and religious practice of* eating soil or clay.

2) D

Detail Question

The professor says that these tribes cannot "hunt or fish for several months each year because of flooding rivers," so they supplement their diet with clay.

3) B

Purpose Question

Here, the professor is *providing a playful response* by implying that the student is asking if geophagy is practiced in America because the student might want to eat dirt herself because she is hungry.

4) C

Detail Question

The professor says that clay "contains important minerals and vitamins that are not available in the local diet."

5) D

Inference Question

Because the professor says that certain clays serve as dietary supplements and act as "ingredients in medicines for nausea and diarrhea," we can infer that he believes that geophagy *is a beneficial and sometimes necessary practice*.

6) B

Purpose Question

The professor mentions geophagy as part of religious practices in separate hemisphere (Central America and Pakistan) in two world religions. Thus, we can infer that the professor wants *to emphasize how widespread the practice of geophagy is*.

ACTUAL PRACTICE 19 - PRACTICE SET 3

Notes

industry terms

→ concentration = how much production comes from few businesses; fewer businesses control most of an industry = high concentration (ex. Proctor and Gamble detergent)

→ economies of scale = increased production lowers production costs (ex. Nike); benefits big businesses

→ entry barriers = obstacles that prevent new businesses from competing in an industry

→ diversified = a business that produces a variety of unrelated goods (ex. Time Warner); diversification = financial security

1) D

Main Idea Question

The professor explains the main topic of the lecture when she says, "I'd like to review some of the terms we will be using to describe industries during this unit."

2) C

Purpose Question

The professor explains, "A highly concentrated industry… is known as an oligopoly," and "Proctor and Gamble… is said to have an oligopoly on that market." From this, we can conclude that Proctor and Gamble serves as *an example of a business in a highly concentrated industry*.

3) B

Purpose Question

Because the professor begins with the word "Basically…" we can infer that what follows will be a *simplified version of the potentially confusing definition* that preceded it.

4) D

Inference Question

The professor says that the detergent industry in America is highly concentrated. She also says that "the amount of concentration in an industry depends on" economies of scale, and economies of scale are entry barriers for new, small businesses trying to enter a concentrated industry. Thus, the detergent industry *does not have room for smaller businesses to compete*.

5) A, C

Detail Question

Some of the entry barriers described by the professor include established firms controlling "the supply of raw materials;" in addition, she cites "large factories and expensive equipment," so *the high cost of equipment and manufacturing space*.

6) A

Inference Question

The professor says that a diversified business "produces a number of largely unrelated goods and services." Thus, selling a wide range of products, such as *cars, computers, televisions, and kitchen appliances*, makes a business diversified.

ACTUAL PRACTICE 20 - PRACTICE SET 1

Notes

stu. has not received loan check, must pay tuition by next week
→ *advisor says check was sent last week*
→ *stu. suspects his roommate lost it*
→ *stu. forgot to change address w/ the office, check sent to wrong house*
two solutions:
  1) wait for check to get forwarded to current address
  2) request check be cancelled; pick up new check at office tomorrow
     stu. prefers this option
advisor asks about previous residence, stu. says landlord good

1) D
   Main Idea Question
   At the beginning of the conversation, the student says, "I'm still waiting to receive my loan check for this semester," so we can conclude that he needs *help locating an important piece of mail*.

2) B
   Detail Question
   The student says, "I must have forgotten to change my address with your office," so the check did not come because it *was sent to his old address*.

3) C
   Detail Question
   The student indicates that canceling the check and picking up a new one latter is the best course because "it is almost a guarantee that I'll get the check before tuition is due."

4) A
   Inference Question
   After the advisor says, "we need to know if a landlord is taking advantage of students," the student says, "No, no problems there." From this, we can infer that the student did not have any problems with his landlord, so *the landlord was satisfactory*.

5) B
   Detail Question
   The student says that his previous house was "just too far from campus."

ACTUAL PRACTICE 20 - PRACTICE SET 2

Notes

Great Gatsby = one of best American novels
→ *about parties and rich people, also ugliness*
→ *Nick moves to NY suburb, visits cousin (Daisy), knows her husband*
→ *Nick's neighbor (Gatsby) throws huge parties, hoping to attract Daisy*
→ *Daisy and Gatsby dated, he hopes she'll come back*
→ *Gatsby dishonest w/ himself (not romantic hero, really gangster)*

1) D
   Main Idea Question
   The professor implies that the novel reflects "our culture" in a way that is beautiful but "honest about ugliness." He then says they will "go through the plot…highlighting the tension between beautiful and ugly;" in other words, *exploring the novel's insights into society*.

2) A
   Detail Question
   The professor says that the narrator, his cousin, and his cousin's husband all know each other; but in spite of his lavish parties, "No one knows Gatsby."

3) D
   Detail Question
   The student says that Gatsby seems to be "living in the past," thinking that Daisy's love for him has not changed, and that she has never really loved her husband.

4) B
   Purpose Question
   The professor says that Gatsby "believes that he is a prince coming to rescue (Daisy) from a tower, like some kind of fairy tale," indicating that *Gatsby has a child-like, naïve view of the situation*.

5) A
   Purpose Question
   The professor describes how Gatsby expects to win Daisy back, but the student says that Daisy and her

husband, Tom, "are never going to break up." *The professor is agreeing with the student* by saying that Gatsby "seems ridiculous" for his expectations.

6) A

Inference Question

The professor implies complexity in the novel when he talks about "tension between beautiful and ugly" in it. He also implies that he agrees that the book is one of the greatest American novels because it "show(s) us our culture in a way that is beautiful, and at the same time, honest about ugliness."

ACTUAL PRACTICE 20 - PRACTICE SET 3

Notes

light bulb enhances modern living, safer than kerosene lamp light bulbs constantly improved
→ *first = carbon-arc lamp: powered by electricity, not fuel (ie. kerosene lamp)*
→ *carbon electrodes heated, glow very bright*
→ *problems: too bright (can't use inside), too hot (caused burns, fires)*
→ *still used outdoors and in projectors*
Edison: first light bulb in glass container
→ *added carbon filament to carbon electrodes*
→ *not as bright or hot*

1) C

Main Idea Question

The professor describes carbon-arc lamps, and Edison's light bulb, both of which were *precursors of the modern light bulb*.

2) A

Purpose Question

The professor mentions the open-glass containers used for both kerosene lamps and carbon-arc lamps, so he uses a *familiar example* to describe carbon-arc lamps' appearance.

3) B

Inference Question

The professor says that light bulbs "provided an alternative to earlier kerosene lamps which can easily cause fires," so we can infer that kerosene lamps *are less safe than light bulbs*.

4) C, D

Detail Question

The professor claims that carbon-arc lamps are "so blindingly bright" that they cannot be used to light the interiors of buildings, so they are *too bright for most places*. Carbon-arc lamps also "become so hot that they can... start fires."

5) C

Purpose Question

The student asks about the steps that led from the carbon-arc lamp to the modern lightbulb. Thus, *he wants to know more about the development of light bulbs*.

6) A

Inference Question

At the end of the lecture, the professor says, "there were problems with this early light bulb as well..." so the class will probably *discuss problems with the early light bulb*.

ACTUAL PRACTICE 21 - PRACTICE SET 1

Notes

stu. wants advice on how to improve grade in anatomy class (freshman)
→ *prof. reveals that most students have "Cs," class supposed to be very difficult*
→ *stu. plans on med. school, needs good grades*
prof. advice for studying:
→ *go to tutoring center for memorization strategies*
→ *study in groups (prof. cites psych. study)*

1) C

Main Idea Question

The student reveals that he wants *advice on improving his grade* when he says "I just was looking for some advice or suggestions" because he has gotten low quiz scores.

2) D

Inference Question

The professor says, "I apologize for not knowing your name. That's a problem with the large lecture courses." Here, she is implying that *it is difficult to learn so many students' names* in large classes.

3) A

Purpose Question

The professor asks the student if he thinks that "doctors are born knowing" complex medical terms to emphasize that all doctors have to spend a lot of time memorizing. Thus, she is *explaining that people become doctors through hard work*.

4) A, D

Detail Question

The professor says to the student, "the university tutoring center can help you with memorization strategies." She also claims, "forming study groups seems to improve grades in my anatomy classes."

5) B

Inference Question

At the end of the conversation, the student says, "I'm glad I came to your office hours," so we can infer that he is *appreciative for the professor's advice*.

ACTUAL PRACTICE 21 - PRACTICE SET 2

Notes

science fiction at least 200 yrs. old
→ *first sci. fi. novel = Frankenstein*
→ *features of sci. fi. = spec. about future, explain mysteries with sci. theory*
late 1800s genre grew
→ *Jules Verne: explore uncharted areas*
→ *H.G. Wells: aliens, time travel, superhuman mutations*
reason for prolif.? industrial rev. (anxiety)
sci. advancements → *inspiration for sci. fi.*
computers → *robot takeovers, virtual realities (Matrix)*

1) B

Main Idea Question

The professor talks about the history (*the development and characteristics*) of science fiction (*a literary genre*).

2) B

Inference Question

The professor offers a definition of science fiction; "a fictionalization of scientific discoveries that may be possible in future." Thus, we can assume that *science fiction stories often include future scientific discoveries*.

3) D

Purpose Question

The professor ties authors' speculations to the huge "growth in a scientific understanding at that time." Therefore, the professor is *explaining the reasons for the proliferation of science fiction*.

4) B, C

Detail Question

The professor mentions some common characteristics of science fiction stories, focusing on "speculating about the future," and "explaining imagined situations using real scientific discoveries." In other words, *speculating about future discoveries, and explaining the unknown using science*.

5) A

Inference Question

Because the professor says, "Some of you have read [*Frankenstein*] without realizing its relationship to science fiction," we can infer that *its science fiction elements often go unrecognized*.

6) C

Detail Question

The professor says that "many modern books and movies deal with the idea of artificial intelligence or robot takeovers."

ACTUAL PRACTICE 21 - PRACTICE SET 3

Notes

Radio waves = energy (like light), travel as sine wave
→ *amplitude, wavelength, frequency*
→ *travel through walls, farther than other forms of energy*
→ *radio waves common to send/receive info. (phones, comp., TV, radio, etc)*
AM and FM = amp. modulation, and freq. mod.
→ *encodes info. by changing amp. or freq.*
→ *transmitter converts song into wave, broadcasts*
→ *receiver in car detects and decodes wave, plays music*

1) B

Main Idea Question

The professor discusses "some of the basics" regarding radio waves, including *how radio waves transmit information*.

2) D

Detail Question

According to the professor, hertz measure "how many waves pass through a point in a second."

3) C

Detail Question

A student claims that "radio waves travel farther than other forms of energy."

4) B

Purpose Question

Here, the professor emphasizes how important radio waves are to daily life by *pointing out some of the numerous applications of radio waves.*

5) A

Purpose Question

Before the professor describes the transmission and reception of a radio signal, he says, "I'd imagine that some of this information is unclear to some of you guys, [so] I want to look at how radio waves… transmit information." Thus, he gives the example to explain *a potentially confusing concept.*

6) D

Inference Question

If a radio station called AM 750 sends out "radio waves at a frequency of 750,000 waves per second," we can infer that AM 425 would *broadcast a radio signal at* 425,000 *waves per second, which is equal to* 425,000 *hertz.*

ACTUAL PRACTICE 22 - PRACTICE SET 1

Notes

stu. looking for part-time job listing (first time in career center, freshman)
→ *listings for part-time local jobs on wall*
→ *uni. tries to check job listings for scammers, advisor says not to give out too much personal info.*
→ *advisor recommends stu. take employment workshop (interview strategies)*
→ *available on-campus jobs on wall (advisor prefers on-campus jobs b/c they're convenient and good for socializing)*
→ *advisor says many bookstore/library jobs available*

1) B

Main Idea Question

The student says, "I just came in because I need to get a part-time job," so she wants *to ask about job opportunities.*

2) C

Detail Question

The advisor explains that "scams are not unheard of" in the career center's job listings; he tells the student not to give too much personal information *to avoid having the information stolen by scammers.*

3) C, D

Detail Question

The advisor explains that the workshop goes over "how to be careful when sending information in response to job offers" and "interviewing strategies."

4) A

Inference Question

The advisor implies that on campus jobs *are more convenient than off-campus jobs* when she says, "campus jobs can work around you class schedule" and that they are closer than off-campus jobs.

5) B, D

Detail Question

The advisor says that the most on-campus job availabilities "are the libraries and the bookstore."

ACTUAL PRACTICE 22 - PRACTICE SET 2

Notes

ADHD diagnosis ↑ in past decade → more ADHD research
→ *ADHD people have unusual dopamine (feelings of happiness, reward) receptors*
→ *ADHD = underactive dopamine receptors, harder to stay focused*
ADHD and evo. bio.
→ *early humans = hunter-gatherers, adapt to changing environments (ADHD good in such environment); agriculture = repetitive tasks, little change (ADHD bad)*
→ *Ariaal tribe (Africa); nomadic ppl., some become farmers*
men in both groups of Ariaal tested: in nomads, ADHD symptoms beneficial; in farmers, bad (malnourished)

1) D

Main Idea Question

Although the professor spends the first part of the lecture describing general characteristics of ADHD, she spends most of the lecture *discussing how ADHD may have benefitted ancient humans* by discussing the Ariaal tribe.

2) B, C

Detail Question

According to a student, dopamine absorption in the brain "leads to feelings of happiness." The professor says that dopamine "tells your brain to focus on an experience, so that you can remember what you did to trigger that reward," so *it improves concentration.*

3) C

Detail Question

The professor says that "people with ADHD often have underactive dopamine receptors," so they don't feel rewarded by accomplishing simple tasks. As a result, they have limited *attentiveness during certain tasks*.

4) A

Purpose Question

Because the professor describes how the symptoms of ADHD may have benefitted humans in the distance past, we can infer that she discusses the hunter-gatherer lifestyle *to link ADHD to human evolution*.

5) D

Detail Question

According to the professor, "hunting and gathering made for an unpredictable, ever-changing lifestyle," and people with ADHD want to "constantly… search for new experiences and environments." Thus, we can infer that ADHD *would have made our ancestors more aware of their environments*, and therefore more likely to survive.

6) A

Detail Question

The professor says, "Today, most schools and jobs require focus." In other words, *most cultures place a high value on one's ability to concentrate*.

ACTUAL PRACTICE 22 - PRACTICE SET 3

Notes

President Johnson (LBJ), began presidency 1963, after Kennedy's assassination
→ *LBJ in Congress 1937, became more conservative to appeal to Texans*
→ *1953, becomes leader of Senate*
→ *1960, joins Kennedy's campaign*
LBJ famous for civil rights and Vietnam War
→ *ensured passing of 1957 Civil Rights Act*
→ *made Civil Rights Act 1964 main goal, got passed*
→ *also passed Voting rights Act (for black vote in the South) and Medicare (health care for seniors)*
→ *LBJ blamed for Vietnam War*
Chose not to run for re-election (radical decision)

1) D

Main Idea Question

The professor talks about President Johnson's important civil rights accomplishments, and he stresses that Johnson is often wrongly held completely responsible for the Vietnam War; in short, the professor argues that *President Johnson was a competent leader*.

2) D

Detail Question

The professor explains, "Johnson became increasingly conservative over the years… to succeed politically in his home state of Texas," so *he wanted to appeal to voters and politicians in his home state*.

3) C

Detail Question

The professor emphasizes Johnson's efforts to pass the Civil Rights Act of 1964, Medicare, and the Voting Rights Act.

4) C

Inference Question

The professor says, "The anti-war movement become as important in the media as the Civil Rights Movement," and the anti-war movement damaged Johnson's "reputation and his power." Thus, we can infer that the successes of Johnson's presidency *were overshadowed by the Vietnam War*.

5) D

Purpose Question

The professor says that many people "blame Johnson for the Vietnam War," but he gives the history of the conflict to show that it began before Johnson's presidency, proving *that Johnson was not completely responsible for the war in Vietnam*.

6) D

Inference Question

The professor says that Kennedy's Civil Rights Act "seemed unlikely to pass through Congress," but because of Johnson's efforts "The Civil Rights Act of 1964 was passed and signed into law."

ACTUAL PRACTICE 23 - PRACTICE SET 1

Notes

stu. visits prof. to ask about paper
→ *topic is too broad, needs help focusing*
→ *thinking about film Birth of a Nation, (silent film)*
→ *falsified history, KKK "heroes", ↑ KKK membership*
stu.: Civil War scenes realistic (1st film w/ scenes of battlefield), good topic?

→ prof.: no, better-measurable effects of film on society; ie. evidence of KKK rise
→ could look at backlash, too (growth of NAACP) + film 1920 In Our Gates (silent film)

1) B

   Main Idea Question

   The professor tells the student that his idea to write about film is "probably a topic that needs to be narrowed down," and then she assists him with ideas for a "focus." Thus, they are discussing *narrowing down a research topic.*

2) D

   Purpose Question

   The professor says that the KKK "really terrorized African Americans," so calling the KKK "dangerous" is "putting it mildly," or *describing the group using a word that was too weak.*

3) B

   Detail Question

   The student says that the filmmaker "tried to show very realistic battle scenes…what combat was really like during the Civil War." Thus, he *strove to make [the battle scenes] look real.*

4) A

   Detail Question

   The professor suggests that the student can "trace the Klan's membership and political clout following the movie's appearance." In other words, data may support the *film inspiring some white Americans to join a violent group.*

5) C

   Inference Question

   The professor and the student are discussing a "research paper." The professor advises the student to avoid simply describing the film, or on the other hand, speculating about its impact. Instead, she says he should focus on "measurable effects." In other words, she implies that *she will give higher grades to papers with factual support.*

ACTUAL PRACTICE 23 - PRACTICE SET 2

Notes

Pres. Nixon resigned in 1973 b/c of criminal activities; yet great environmental president
→ *stu. compares T. Roosevelt to Nixon; prof. says Nixon greater environmental president*
→ *Nixon = Republican, term when industry in U.S. ↓ esp. mining, manufact.*
National Env. Policy Act of 1969 → Environ. Impact Reports for federal projects
→ *1970, establishes EPA (agency) = regulations on health, env.*
→ *1973, Endangered Species Act → gov. power to protect wild species*
→ *1974, Safe Drinking Water Act*

1) D

   Main Idea Question

   Early in the lecture, the professor claims, "Nixon was our greatest environmental president," and then she spends the rest of the lecture describing *the environmental accomplishments of President Nixon.*

2) B

   Detail Question

   The professor says, "the Endangered Species Act… has been called the Magna Carta of the environmental movement."

3) C

   Detail Question

   In regards to the Environmental Policy Act of 1969, the professor says, "Most importantly, this act required that Environmental Impact Reports be done for most federally funded projects."

4) C

   Purpose Question

   Throughout the lecture, the professor is trying to stress that *Nixon cared very much about environmental issues* by listing some of his actions regarding the environment.

5) B

   Detail Question

   The professor describes the "huge companies" in the mining and manufacturing sectors that "wanted nothing to stand in their way," such as environmental laws. Thus, the professor is *explaining the fierce opposition* that Nixon withstood.

6) B

   Inference Question

   Because Nixon's name has "become synonymous with abuse of power," the professor suggests that it does not occur to historians to consider his environmental accomplishments. Thus, it is "difficult to see" positive because of Nixon's *bad reputation.*

ACTUAL PRACTICE 23 - PRACTICE SET 3

Notes

Sami = only indigenous Europeans (Finland, Norway, etc pushed into Arctic Circle)
→ *reindeer to pull sleds; culture part of Santa Claus story*
→ *Sami adapted to climate: eat fish, meat; clothes from hides, antlers*
→ *hunted in winter w/ skis, dogs w/double fur (track, keep watch)*
→ *language = very specific to env. (100s of words for "snow")*
→ *homes = tents, sod, small community = siida*
→ *strong storytelling tradition, incl. "yoik" (like musical name for person)*

1) A

Main Idea Question

After a basic introduction to the Sami, the professor says, "This is a culture that, for thousands of years, helped people adapt to living in a harsh environment…" For the remainder of the lecture, he explains how *cultural adaptations have helped people thrive in a challenging habitat.*

2) A

Inference Question

The student indicates that he had never heard about the real Sami people or their lifestyle, but he was familiar with reindeer as characters in the Santa Claus story. The professor implies that the "cute" stories have minimized or *trivialized a complex culture.*

3) C

Purpose Question

The professor agrees with the student that skiing enabled the Sami "to hunt, fish, and trap animals in winter, when there was deep snow on the ground." He also says that dogs "helped keep watch, discourage wolves and bears, and track game." In other words, he discusses skis and dogs to explain *how the Sami managed to hunt for food.*

4) D

Detail Question

The professor indicates that Sami languages adapted in such a way that speakers could compress a great deal of information about snow into one word, because they had "literally hundreds of words for 'snow'." Thus, the professor focuses on the languages' *ability to express highly specific conditions with words for "snow."*

5) C

Detail Question

The professor introduces yoikking by saying that it was part of a "beautiful storytelling and singing tradition" that helped people through the long winters and "fostered strong social ties within the siida (community.)" He also says that yoiks can refer to people and events, and can be joined together in a storyline that will "be understood only by one's own inner circle." Thus, yoikking *has helped foster close bonds in the community.*

6) B

Inference Question

The professor first describes the traditional food and clothing of the Sami people, and then their means of obtaining the food; then he moves on to describing language, storytelling, and singing. Thus, his description shifts from *practical to social adaptations.*

ACTUAL PRACTICE 24 - PRACTICE SET 1

Notes

Stu.: assigned to analyze/evaluate writer's strategy in opinion article
Tutor: problem = stu. summarized article, gave on own opinion
→ *Writer supports high school algebra, compares to ABCs in kindergarten*
→ *Name the strategy (analogy)*
   labeling = analyzing, but must also evaluate
   + explain ie., convincing information = facts, details

1) C

Main Idea Question

The speakers spend the conversation discussing *how to complete the student's writing assignment,* which involves "analyzing and evaluating the writer's strategies."

2) A, C

Detail Question

The tutor says to the student, "you have to analyze *how* she is making her point," so *the student must analyze the author's writing strategies,* and judge how well they work (*comment on the effectiveness of the ... strategies*).

3) A

Detail Question

The tutor says that the author of the article "makes an analogy between learning algebra and learning the alphabet."

4) D

Purpose Question

The tutor says that the student should label the author's strategies because "that is analyzing." Thus, labeling will *help the student understand how to analyze an author's writing*.

5) B

Inference Question

Because the student asks the tutor, "can I come back on Thursday with a new draft?" we can infer that she will *rewrite the assignment, and then return to the tutor*.

ACTUAL PRACTICE 24 - PRACTICE SET 2

Notes

neuroscience = study of brain/nervous system
→ *glial cells (glia) important part of neurology*
→ *glia initially assumed to be "support cells"*
structure of neurons = dendrites, cell body, axon
→ *neurons surrounded by sodium/potassium*
→ *+ charge outside neuron, - charge inside*
→ *Neuron sends signals by letting + charges into cell, then pushes + charges to next neuron; signal = relay of + charges*
types of glia:
→ *astroglia: star-shaped; connect neuron to blood supply, remove extra potassium*
→ *oligodendroglia: surround axon, myelin sheath helps send signals*

1) B

Main Idea Question

The professor discusses the *functions* of neurons, astroglia, and oligodendroglia, which are *different types of cells found in the nervous system*.

2) D

Detail Question

The professor thinks that the term "neuroscience" "is misleading because it leaves out a group of cells that are absolutely crucial to the... central nervous system."

3) A

Inference Question

Because the professor needs to describe neurons "before... discussing the types and functions of glial cells," we can infer that *understanding glia required knowledge of neurons*.

4) C

Purpose Question

The professor suggests that "astroglia... make neurons look downright lazy" because glia have important roles in the nervous system. Thus, he is *emphasizing the numerous functions of astroglia*.

5) B

Detail Question

The professor says, "To send a signal, a neuron's cell membrane will let in some of the positively charged sodium and potassium into the cell body."

6) D

Detail Question

According to the professor, oligodendroglia form myelin sheaths around axons, allowing "electrochemical signals [to] travel more efficiently from one neuron to the next." In other words, oligodendroglia *help axons send electrochemical signals*.

ACTUAL PRACTICE 24 - PRACTICE SET 3

Notes

Surprisingly complex: why is the sky blue?
→ *light = electromagnetic radiation*
  like a river → narrow = fast, wider = slow
  speed (freq), width (wavelength)
→ *people see diff. freq. light as diff. color (blue = short, red = long)*
light enters atmosphere, reacts with gases: Rayleigh Scattering (mostly blue light)
→ *gas doesn't absorb light, just scatters back out*
→ *people see scattered light, sky = blue*

1) A

Main Idea Question

The professor explains the main topic when he says, "today, we're going to explore a very simple question... 'Why is the sky blue?'" Thus, the class is discussing *the reasons for the colors of Earth's sky*.

2) C

Purpose Question

The lectures discusses abstract concept about light waves. Because students can not see what he describes, the professor uses *analogies to help them understand*.

3) D

Detail Question

The professor uses an analogy to a river when he discusses wavelengths of light. He says, "At the other end, reds and oranges flow gently by across great leagues." In other words, *red and orange have the greatest wavelengths*.

4) B

Detail Question

When discussing Rayleigh Scattering, the professor says, "Unlike an opaque solid or liquid, the transparent gases in our atmosphere don't react chemically with incoming light," which explains why light radiates back out.

5) C

Detail Question

The professor explains that all colors of light get absorbed by atmospheric gases, "but blue is retained more often than any other color of light." Therefore, *blue light interacts the most with the gases in Earth's atmosphere*.

6) A

Inference Question

The professor explains that different wavelengths produce different colors of light. He also mentions that the sun produces many wavelengths of light. Therefore, *we can infer that sunlight produces different colors when it interacts with different objects*.

ACTUAL PRACTICE 25 - PRACTICE SET 1

Notes

stu. confused about test score (65% = B, not D)
prof. explains that he grades on a curve
→ *prof.'s calc. class = hard*
→ *prof. bases all grades off highest grade in class (if top grade = 86%, then 86% = A+)*
→ *ensures that those who know the most will succeed in class; grades still 10 points apart from e/o*
→ *prof.'s system is "kinder" than other grading curves*

1) C

Main Idea Question

The student visits the professor because she's "wondering if maybe there was a mistake" with grading her quiz. Thus, she wants *to ask about the grade she received on a quiz*.

2) B

Detail Question

The student says, "I got a 'B' on the quiz even though my score was only 65 percent."

3) D

Purpose Question

Before the professor explains his grading system, he says, "this calculus class is tough," so we can infer that this statement is related to his grading system. Thus, he says this *to explain why he uses an alternative grading system*.

4) B

Purpose Question

The student remarks that some professors' grading systems "seem harsh" because a slightly lower-than-average score could receive an "F." Thus, her comment conveys her opinion that such a "harsh" grading system *would be unfair*.

5) A

Inference Question

The professor says, "even if the quiz or test is insanely difficult, the students who demonstrated the most knowledge will still get 'As' and 'Bs'," instead of "Ds" and "Fs." This implies that the professor's grading system *allows many students to receive better grades*.

ACTUAL PRACTICE 25 - PRACTICE SET 2

Notes

Income tax only 100 years old (1913 amendment)
until 1900s, gov't had few expenses (no highways, schools, military)
→ *used other taxes: tariffs, excises, property tax (tariffs much higher rate in past)*
→ *excise: a sale tax on specific products, unpopular (Whiskey Rebellion)*
20th century changing perceptions
Industrial Rev. led to inequality and new ideas (ie. communism)
→ *need for greater education, public services/attempt*

social justice

→ *Congress approved income tax*

1) A

   Main Idea Question

   The professor introduces the topic of income tax at the beginning of the lecture and spends some time describing its origins. Therefore, the main topic is *how the modern income tax system evolved in the U.S.*

2) B, C

   Detail Question

   The professor spends some time discussing different types of taxes. He explains that, "following the Revolutionary War, the U.S. relied heavily on tariffs." In addition, "property taxes have always been a popular method for states to meet their budgetary needs." Thus, *property tax and tariffs were used prior to an income tax.*

3) C

   Detail Question

   The professor explains: "in order to pay for the increased services offered to the public, the U.S. government had to increase taxes." He specifically mentions schools as one public service that required government funding. Therefore, *the U.S. government implemented an income tax to pay for public services, such as schools.*

4) D

   Detail Question

   The professor explains that an excise was added to domestically distilled spirits. He adds, "this tax was so unpopular it eventually led to a minor insurrection known as the 'Whiskey Rebellion.'" Therefore, *the cause of the Whiskey Rebellion was an excise on domestically distilled spirits.*

5) A

   Purpose Question

   The professor discusses several reasons for the income tax amendment, including changing perceptions. He mentions labor unions and socialism as *examples of ideas that helped make income tax publicly acceptable.*

6) C

   Inference Question

   The professor describes public schools as one public service that the U.S. government began funding in the early 20th century. He adds that "the downside to all this social reform is its cost," implying that public services, including schools, *are expensive.*

ACTUAL PRACTICE 25 - PRACTICE SET 3

Notes

Philae = 1st spacecraft to land on a comet; looking for organic compounds (hydrogen + carbon)

abiogenesis = life from non-living matter

→ *in ancient times, ppl. believed in abio. (maggots from food, frogs from mud) but 1st questioned in 1600s*

→ *now, back to abiogen. (1st life created from organic compounds)*

sci. replicate Earth 4 bil. years ago

1950s, Miller and Urey combine elements, electricity → created complex organic compounds (not life)

1) B

   Main Idea Question

   The professor says that "our main topic for today" is abiogenesis, *a theory about the origins of life on Earth.*

2) A, C

   Detail Question

   The professor says, "organic compounds are combinations of chemical elements that contain hydrogen and carbon."

3) B

   Inference Question

   Because watching maggots hatch in rotten food or frogs emerge from mud does not require any *experimentation*, we can infer that *acceptance of abiogenesis was based on observation.*

4) D

   Detail Question

   According to the professor, Miller and Urey tried to "replicate the chemical and environmental conditions on Earth about 4 billion years ago" to prove that *life on Earth originated from reactions between non-living organic compounds.*

5) A

   Inference Question

   We can infer that *scientists have not yet replicated abiogenesis in their experiments* because their experiments have "produced complex organic compounds," but "not life," and abiogenesis requires the creation of life.

6) B

Purpose Question

The professor explains that "if organic compounds present on the comet match those found on Earth," the theory of abiogenesis would be supported by indicating comets as the source of organic compounds.

APPENDIX

Simple Answers

TOEFL PATTERN LISTENING 3

CHAPTER 2

● ACTUAL PRACTICE 1

Practice Set 1
1) A
2) C
3) D
4) A
5) B

Practice 2
1) B
2) C, D
3) A
4) D
5) A, C, D
6) C

Practice 3
1) D
2) B, C
3) A
4) D
5) C
6) B

● ACTUAL PRACTICE 2

Practice 1
1) D
2) B
3) A
4) B, C
5) C

Practice 2
1) D
2) B
3) B
4) A
5) B, C, E
6) D

Practice 3
1) C
2) B
3) D
4) B
5) B
6) A

● ACTUAL PRACTICE 3

Practice 1
1) C
2) B
3) D
4) C
5) B

Practice 2
1) D
2) A
3) B
4) C
5) B, D
6) D

Practice 3
1) B
2) A
3) C
4) A
5)

Auxins	Cytokinins	Gibberellins
		✓
✓		
	✓	

● ACTUAL PRACTICE 4

Practice 1
1) B
2) A
3) C
4) B, D
5) D

Practice 2
1) C
2) A
3) C
4) D
5) B
6) C, D

Practice 3
1) C
2) A, B
3) C
4) D
5) C
6) B

● ACTUAL PRACTICE 5

Practice 1
1) B
2) C
3) A
4) D
5) A, D
6) C

Practice 2
1) C
2) A
3) D
4) B
5) B
6) B, C

Practice 3
1) B
2) C
3) D
4) A
5) A, B
6) B

● ACTUAL PRACTICE 6

Practice 1
1) C
2) D
3) A
4) B
5) A, D

Practice 2

1) C
2) A
3) D
4) A
5) B
6) D

Practice 3
1) D
2) A
3) B
4) B
5)

Lepidop-tera	Braconid Wasp	Chalcid Wasp
✓	✓	
	✓	✓
		✓

● ACTUAL PRACTICE 7
Practice 1
1) B
2) D
3) A
4) C
5) B

Practice 2
1) B
2) B, C
3) D
4) D
5) B
6) D

Practice 3
1) A
2) C
3) A, C
4) B
5) C, D
6) D

● ACTUAL PRACTICE 8

Practice 1
1) A
2) D
3) A, D
4) B
5) D

Practice 2
1) B
2) A
3) A, C
4) B
5) C
6) D

Practice 3
1) B
2) D
3) B
4) B
5) D
6) C

● ACTUAL PRACTICE 9
Practice 1
1) C
2) C
3) A
4) A
5) D

Practice 2
1) B
2) B, D
3) D
4) C
5) A
6) B

Practice 3
1) B
2) C, D
3) B
4) A
5) D
6) C

● ACTUAL PRACTICE 10
Practice 1
1) B
2) C, D
3) C
4) A
5) D

Practice 2
1) C
2) B
3) A
4) B, D
5) C
6) D

Practice 3
1) C
2) A
3) C
4) B
5) D
6) D

● ACTUAL PRACTICE 11
Practice 1
1) B
2) A
3) C
4) A
5) D

Practice 2
1) C
2) D
3) B
4) C, D
5) A
6) A

Practice 3
1) D
2) B, C
3) C

4) A
   5) B
   6) C

● ACTUAL PRACTICE 12
Practice 1
   1) D
   2) A, C
   3) B
   4) C
   5) B

Practice 2
   1) D
   2) B
   3) B
   4) A
   5) D
   6) C

Practice 3
   1) C
   2) C
   3) D
   4) A, C
   5) D
   6) B

● ACTUAL PRACTICE 13
Practice 1
   1) B
   2) C
   3) D
   4) A, B
   5) A

Practice 2
   1) C
   2) B
   3) D
   4) B
   5) A
   6) A

Practice 3
   1) A

   2) C, D
   3) D
   4) D
   5)

| A, F | B, E | C, D |

● ACTUAL PRACTICE 14
Practice 1
   1) A
   2) D
   3) A
   4) B
   5) D

Practice 2
   1) D
   2) B
   3) D
   4) C
   5) B
   6) A

Practice 3
   1) B
   2) A
   3) C
   4) B, D
   5) C
   6) B

● ACTUAL PRACTICE 15
Practice 1
   1) C
   2) B
   3) A
   4) D
   5) C

Practice 2
   1) B
   2) A, B
   3) D
   4) C
   5) B
   6) A

Practice 3
   1) D
   2) B
   3) A
   4) A, D
   5) C
   6) A

● ACTUAL PRACTICE 16
Practice 1
   1) D
   2) C
   3) D
   4) A
   5) B

Practice 2
   1) D
   2) C
   3) B
   4) A
   5) C
   6) D

Practice 3
   1) C
   2) D
   3) B, C
   4) B
   5) A
   6) A, D

● ACTUAL PRACTICE 17
Practice 1
   1) A
   2) C
   3) C
   4) B, C
   5) D

Practice 2
   1) D
   2) B
   3) B
   4) C
   5) B, D

Practice 3
1) B
2) A
3) D
4) C
5) C
6) B, D

• ACTUAL PRACTICE 18
Practice 1
1) C
2) A
3) A, C
4) C, D
5) B

Practice 2
1) A
2) C
3) B
4) B, C
5) D
6) B

Practice 3
1) D
2) B
3) A
4) A, C
5) C
6) D

• ACTUAL PRACTICE 19
Practice 1
1) A
2) B, C
3) A
4) D
5) B

Practice 2
1) C
2) D
3) B
4) C
5) D

6) B

Practice 3
1) D
2) C
3) B
4) D
5) A, C
6) A

• ACTUAL PRACTICE 20
Practice 1
1) D
2) B
3) C
4) A
5) B

Practice 2
1) D
2) A
3) D
4) B
5) A
6) A

Practice 3
1) C
2) A
3) B
4) C, D
5) C
6) A

• ACTUAL PRACTICE 21
Practice 1
1) C
2) D
3) A
4) A, D
5) B

Practice 2
1) B
2) B
3) D

4) C, B
5) A
6) C

Practice 3
1) B
2) D
3) C
4) B
5) A
6) D

• ACTUAL PRACTICE 22
Practice 1
1) B
2) C
3) C, D
4) A
5) B, D

Practice 2
1) D
2) B, C
3) C
4) A
5) D
6) A

Practice 3
1) D
2) D
3) C
4) C
5) D
6) D

• ACTUAL PRACTICE 23
Practice 1

1) B
2) D
3) B
4) A
5) C

Practice 2
1) D
2) B
3) C
4) C
5) B
6) B

Practice 3
1) A
2) A
3) C
4) D
5) C
6) B

● **ACTUAL PRACTICE 24**
Practice 1
1) C
2) A, C
3) A
4) D
5) B

Practice 2
1) B
2) D
3) A
4) C
5) B
6) D

Practice 3
1) A
2) C
3) D
4) B
5) C
6) A

● **ACTUAL PRACTICE 25**
Practice 1
1) C
2) B
3) D
4) B
5) A

Practice 2
1) A
2) B, C
3) C
4) D
5) A
6) C

Practice 3
1) B
2) A, C
3) B
4) D
5) A
6) B